The
C++
Programming
Language

Bjarne Stroustrup

AT&T Bell Laboratories
Murray Hill, New Jersey

ADDISON-WESLEY PUBLISHING COMPANY

Reading, Massachusetts • Menlo Park, California
Don Mills, Ontario • Wokingham, England • Amsterdam
Sydney • Singapore • Tokyo • Mexico City
Bogotá • Santiago • San Juan

This book is in the **Addison-Wesley Series in Computer Science**

Michael A. Harrison
Consulting Editor

Library of Congress Cataloging-in-Publication Data

Stroustrup, Bjarne.
  The C++ Programming Language.

  Includes bibliographies and index.
  1. C++ (Computer program language)   I. Title.
II. Title: C plus plus programming language.
QA76.73.C153S77 1986   005.13'3   85-20087
ISBN 0-201-12078-X

Reprinted with corrections March, 1986

This book was typeset in Times Roman and Courier by the author, using a Mergenthaler Linotron 202 phototypesetter driven by a VAX-11/750 running the 8th Edition of the UNIX operating system.

DEC, PDP and VAX are trademarks of Digital Equipment Corporation. Power 6/32 is a trademark of Computer Consoles, Incorporated. UNIX is a trademark of AT&T Bell Laboratories.

BCDEFGHIJK-DO-89876

Preface

Language shapes the way we think,
and determines what we can think about.
– B.L.Whorf

C++ is a general purpose programming language designed to make programming more enjoyable for the serious programmer. Except for minor details, C++ is a superset of the C programming language. In addition to the facilities provided by C, C++ provides flexible and efficient facilities for defining new types. A programmer can partition an application into manageable pieces by defining new types that closely match the concepts of the application. This technique for program construction is often called *data abstraction*. Objects of some user-defined types contain type information. Such objects can be used conveniently and safely in contexts in which their type cannot be determined at compile time. Programs using objects of such types are often called *object based*. When used well, these techniques result shorter, easier to understand, and easier to maintain programs.

The key concept in C++ is *class*. A class is a user-defined type. Classes provide data hiding, guaranteed initialization of data, implicit type conversion for user-defined types, dynamic typing, user-controlled memory management, and mechanisms for overloading operators. C++ provides much better facilities for type checking and for expressing modularity than C does. It also contains improvements that are not directly related to classes, including symbolic constants, inline substitution of functions, default function arguments, overloaded function names, free store management operators, and a reference type. C++ retains C's ability to deal efficiently with the fundamental objects of the hardware (bits, bytes, words, addresses, etc.). This allows the user-defined types to be implemented with a pleasing degree of efficiency.

C++ and its standard libraries are designed for portability. The current implementation will run on most systems that support C. C libraries can be used from a C++ program, and most tools that support programming in C can be used with C++.

This book is primarily intended to help serious programmers learn the language and use it for nontrivial projects. It provides a complete description of C++, many complete examples, and many more program fragments.

Acknowledgments

C++ could never have matured without the constant use, suggestions, and constructive criticism of many friends and colleagues. In particular, Tom Cargill, Jim Coplien, Stu Feldman, Sandy Fraser, Steve Johnson, Brian Kernighan, Bart Locanthi, Doug McIlroy, Dennis Ritchie, Larry Rosler, Jerry Schwarz, and Jon Shopiro provided important ideas for development of the language. Dave Presotto wrote the current implementation of the stream I/O library.

In addition, hundreds of people contributed to the development of C++ and its compiler by sending me suggestions for improvements, descriptions of problems they had encountered, and compiler errors. I can mention only a few: Gary Bishop, Andrew Hume, Tom Karzes, Victor Milenkovic, Rob Murray, Leonie Rose, Brian Schmult, and Gary Walker.

Many people have also helped with the production of this book, in particular, Jon Bentley, Laura Eaves, Brian Kernighan, Ted Kowalski, Steve Mahaney, Jon Shopiro, and the participants in the C++ course held at Bell Labs, Columbus, Ohio, June 26-27, 1985.

Murray Hill, New Jersey   *Bjarne Stroustrup*

Contents

Chapter 2: Declarations and Constants   39

Chapter 3: Expressions and Statements   71

Chapter 4: Functions and Files   103

Reference Manual   245

Index   313

Notes to the Reader

"The time has come," the Walrus said,
"to talk of many things."
– L.Carroll

This chapter consists of an overview of this book, a list of references, and some ancillary notes on C++. The notes concern the history of C++, ideas that influenced the design of C++, and thoughts about programming in C++. This chapter is not an introduction: the notes are not a prerequisite for understanding the following chapters, and some notes assume knowledge of C++.

The Structure of This Book

Chapter 1 is a quick tour of the major features of C++ intended to give the reader a feel for the language. C programmers can read the first half of the chapter very quickly; it primarily covers features common to C and C++. The second half describes C++'s facilities for defining new types; a novice may postpone a more detailed study of this until after Chapters 2, 3 and 4.

Chapters 2, 3, and 4 describe features of C++ that are not involved in defining new types: the fundamental types, expressions, and control structures for C++ programs. In other words, they describe the subset of C++ that is essentially C. They go into considerably greater detail than Chapter 1, but the complete information can be found only in the reference manual. However, these chapters provide examples, opinions, recommendations, warnings, and exercises that have no place in a manual.

Chapters 5, 6, and 7 describe C++'s facilities for defining new types, features that do not have counterparts in C. Chapter 5 presents the basic class concept, showing how objects of a user-defined type can be initialized, accessed, and finally cleaned up. Chapter 6 explains how to define unary and binary operators for a user-defined type, how to specify conversions between user-defined types, and how to specify the way every creation, deletion, and copying of a value of a user-defined type is to be handled. Chapter 7 describes the concept of a derived class, which enables a programmer to build more complex classes from simpler ones, to provide alternative interfaces to a class, and to handle objects in an efficient and type-secure manner in contexts in which their type cannot be known at compile time.

Chapter 8 presents the `ostream` and `istream` classes provided for input and output in the *standard library*. This chapter has a dual purpose; it presents a useful facility that is also a realistic example of C++ use.

Finally, the C++ reference manual is included.

References to parts of this book are of the form §2.3.4 (Chapter 2 subsection 3.4). Chapter *r* is the reference manual; for example §r.8.5.5.

Implementation Notes

At the time of writing, all C++ implementations use versions of a single compiler front-end†. It is used on a large number of architectures, including AT&T 3B, DEC VAX, IBM 370, and Motorola 68000 running versions of the UNIX operating system. The program fragments in this book were directly taken from source files that were compiled on a 3B20 running UNIX System V release 2^{15}, a VAX11/750 running 8th Edition UNIX[16], and a CCI Power 6/32 running BSD4.2 UNIX[17]. The language described in this book is "pure C++", but the current compiler also implements a number of "anachronisms" (described in §r.15.3) that should ease a transition from C to C++.

Exercises

Exercises can be found at the end of chapters. The exercises are mainly of the write-a-program variety. Always write enough code for a solution to be compiled and run with at least a few test cases. The exercises vary considerably in difficulty, so they are marked with an estimate of their difficulty. The scale is exponential so that if a (∗1) exercise takes you about five minutes, a (∗2) might take an hour, and a (∗3) might take a day. The time needed to write and test a program depends more on the reader's experience than on the exercise itself. A (∗1) exercise might take a day if the reader first has to get acquainted with a new computer system to run it. On the other hand, a (∗5) exercise might be done in an hour by someone who happens to have the right collection of programs handy. Any book on programming in C can be used as

---

† C++ is available from AT&T, Software Sales and Marketing, PO Box 25000, Greensboro, NC 27420, USA (telephone 800-828-UNIX) or from your local sales organization for the UNIX System.

a source of exercises for Chapters 2-4. Aho et. al.[1] present many common data structures and algorithms in terms of abstract data types. It can therefore be used as a source of exercises for Chapters 5-7. However, the language used in that book lacks both member functions and derived classes. Consequently, the user-defined types can often be expressed more elegantly in C++.

Design Notes

Simplicity was an important design criterion; where there was a choice between simplifying the manual and other documentation or simplifying the compiler, the former was chosen. Great importance was also attached to retaining compatibility with C; this precluded cleaning up C syntax.

C++ has no high-level data types and no high-level primitive operations. For example, there is no matrix type with an inversion operator or a string type with a concatenation operator. If a user wants such a type, it can be defined in the language itself. In fact, defining a new general-purpose or application-specific type is the most fundamental programming activity in C++. A well designed user-defined type differs from a built-in type only in the way it is defined and not in the way it is used.

Features that would incur run-time or memory overheads even when not used were avoided. For example, ideas that would make it necessary to store "housekeeping information" in every object were rejected; if a user declares a structure consisting of two 16-bit quantities, that structure will fit into a 32-bit register.

C++ was designed to be used in a rather traditional compilation and run-time environment, the C programming environment on the UNIX system. Facilities such as exception handling or concurrent programming that require nontrivial loader and run-time support are not included in C++. Consequently, a C++ implementation can be very easily ported. There are, however, good reasons for using C++ in an environment with significantly more support available. Facilities such as dynamic loading, incremental compilation, and a database of type definitions can be put to good use without affecting the language.

C++ types and data-hiding features rely on compile-time analysis of programs to prevent accidental corruption of data. They do not provide secrecy or protection against someone deliberately breaking the rules. They can, however, be used freely without incurring run-time or space overheads.

Historical Note

Clearly C++ owes most to C[7]. C is retained as a subset, and so is C's emphasis on facilities that are low-level enough to cope with the most demanding systems programming tasks. C in turn owes much to its predecessor BCPL[9]; in fact, BCPL's // comment convention has been (re)introduced in

C++. If you know BCPL you will notice that C++ still lacks a VALOF block. The other main source of inspiration was Simula67[2,3]; the class concept (with derived classes and virtual functions) was borrowed from it. The Simula67 inspect statement was deliberately not introduced into C++. The reason for that is to encourage modularity through the use of virtual functions. C++'s facility for overloading operators and the freedom to place a declaration wherever a statement can occur resembles Algol68[14].

The name C++ is a quite recent invention (summer of 1983). Earlier versions of the language collectively known as "C with Classes"[13] have been in use since 1980. The language was originally invented because the author wanted to write some event-driven simulations for which Simula67 would have been ideal, except for efficiency considerations. "C with Classes" was used for major simulation projects in which the facilities for writing programs that use (only) minimal time and space were severely tested. "C with Classes" lacked operator overloading, references, virtual functions, and many details. C++ was first installed outside the author's research group in July, 1983; quite a few current C++ features had not yet been invented, however.

The name C++ was coined by Rick Mascitti. The name signifies the evolutionary nature of the changes from C. "++" is the C increment operator. The slightly shorter name C+ is a syntax error; it has also been used as the name of an unrelated language. Connoisseurs of C semantics find C++ inferior to ++C. The language is not called D, since it is an extension of C and does not attempt to remedy problems by removing features. For yet another interpretation of the name C++, see the appendix of Orwell[8].

C++ was primarily designed so that the author and his friends would not have to program in assembler, C, or various modern high-level languages. Its main purpose is to make writing good programs easier and more pleasant for the individual programmer. There never was a C++ paper design; design, documentation, and implementation went on simultaneously. Naturally, the C++ front-end is written in C++. There never was a "C++ project" either, or a "C++ design committee". Throughout, C++ evolved, and continues to evolve, to cope with problems encountered by users, and through discussions between the author and his friends and colleagues.

C was chosen as the base language for C++ because it (1) is versatile, terse, and relatively low-level; (2) is adequate for most system programming tasks; (3) runs everywhere and on everything; and (4) fits into the UNIX programming environment. C has its problems, but a language designed from scratch would have some too, and we know C's problems. Most important, working with C enabled "C with Classes" to be a useful (if awkward) tool within months of the first thought of adding Simula-like classes to C.

As C++ became more widely used, and as the facilities it provided over and above those of C became more significant, the question of whether to retain compatibility was raised again and again. Clearly some problems could be avoided if some of the C heritage was rejected (see, for example, Sethi[12]).

This was not done because (1) there are millions of lines of C code that might benefit from C++, provided that a complete rewrite from C to C++ were unnecessary; (2) there are hundreds of thousands of lines of library functions and utility software code written in C that could be used from/on C++ programs provided C++ were completely link compatible and syntactically very similar to C; (3) there are tens of thousands of programmers who know C and therefore need only learn to use the new features of C++ and not relearn the basics; and (4) since C++ and C will be used on the same systems by the same people for years, the differences should be either very large or very small to minimize mistakes and confusion. Lately, the definition of C++ has been revised to ensure that any construct that is both legal C and legal C++ actually has the same meaning in both languages.

The C language has itself evolved over the last few years, partly under the influence of the development of C++ (see Rosler[11]). The preliminary draft ANSI C standard[10] contains a function declaration syntax borrowed from "C with classes." Borrowing works both ways; for example, the void* pointer type was invented for ANSI C and first implemented in C++. When the ANSI standard has developed a bit further, it will be time to review C++ to remove gratuitous incompatibilities. For example, the preprocessor (§r.11) will be modernized, and the rules for doing floating point arithmetic will probably have to be adjusted. That should not be painful; both C and ANSI C are very close to being subsets of C++ (see §r.15).

Efficiency and Structure

C++ was developed from the C programming language and with very few exceptions retains C as a subset. The base language, the C subset of C++, is designed so that there is a very close correspondence between its types, operators, and statements and the objects computers deal with directly: numbers, characters, and addresses. Except for the free store operators new and delete, individual C++ expressions and statements typically need no hidden run-time support or subroutines.

C++ uses the same function call and return sequences as C. When even this relatively efficient mechanism is too expensive, a C++ function can be substituted inline, thus enjoying the notational convenience of functions without run-time overhead.

One of the original aims for C was to replace assembly coding for the most demanding systems programming tasks. When C++ was designed, care was taken not to compromise the gains in this area. The difference between C and C++ is primarily in the degree of emphasis on types and structure. C is expressive and permissive. C++ is even more expressive, but to gain that increase in expressiveness, the programmer must pay more attention to the types of objects. Knowing the types of objects, the compiler can deal correctly with expressions when the programmer would otherwise have had to specify operations in painful detail. Knowing the types of objects also enables the compiler to detect errors that would otherwise have persisted until testing. Note that using the type system to get function argument checking, to protect data from accidental corruption, to provide new types, to provide new operators, etc., does not in itself increase run-time or space overheads.

The emphasis on structure in the design of C++ reflects the increase in the scale of programs written since C was designed. You can make a small program (less than 1000 lines) work through brute force even when breaking every rule of good style. For a larger program, this is simply not so. If the structure of a 10,000 line program is bad, you will find that new errors are introduced as fast as old ones are removed. C++ was designed to enable larger programs to be structured in a rational way so that it would not be unreasonable for a single person to cope with 25,000 lines of code. Much larger programs exist, but the ones that work generally turn out to consist of many nearly independent parts, each one well below the limits previously mentioned. Naturally, the difficulty of writing and maintaining a program depends on the complexity of the application and not simply on the number of lines of program text, so the exact numbers used to express the preceding ideas should not be taken too seriously.

However, not every piece of code can be well structured, hardware independent, easy to read, etc. C++ possesses features that are intended for manipulating hardware facilities in a direct and efficient way without regard for safety or ease of comprehension. It also possesses facilities for hiding such code behind elegant and safe interfaces.

This book emphasizes techniques for providing general-purpose facilities, generally useful types, libraries, etc. These techniques will serve programmers of small programs as well as programmers of large ones. Furthermore, since all nontrivial programs consist of many semi-independent parts, the techniques for writing such parts serve programmers of both systems and applications.

One might suspect that specifying a program using a more detailed type structure would lead to a larger program source text. With C++ this is not so; a C++ program declaring functions argument types, using classes, etc., is typically a bit shorter than the equivalent C program not using these facilities.

Philosophical Note

A programming language serves two related purposes: it provides a vehicle for the programmer to specify actions to be executed and a set of concepts for the programmer to use when thinking about what can be done. The first aspect ideally requires a language that is "close to the machine", so that all important aspects of a machine are handled simply and efficiently in a way that is reasonably obvious to the programmer. The C language was primarily designed with this in mind. The second aspect ideally requires a language that is "close to the problem to be solved" so that the concepts of a solution can be expressed directly and concisely. The facilities added to C to create C++ were primarily designed with this in mind.

The connection between the language in which we think/program and the problems and solutions we can imagine is very close. For this reason restricting language features with the intent of eliminating programmer errors is at best dangerous. As with natural languages, there are great benefits from being at least bilingual. The language provides a programmer with a set of conceptual tools; if these are inadequate for a task, they will simply be ignored. For example, seriously restricting the concept of a pointer simply forces the programmer to use a vector plus integer arithmetic to implement structures, pointers, etc. Good design and the absence of errors cannot be guaranteed by mere language features.

The type system should be especially helpful for nontrivial tasks. The C++ class concept has, in fact, proven itself as a powerful conceptual tool.

Thinking about Programming in C++

Ideally one approaches the task of designing a program in three stages: first gain a clear understanding of the problem, then identify the key concepts involved in a solution, and finally express that solution in a program. However, the details of the problem and the concepts of the solution often become clearly understood only through the effort to express them in the program – this is where the choice of programming language matters.

In most applications there are concepts that are not easily represented in a program as either one of the fundamental types or as a function without associated static data. Given such a concept, declare a class to represent it in the program. A class is a type; that is, it specifies how objects of its class behave: how they are created, how they can be manipulated, how they are destroyed. A class also specifies how objects are represented, but at the early stages of the design of a program, that is not (should not be) the major concern. The key to writing a good program is to design classes so that each cleanly represents a single concept. Often this means that the programmer must focus on the questions: How are objects of this class created? Can objects of this class be copied and/or destroyed? What operations can be done on such objects? If there are no good answers to such questions, the concept probably wasn't "clean" in the first place, and it might be a good idea to think a bit more about the problem and the proposed solution instead of immediately starting to "code around" the problems.

The concepts that are easiest to deal with are the ones that have a traditional mathematical formalism: numbers of all sorts, sets, geometric shapes, etc. There really ought to be standard libraries of classes representing such concepts, but this is not the case at the time of writing. C++ is still young, and its libraries have not yet matured to the same degree as the language itself.

A concept does not exist in a vacuum; there are always clusters of related concepts. Organizing the relationship between classes in a program, that is, determining the exact relationship between the different concepts involved in a solution, is often harder than laying out the individual classes in the first place. The result had better not be a muddle in which every class (concept) depends on every other. Consider two classes, A and B: Relationships such as "A calls functions from B," "A creates Bs," and "A has a B member" seldom cause major problems, and relationships such as "A uses data from B" can typically be eliminated (simply don't use public data members). The trouble spots are most often relations that are naturally expressed as "A is a B and ... ."

One of the most powerful intellectual tools for managing complexity is hierarchical ordering; that is, organizing related concepts into a tree structure with the most general concept at the root. In C++, derived classes represent such structures. A program can often be organized as a set of trees (a forest?). That is, the programmer specifies a number of base classes, each with its own set of derived classes. Virtual functions (§7.2.8) can often be used to define a set of operations for the most general version of a concept (a base class). When necessary, the interpretation of these operations can be refined for particular special cases (derived classes).

Naturally, this organization has its limits. In particular, a set of concepts is sometimes better organized as a directed acyclic graph in which a concept can directly depend on more than one other concept; for example, "A is a B and a C and ... ." There is no direct support for this in C++, but such relations can be represented with some loss of elegance and a bit of extra work (§7.2.5).

Sometimes even a directed acyclic graph seems insufficient for organizing the concepts of a program; some concepts seem to be inherently mutually dependent. If a set of mutually dependent classes is so small that it is easy to understand, the cyclic dependencies need not be a problem. The idea of `friend` classes (§5.4.1) can be used to represent sets of mutually dependent classes in C++.

If you can organize the concepts of a program only into a general graph (and not a tree or a directed acyclic graph), and if you cannot localize the mutual dependencies, then you are most likely in a predicament that no programming language can help you out of. Unless you can conceive of some easily stated relationships between the basic concepts, the program is likely to become unmanageable.

Remember that much programming can be simply and clearly done using only primitive types, data structures, plain functions, and a few classes from a standard library. The whole apparatus involved in defining new types should not be used except when there is a real need.

The question "How does one write good programs in C++?" is very similar to the question "How does one write good English prose?" There are two kinds of answers: "Know what you want to say" and "Practice. Imitate good writing." Both kinds of advice appear to be as appropriate for C++ as they are for English – and as hard to follow.

Rules of Thumb

Here is a set of "rules" you might consider while learning C++. As you get more proficient you can evolve them into something suitable for your kind of applications and your style of programming. They are deliberately very simple, so they lack detail. Don't take them too literally. To write a good program takes intelligence, taste, and patience. You are not going to get it right the first time; experiment!

[1] When you program, you create a concrete representation of the ideas in your solution to some problem. Let the structure of the program reflect those ideas as directly as possible:

    [a] If you can think of "it" as a separate idea, make it a class.

    [b] If you can think of "it" as a separate entity, make it an object of some class.

    [c] If two classes have something significant in common, make that a base class. Most classes in your program will have something in common; have a (nearly) universal base class, and design it most carefully.

[2] When you are defining a class that does not implement a mathematical entity like a matrix or a complex number, or a low-level type like a linked list:

    [a] Don't use global data.

    [b] Don't use global (nonmember) functions.

    [c] Don't use public data members.

    [d] Don't use friends, except to avoid [a], [b] or [c].

    [e] Don't access data members of another object directly.

    [f] Don't put a "type field" in a class; use virtual functions.

    [g] Don't use inline functions; except as a significant optimization.

Note to C Programmers

The better one knows C, the harder it seems to avoid writing C++ in C style, and thereby lose some of the potential benefits of C++. So please take a look at the "Differences from C" section of the reference manual (§r.15). Here are a few pointers to the areas in which C++ has better ways of doing something than C has. Macros (#define) are almost never necessary in C++; use const (§2.4.6) or enum (§2.4.7) to define manifest constants, and inline (§1.12) to avoid function-calling overhead. Try to declare all functions and to specify the type of all arguments – there are very few good reasons not to. Similarly, there are very few good reasons for declaring a local variable without initializing it since a declaration can occur anywhere a statement can – don't declare a variable before you need it. Don't use malloc() – the new operator (§3.2.6) does the same job better. Many unions do not need a name – try anonymous unions (§2.5.2).

References

There are few direct references in the text, but here is a short list of books and papers that are mentioned directly or indirectly.

[1] A.V. Aho, J.E. Hopcroft, and J.D. Ullman: *Data Structures and Algorithms.* Addison-Wesley, Reading, Massachusetts. 1983.

[2] O-J. Dahl, B. Myrhaug, and K. Nygaard: *SIMULA Common Base Language.* Norwegian Computing Center S-22. Oslo, Norway. 1970.

[3] O-J. Dahl and C.A.R. Hoare: *Hierarchical Program Construction* in *"Structured Programming."* Academic Press, New York. 1972. pp 174-220.

[4] A. Goldberg and D. Robson: *SMALLTALK-80 The Language and Its Implementation.* Addison Wesley, Reading, Massachusetts. 1983.

[5] R.E. Griswold et.al.: *The Snobol4 Programming Language.* Prentice-Hall, Englewood Cliffs, New Jersey. 1970.

[6] R.E. Griswold and M.T. Griswold: *The ICON Programming Language.* Prentice-Hall, Englewood Cliffs, New Jersey. 1983.

[7] Brian W. Kernighan and Dennis M. Ritchie: *The C Programming Language.* Prentice-Hall, Englewood Cliffs, New Jersey. 1978.

[8] George Orwell: *1984.* Secker and Warburg, London. 1949.

[9] Martin Richards and Colin Whitby-Strevens: *BCPL - The Language and Its Compiler.* Cambridge University Press. 1980.

[10] L. Rosler (Chairman, ANSI X3J11 Language Subcommittee): *Preliminary Draft Proposed Standard - The C Language.* X3 Secretariat: Computer and Business Equipment Manufactures Association, 311 First Street, NW, Suite 500, Washington, DC 20001, USA.

[11] L. Rosler: *The Evolution of C - Past and Future.* AT&T Bell Laboratories Technical Journal. Vol.63 No.8 Part 2. October 1984. pp 1685-1700.

[12] Ravi Sethi: *Uniform Syntax for Type Expressions and Declarations.* Software Practice & Experience, Vol 11 (1981), pp 623-628.

[13] Bjarne Stroustrup: *Adding Classes to C: An Exercise in Language Evolution.* Software Practice & Experience, 13 (1983), pp 139-61.

[14] P.M. Woodward and S.G. Bond: *Algol 68-R Users Guide.* Her Majesty's Stationery Office, London. 1974.

[15] *UNIX System V Release 2.0. User Reference Manual.* AT&T Bell Laboratories, Murray Hill, New Jersey. December 1983.

[16] *UNIX Time-Sharing System: Programmer's Manual. Research Version, Eighth Edition.* AT&T Bell Laboratories, Murray Hill, New Jersey. February 1985.

[17] *UNIX Programmer's Manual.* 4.2 Berkeley Software Distribution University of California, Berkeley, California. March 1984.

Chapter 1

A Tour of C++

The only way to learn
a new programming language
is by writing programs in it.
– Brian Kernighan

This chapter is a quick tour of the major features of the C++ programming language. First a C++ program is presented, and it is shown how it can be compiled and run, and how such a program can produce output and read input. After the introduction, about a third of the chapter presents the more conventional features of C++: fundamental types, declarations, expressions, statements, functions, and program structure. The remainder concentrates on C++'s facilities for defining new types, data hiding, user-defined operators, and hierarchies of user-defined types.

1.1 Introduction

This tour will guide you through a sequence of C++ programs and program fragments. At the end you should have a general idea about the facilities of C++ and enough information to write simple programs. A precise and complete explanation of the concepts involved in even the smallest complete example requires pages of definitions. To avoid this chapter turning into a manual or a discussion of general ideas, examples are presented with only the briefest definitions of the terms used. Terms are reviewed later when a larger body of examples is available to aid the discussion.

1.1.1 Output

Let us first of all write a program to write a line of output:

```
#include <stream.h>

main()
{
    cout << "Hello, world\n";
}
```

The line #include <stream.h> instructs the compiler to *include* the declarations of the standard stream input and output facilities as found in the file stream.h. Without these declarations, the expression cout<<"Hello, world\n" would make no sense. The operator << ("put to"†) writes its second argument onto its first (in this case, the string "Hello, world\n" onto the standard output stream cout). A string is a sequence of characters surrounded by double quotes. In a string the backslash character \ followed by another character denotes a single special character; in this case, \n is the newline character, so that the characters written are Hello, world and a newline.

The rest of the program

```
main() { ... }
```

defines a function called main. Every program must have a function named main, and the program is started by executing that function.

1.1.2 Compilation

Where did the output stream cout and the code implementing the output operator << come from? A C++ program must be compiled to produce executable code; the compilation process is essentially the same as for C and shares most of the programs involved. The program text is read and analyzed, and if no error is found, code is generated. Then the program is examined to find names and operators that have been used but not defined (in our case cout and <<). If possible, the program is then completed by adding the missing definitions from a library (there is a standard library and users can provide their own). In our case cout and << were declared in stream.h; that is, their types were given, but no details of their implementation were provided. The standard library contains the specification of the space and initialization code for cout and the code for <<. Naturally there are many other things in that library, some of which are declared in stream.h, but only the subset of the library needed to complete our program is added to the compiled version.

---

† C programmers know << as the left shift operator for integers. This use of << is not lost; << has simply been further defined for the case in which it has an output stream as its left hand operand. How that is done is described in §1.8.

The C++ compile command is typically called CC. It is used like cc for C programs; see your manual for details. Assuming that the "Hello, world" program is stored in a file called hello.c, you can compile and run it like this (**$** is the system's prompt):

```
$ CC hello.c
$ a.out
Hello, world
$
```

a.out is the default name for an executable result of a compilation; if you want to name your program you can do it using the –o option:

```
$ CC hello.c -o hello
$ hello
Hello, world
$
```

1.1.3 Input

The following (rather verbose) conversion program prompts you to enter a number of inches. When you have done this it will print the corresponding number of centimeters.

```
#include <stream.h>

main()
{
    int inch = 0;
    cout << "inches=";
    cin  >> inch;
    cout << inch;
    cout << " in = ";
    cout << inch*2.54;
    cout << " cm\n";
}
```

The first line of main() declares an integer variable inch. Its value is read in using the operator >> ("get from") on the standard input stream cin. The declarations of cin and >> are of course found in <stream.h>. After running it, your terminal might look like this:

```
$ a.out
inches=12
12 in = 30.48 cm
$
```

This example has one statement per output operation; this is unnecessarily verbose. The output operator << can be applied to its own result so that the last four output operations could be written in a single statement:

```
cout << inch << " in = " << inch*2.54 << " cm\n";
```

Input and output are described in greater detail in the following sections. In fact, this whole chapter can be seen as an explanation of how it is possible to write the preceding programs in a language that does not provide an input or an output operator! The programs presented previously are in fact written in C++ "extended" with I/O operations through the use of libraries and #include files. In other words, the C++ language as described in the reference manual does not define facilities for input and output; instead, the operators >> and << are defined using only facilities available to every programmer.

1.2   Comments

It is often useful to insert text that is intended only as a comment for a human reader and should be ignored by the compiler into a program. In C++, this can be done in one of two ways.

The characters /* start a comment that terminates with the characters */. The whole sequence is equivalent to a whitespace character (for example, a space). This is most useful for multiline comments and for editing out code, but note that /* */ comments do not nest.

The characters // start a comment that terminates at the end of the line on which they occur. Again, the whole sequence is equivalent to a whitespace character. This is most useful for short comments. A // can be used to comment out a /* or a */, and a /* can be used to comment out a //.

1.3   Types and Declarations

Every name and every expression has a type that determines the operations that may be performed on it. For example, the declaration

```
int inch;
```

specifies that inch is of type int; that is, inch is an integer variable.

A declaration is a statement that introduces a name into the program. A declaration specifies a type for that name. A type defines the proper use of a name or an expression. Operations such as +, -, *, and / are defined for integers. After stream.h has been included, an int can also be the second operand to << when the first argument is an ostream.

The type of an object determines not only which operations can be applied to it, but also the meaning of those operations. For example, the statement

```
cout << inch << " in = " << inch*2.54 << " cm\n";
```

correctly treats the four output values differently. The strings are printed literally, whereas the integer inch and the floating point value of inch*2.54

are converted from their internal representations to character representations fit for human eyes.

C++ has several basic types and several ways of creating new ones. The simplest forms of C++ types are presented in subsequent sections; the more interesting ones are saved for later.

1.3.1 Fundamental Types

The fundamental types, corresponding most directly to hardware facilities, are:

```
char   short   int   long   float   double
```

The first four types are used to represent integers, the last two to represent floating point numbers. A variable of type char is of the natural size to hold a character on a given machine (typically a byte), and a variable int is of the natural size for integer arithmetic on a given machine (typically a word). The range of integers that can be represented by a type depends on its size. In C++, sizes are measured in multiples of the size of a char, so by definition char has size one. The relation between the fundamental types can be written like this:

$$1 \equiv sizeof(char) \leq sizeof(short) \leq sizeof(int) \leq sizeof(long)$$

$$sizeof(float) \leq sizeof(double)$$

In general, it is unwise to assume more about the sizes of fundamental types. In particular, it is not true for all machines that an integer is large enough to hold a pointer.

The adjective const can be applied to a basic type to yield a type that has identical properties to the original, except that the value of variables of a const type cannot be changed after initialization.

```
const float pi = 3.14;
const char plus = '+';
```

A character enclosed in single quotes is a character constant. Note that often a constant defined like this need not occupy storage; its value can simply be used directly where needed. A constant *must* be initialized at the point of declaration. For variables, the initialization is optional, but strongly recommended. There are very few good reasons for introducing a local variable without initializing it.

The arithmetic operators can be used for any combination of these types:

```
+    (plus, both unary and binary)
-    (minus, both unary and binary)
*    (multiply)
/    (divide)
```

1.4.3 Null Statements

The simplest statement is the null statement:

```
;
```

It does nothing. It can be useful, however, when the syntax requires a statement but you have no need for one.

1.4.4 Blocks

A block is a possibly empty list of statements enclosed in curly braces:

```
{ a=b+2;  b++;  }
```

A block lets you treat several statements as one. The scope of a name declared in a block extends from the point of declaration to the end of the block. The name can be hidden by declarations of the same name in inner blocks.

1.4.5 If Statements

The following example performs both inch-to-centimeter and centimeter-to-inch conversion; you are supposed to indicate the unit of the input by appending i for inches or c for centimeters:

```
#include <stream.h>

main( )
{
    const float fac = 2.54;
    float x, in, cm;
    char ch = 0;

    cout << "enter length: ";
    cin >> x >> ch;

    if (ch == 'i') {        // inch
        in = x;
        cm = x*fac;
    }
    else if (ch == 'c') { // cm
        in = x/fac;
        cm = x;
    }
    else
        in = cm = 0;

    cout << in << " in = " << cm << " cm\n";
}
```

Note that the condition in an if statement must be parenthesized.

1.4.6 Switch Statements

A switch statement tests a value against a set of constants. The tests in the preceding example could be written like this:

```
switch (ch) {
case 'i':
    in = x;
    cm = x*fac;
    break;
case 'c':
    in = x/fac;
    cm = x;
    break;
default:
    in = cm = 0;
    break;
}
```

The break statements are used to exit the switch statement. The case constants must be distinct, and if the value tested does not match any of them, the default is chosen. The programmer need not provide a default.

1.4.7 While Statements

Consider copying a string given a pointer p to its first character and a pointer q to the target. By convention a string is terminated by the character with the integer value 0.

```
while (*p != 0) {
    *q = *p;        // copy character
    q = q+1;
    p = p+1;
}
*q = 0;                 // terminating 0 not copied
```

The condition following while must be parenthesized. The condition is evaluated, and if its value is nonzero, the statement directly following is executed. This is repeated until the condition evaluates to zero.

This example is rather verbose. The operator ++ can be used to express incrementing directly, and the test can be simplified:

```
while (*p) *q++ = *p++;
*q = 0;
```

where the construct *p++ means: "take the character pointed to by p then increment p."

The example can be further compressed since the pointer p is dereferenced twice each time around the loop. The character copy can be performed at the same time as the condition is tested:

```
while (*q++ = *p++) ;
```

which takes the character pointed to by p, increments p, copies that character
to the location pointed to by q and increments q. If the character is nonzero,
the loop is repeated. Since all the work is done in the condition, no statement
is needed. The null statement is used to indicate this. C++ (like C) is both
loved and hated for enabling such extremely terse expression-oriented coding.

1.4.8 For Statements

Consider copying 10 elements from one vector to another:

```
for (int i=0; i<10; i++) q[i]=p[i];
```

This is equivalent to

```
int i = 0;
while (i<10) {
    q[i] = p[i];
    i++;
}
```

but more readable since all the information controlling the loop is localized.
When applied to an integer variable, the increment operator ++ simply adds
one. The first part of a for statement need not be a declaration; any statement will do. For example:

```
for (i=0; i<10; i++) q[i]=p[i];
```

is again equivalent provided i is suitably declared earlier.

1.4.9 Declarations

A declaration is a statement that introduces a name into the program; it may
also initialize the object of that name. The declaration is executed, that is the
initializer is evaluated and the initialization is performed, when the flow of
control reaches the declaration. For example:

```
for (int i = 1; i<MAX; i++) {
    int t = v[i-1];
    v[i-1] = v[i];
    v[i] = t;
}
```

For each execution of the for statement, i will be initialized once and t will
be initialized MAX-1 times.

1.5   Functions

A function is a named part of a program that can be invoked from other parts of the program as often as needed. Consider a program writing powers of 2:

```
extern float pow(float, int); // pow() defined elsewhere

main()
{
    for (int i=0; i<10; i++) cout << pow(2,i) << "\n";
}
```

The first line is a function declaration that specifies pow to be a function taking a `float` and an `int` argument and returning a `float`. A function declaration is used to enable calls to a function defined elsewhere.

In a call each function argument is checked against its expected type exactly as if a variable of the declared type were being initialized. This ensures proper type checking and type conversion. For example, a call `pow(12.3,"abcd")` causes the compiler to complain because `"abcd"` is a string and not an `int`. For the call `pow(2,i)`, the compiler converts the integer constant 2 to a `float`, as expected by the function. Pow might be defined like this:

```
float pow(float x, int n)
{
    if (n < 0) error("sorry, negative exponent to pow()");

    switch (n) {
    case 0:    return 1;
    case 1:    return x;
    default:   return x*pow(x,n-1);
    }
}
```

The first part of a function definition specifies the name of the function, the type of the value it returns (if any), and the types and names of its arguments (if any). A value is returned from a function using a `return` statement.

Different functions typically have different names, but for functions performing similar tasks on different types of objects it is sometimes better to let these functions have the same name. When their argument types are different the compiler can distinguish them anyway and chose the right function to call. For example, one could have one power function for integers and another for floating point variables:

```
overload pow;
int pow(int, int);
double pow(double, double);
//...
x = pow(2,10);
y = pow(2.0,10.0);
```

The declaration

```
overload pow;
```

informs the compiler that the use of the name pow for more than one function is intentional.

If a function does not return a value it should be declared void:

```
void swap(int* p, int* q)
{
    int t = *p;
    *p = *q;
    *q = t;
}
```

1.6 Program Structure

A C++ program typically consists of many source files, each containing a sequence of declarations of types, functions, variables, and constants. For a name to be used to refer to the same thing in two source files, it must be declared to be external. For example:

```
extern double sqrt(double);
extern istream cin;
```

The most common way of guaranteeing consistency between source files is to place such declarations in separate files, called *header files*, and then *include*, that is copy, those header files in all files needing the declarations. For example, if the declaration of sqrt is stored in the header file for the standard mathematical functions math.h, and you want to take the square root of 4, you could write:

```
#include <math.h>
//...
x = sqrt(4);
```

Since a typical header file is included in many source files, it does not contain declarations that should not be replicated. For example, function bodies are provided only for inline functions (§1.12) and initializers only for constants (§1.3.1). Except for those cases, a header file is a repository for type information; it provides an interface between separately compiled parts of a program.

In an include directive, a file name enclosed in angle brackets, such as <math.h>, refers to the file of that name in a *standard include directory* (often /usr/include/CC); files elsewhere are referred to by names enclosed in double quotes. For example:

```
#include "math1.h"
#include "/usr/bs/math2.h"
```

would include `math1.h` from the user's current directory and `math2.h` from the directory `/usr/bs`.

Here is a very small complete example in which a string is defined in one file and printed out in another. The file `header.h` defines the types needed:

```
// header.h

extern char* prog_name;
extern void f();
```

The file `main.c` is the main program:

```
// main.c

#include "header.h"
char* prog_name = "silly, but complete";
main()
{
    f();
}
```

and the file `f.c` prints the string:

```
// f.c

#include <stream.h>
#include "header.h"
void f()
{
    cout << prog_name << "\n";
}
```

You can compile and run this program like this:

```
$ CC main.c f.c -o silly
$ silly
silly, but complete
$
```

1.7 Classes

Let us look at how we might define the type ostream. To simplify this task, assume that a type streambuf has been defined for buffering characters. A type `streambuf` actually is defined in `<stream.h>` where the real definition of `ostream` is also found. Please do not try out the examples defining `ostream` in this and the following sections; unless you avoid using `<stream.h>` completely, the compiler will complain about redefinitions.

The definition of a user-defined type (called a `class` in C++) contains a specification of the data needed to represent an object of the type and a set of operations for manipulating such objects. The definition has two parts: a private part holding information that can only be used by its implementer, and a public part presenting an interface to users of the type:

```
class ostream {
    streambuf* buf;
    int state;
public:
    void put(char*);
    void put(long);
    void put(double);
};
```

The declarations after the `public` label specify the interface: a user can call only the three `put()` functions. The declarations before the `public` label specify the representation of an object of class `ostream`; the names `buf` and `state` can be used only by the `put()` functions declared in the public part.

A `class` defines a type, not a data object, so to use an `ostream` we must declare one (in the same way we declare variables of type `int`):

```
ostream my_out;
```

Assuming `my_out` has been appropriately initialized (as is explained in §1.10), it can now be used like this:

```
my_out.put("Hello, world\n");
```

The dot operator is used to select a member of a class for a given object of that class. Here the member function `put()` is called for the object `my_out`.

The function might be defined like this:

```
void ostream::put(char* p)
{
    while (*p) buf.sputc(*p++);
}
```

where `sputc()` is a function that puts a character into a `streambuf`. The `ostream` prefix is necessary to distinguish `ostream`'s `put()` from other functions called `put`.

To call a member function, an object of the class must be specified. In the member function, this object can be implicitly referred to, as is done in `ostream::put()` above: in each call, `buf` refers to the member `buf` of the object for which the function is called.

It is also possible to refer explicitly to that object through a pointer called `this`. In a member function of a class `X`, `this` is implicitly declared as an `X*` (pointer to `X`) and initialized with a pointer to the object for which the function is called. The definition of `ostream::put()` might also be written like this:

```
void ostream::put(char* p)
{
    while (*p) this->buf.sputc(*p++);
}
```

The -> operator is used to select a member of an object given a pointer.

1.8   Operator Overloading

The real class ostream defines the operator << to make it convenient to out-put several objects with a single statement. Let us now see how that is done.

To define @, where @ is any C++ operator, for a user-defined type you define a function called operator@, which takes arguments of the appropriate type. For example:

```
class ostream {
    //...
    ostream operator<<(char*);
};

ostream ostream::operator<<(char* p)
{
    while (*p) buf.sputc(*p++);
    return *this;
}
```

defines the << operator as a member of class ostream, so that s<<p is inter-preted as s.operator<<(p) when s is an ostream and p is a character pointer. The operator << is binary, but the function operator<<(char*) appears at first glance to take only one argument; it does, however, also have its standard implicit argument this.

Returning the ostream as the return value enables you to apply << to the result of an output operation. For example s<<p<<q is interpreted as (s.operator<<(p)).operator<<(q). This is the way output operations are provided for the built-in types.

Using the set of operations provided as public members of class ostream, you can now define << for a user-defined type such as complex without modi-fying the declaration of class ostream:

```
ostream operator<<(ostream s, complex z)
// a complex has two parts: real and imag
// print a complex as (real,imag)
{
    return s << "(" << z.real << "," << z.imag << ")";
}
```

Since operator<<(ostream,complex) is not a member function, it needs two explicit arguments to be binary. It will write the values out in the right order since <<, like most C++ operators, groups left-to-right; that is, a<<b<<c means (a<<b)<<c. The compiler knows the difference between member functions and nonmember functions when interpreting operators. For example, if z is a complex variable, s<<z will be expanded using the standard (nonmember) function call operator<<(s,z).

1.9   References

This last version of ostream unfortunately contains a serious error and is furthermore very inefficient. The problem is that the ostream is copied twice for each use of <<: once as an argument and once as the return value. This leaves state unchanged after every call. A facility for passing a pointer to the ostream rather than passing the ostream itself is needed.

This can be achieved using *references*. A reference acts as a name for an object; T& means reference to T. A reference must be initialized and becomes an alternative name for the object it is initialized with. For example:

```
ostream& s1 = my_out;
ostream& s2 = cout;
```

The reference s1 and my_out can now be used in the same way and with the same meaning. For example, assignment

```
s1 = s2;
```

copies the object referred to by s2 (that is, cout) into the object referred to by s1 (that is, my_out). Members are selected using the dot operator

```
s1.put("don't use ->");
```

and if you apply the address operator, you get the address of the object referred to:

```
&s1 == &my_out
```

The first obvious use of references is to ensure that the address of an object, rather than the object itself, is passed to an output function (this is called *call by reference* in some languages):

```
ostream& operator<<(ostream& s, complex z) {
    return s << "(" << z.real << "," << z.imag << ")";
}
```

Interestingly enough, the body of this function is unchanged, but had you assigned to s, you would now have affected the object given as the argument itself rather than a copy. In this case, returning a reference also improves efficiency, since the obvious way of implementing a reference is as a pointer, and a pointer is much cheaper to pass around than is a large data structure.

References are also essential for the definition of input streams because the input operator is given the variable to read into as an operand. Had references not been used, the user would have been required to pass pointers explicitly to the input functions.

```
class istream {
    //...
    int state;
public:
    istream& operator>>(char&);
    istream& operator>>(char*);
    istream& operator>>(int&);
    istream& operator>>(long&);
    //...
};
```

Note that two separate functions are used to read in a long and an int, whereas only one was needed to print them. This is typical, and the reason is that an int can be converted to a long by the standard implicit conversion rules (§r.6.6), thus saving the programmer the bother of writing both output functions.

1.10   Constructors

The definition of ostream as a class made the data members private. Only a member function can access the private members, so you must provide one for initialization. Such a function is called a constructor and is distinguished by having the same name as its class:

```
class ostream {
    //...
    ostream(streambuf*);
    ostream(int size, char* s);
};
```

Here two constructors are provided. One takes a streambuf above for real output; the other takes a size and a character pointer for string formatting. In a declaration, the argument list needed for a constructor is appended to the name. You can now declare streams like this:

```
ostream my_out(&some_stream_buffer);
char xx[256];
ostream xx_stream(256,xx);
```

The declaration of my_out not only sets aside the appropriate amount of store; it also calls the constructor ostream::ostream(streambuf*) to initialize it with the argument &some_stream_buffer, presumably a pointer to a suitable object of class streambuf. The declaration of xx_stream is handled similarly, but uses the other constructor. Declaring constructors for a class not only provides a way of initializing objects, but also ensures that all objects of that class will be initialized. When constructors have been declared for a class, it is not possible to declare a variable of that class without a constructor being called. If a class has a constructor that does not take arguments, that constructor will be called if no arguments are given in the declaration.

1.11   Vectors

The vector concept built into C++ was designed to allow maximal run-time efficiency and minimal store overhead. It is also, especially when used together with pointers, an extremely versatile tool for building higher-level facilities. You could, however, complain that a vector size must be specified as a constant, that there is no vector bounds checking, etc. An answer to such complaints is: "you can program that yourself." Let us see if this is a reasonable answer; in other words, test C++'s abstraction facilities by trying to provide these features for vector types of our own design and observe the difficulties involved, the costs incurred, and the convenience of use of the resulting vector types.

```
class vector {
    int* v;
    int  sz;
public:
          vector(int);    // constructor
          ~vector();      // destructor
    int   size() { return sz; }
    void  set_size(int);
    int&  operator[](int);
    int&  elem(int i) { return v[i]; }
};
```

The function `size` returns the number of elements of the vector; that is, indices must be in the range `0..size()-1`. The function `set_size` is provided to change that size, `elem` provides access to members without checking the index, and `operator[]` provides access with bounds check.

The idea is to have the class itself be a fixed sized structure that controls access to the actual vector storage, which is allocated by the vector constructor using the free store allocator operator `new`:

```
vector::vector(int s)
{
    if (s<=0) error("bad vector size");
    sz = s;
    v = new int[s];
}
```

You can now declare `vectors` very nearly as elegantly as the vectors that are built into the language itself:

```
vector v1(100);
vector v2(nelem*2-4);
```

The access operation can be defined as

```
int& vector::operator[](int i)
{
    if (i<0 || sz<=i) error("vector index out of range");
    return v[i];
}
```

The operator || (oror) is a logical-or operator. Its right-hand operand is only evaluated if necessary; that is, provided its left-hand operand evaluates to zero. Returning a reference ensures that the [ ] notation can be used on either side of an assignment:

```
vi[x] = v2[y];
```

The function with the funny name ~vector is a destructor; that is, a function declared to be called implicitly when a class object goes out of scope. The destructor for a class C is called ~C. If you define it like this:

```
vector::~vector()
{
    delete v;
}
```

it will, using the delete operator, de-allocate the space allocated by the constructor, so that when a vector goes out of scope, all its space is reclaimed for potential reuse.

1.12   Inline Expansion

Given the frequency of very small functions, you might worry about the cost of function calls. A member function is no more expensive to call than a non-member function with the same number of arguments (remembering that a member function always has at least one argument), and C++ function calls are about as efficient as you can get for any language. However, for extremely small functions, the call overhead can become an issue. If so, you might consider specifying a function to be *inline expanded*. If you do, the compiler will generate the proper code for the function at the place of the call. The semantics of the call are unchanged. For example, if size() and elem() are inline substituted:

```
vector s(100);
//...
i = s.size()
x = elem(i-1);
```

generates code equivalent to

```
//...
i = 100;
x = s.v[i-1];
```

The C++ compiler is usually smart enough to generate code that is as good as you get from straightforward macro expansion. Naturally, the compiler sometimes has to use temporary variables and other little tricks to preserve the semantics.

You can indicate that you want a function inline expanded by preceding its definition by the keyword inline, or, for a member function, simply by including the function definition in the class declaration, as is done for size( ) and elem( ) in the preceding example.

When used well, inline functions simultaneously increase the running speed and decrease the object code size. However, inline functions clutter class declarations and may slow down compilation, so they should be avoided when they are not necessary. For inline substitution to be a significant benefit for a function, the function must be very small.

1.13   Derived Classes

Now let us define a vector for which a user can define the index bounds:

```
class vec: public vector {
    int low, high;
public:
    vec(int, int);
    int& elem(int);
    int& operator[](int);
};
```

Defining vec as

```
    : public vector
```

means first of all that a vec is a vector. That is, type vec has (inherits) all the properties of type vector in addition to the ones declared specifically for it. Class vector is said to be the *base* class for vec, and conversely vec is said to be *derived* from vector.

Class vec modifies class vector by providing a different constructor that requires the user to specify the two index bounds rather than the size, and by providing its own access functions elem(int) and operator[](int). A vec's elem( ) is easily expressed in terms of vector's elem( ):

```
int& vec::elem(int i)
{
    return vector::elem(i-low);
}
```

The scope resolution operator `::` is used to avoid an infinite recursion by calling `vec::elem()` from itself. Unary `::` can be used to refer to nonlocal names. It would be reasonable to declare `vec::elem()` inline since efficiency presumably matters, but it is not necessary, reasonable, or possible to write it so that it uses the private member `v` of class `vector` directly. Functions of a derived class have no special access to the private members of its base class.

The constructor can be written like this:

```
vec::vec(int lb, int hb) : (hb-lb+1)
{
    if (hb-lb<0) hb = lb;
    low = lb;
    high = hb;
}
```

The construct `:(hb-lb+1)` is used to specify the argument list needed for the base class constructor `vector::vector()`. This constructor is called before the body of `vec::vec()`. Here is a small example that can be run if compiled with the rest of the `vector` declarations:

```
#include <stream.h>

void error(char* p)
{
    cerr << p << "\n"; // cerr is the error output stream
    exit(1);
}

void vector::set_size(int) { /* dummy */ }

int& vec::operator[](int i)
{
    if (i<low || high<i) error("vec index out of range");
    return elem(i);
}

main()
{
    vector a(10);
    for (int i=0; i<a.size(); i++) {
        a[i] = i;
        cout << a[i] << " ";
    }
    cout << "\n";
```

```
        vec b( 10, 19);
        for (i=0; i<b.size(); i++) b[i+10] = a[i];
        for (i=0; i<b.size(); i++) cout << b[i+10] << " ";
        cout << "\n";
    }
```

This produces

```
    0  1  2  3  4  5  6  7  8  9
    0  1  2  3  4  5  6  7  8  9
```

This line of development of the vector type can be explored further. It is quite simple to provide multidimensional arrays, arrays in which the number of dimensions is specified as an argument to a constructor, Fortran-style arrays that can be accessed both as having two and three dimensions, etc.

Such a class controls access to some data. Since all access is through the interface provided by the public part of the class, the representation of the data can be changed to suit the needs of the implementer. For example, it would be trivial to change the representation of a vector to a linked list. The other side of this coin is that any suitable interface for a given implementation can be provided.

1.14 More about Operators

Another direction of development is to provide vectors with operations:

```
    class Vec : public vector {
    public:
        Vec(int s) : (s) {}
        Vec(Vec&);
        ~Vec() {}
        void operator=(Vec&);
        void operator*=(Vec&);
        void operator*=(int);
        //...
    };
```

Note the way the constructor for the derived class, Vec::Vec( ), is defined to pass its argument to the constructor for the base class, vector::vector( ), and to do nothing else. This is a useful paradigm. The assignment operator is overloaded, and can be defined like this:

```
    void Vec::operator=(Vec& a)
    {
        int s = size();
        if (s!=a.size()) error("bad vector size for =");
        for (int i = 0; i<s; i++) elem(i) = a.elem(i);
    }
```

Assignment of Vecs now truly copies the elements, whereas assignment of vectors simply copies the structure controlling access to the elements. However, the latter also happens when a vector is copied without explicit use of the assignment operator: (1) when a vector is initialized by assignment of another vector; (2) when a vector is passed as an argument; and (3) when a vector is passed as the return value from a function. To gain control in these cases for Vec vectors, you define the constructor Vec(Vec&):

```
Vec::Vec(Vec& a) : (a.size())
{
    int sz = a.size();
    for (int i = 0; i<sz; i++) elem(i) = a.elem(i);
}
```

This constructor initializes a Vec as the copy of another, and will be called in the cases previously mentioned.

For operators such as = and +=, the expression on the left is clearly special, and it seems natural to implement them as operations on the object denoted by that expression. In particular, it is then possible for them to change the value of their first operand. For operators such as + and -, the left-hand operand typically needs no special attention. You could, for example, pass both arguments by value and still get a correct implementation of vector addition. Vectors can be large, however, so to avoid unnecessary copying, the operands of + are passed to operator+() by reference:

```
Vec operator+(Vec& a, Vec& b)
{
    int s = a.size();
    if (s != b.size()) error("bad vector size for +");
    Vec sum(s);
    for (int i=0; i<s; i++)
        sum.elem(i) = a.elem(i) + b.elem(i);
    return sum;
}
```

Here is a small example that can be executed if compiled with the vector declarations previously presented:

```
#include <stream.h>

void error(char* p) {
    cerr << p << "\n";
    exit(1);
}

void vector::set_size(int) { /* ... */ }

int& vec::operator[](int i) { /* ... */ }
```

```
main()
{
    Vec a(10);
    Vec b(10);
    for (int i=0; i<a.size(); i++) a[i] = i;
    b = a;
    Vec c = a+b;
    for (i=0; i<c.size(); i++) cout << c[i] << "\n";
}
```

1.15   Friends

The function operator+() does not operate directly on the representation of
a vector; indeed, it couldn't, since it is not a member. However, it is sometimes desirable to allow nonmember functions to access the private part of a
class object. For example, had there been no "unchecked access" function,
vector::elem(), you would have been forced to check the index i against
the vector bounds three times every time round the loop. This problem was
avoided here, but it is typical, so there is a mechanism for a class to grant
access to its private part to a nonmember function. A declaration of the function preceded by the keyword friend is simply placed in the declaration of
the class. For example, given

```
class Vec;        // Vec is a class name

class vector {
    friend Vec operator+(Vec, Vec);
    //...
};
```

you could have written:

```
Vec operator+(Vec a, Vec b)
{
    int s = a.size();
    if (s != b.size()) error("bad vector size for +");
    Vec& sum = *new Vec(s);
    int* sp = sum.v;
    int* ap = a.v;
    int* bp = b.v;
    while (s--) *sp++ = *ap++ + *bp++;
    return sum;
}
```

One particularly useful aspect of the friend mechanism is that a function can
be the friend of two or more classes. To see this, consider defining a vector
and matrix and then defining a multiplication function (see §r.8.8).

1.16   Generic Vectors

"So far so good", you might say, "but I want one of those vectors for the type `matrix` I just defined." Unfortunately, C++ does not provide a facility for defining a class vector with the type of the elements as an argument. One way to proceed is to replicate the definition of both the class and its member functions. This is not ideal, but often acceptable.

You can use a macro processor (§4.7) to mechanize that task. For example, class `vector` is a simplified version of a class that can be found in a standard header file. You could write:

```
#include <vector.h>

declare(vector,int);

main()
{
    vector(int) vv(10);
    vv[2] = 3;
    vv[10] = 4;      // range error
}
```

The file `vector.h` defines macros so that `declare(vector,int)` expands to the declaration of a class `vector` very much like the one just defined, and `implement(vector,int)` expands to the definitions of the functions of that class. Since `implement(vector,int)` expands into function definitions, it can be used only once in a program, whereas `declare(vector,int)` must be used once in every file manipulating this kind of integer vectors.

```
declare(vector,char);
//...
implement(vector,char);
```

would give you a (separate) type "vector of characters." An example of a macro implementing a generic class is presented in §7.3.5.

1.17   Polymorphic Vectors

Alternatively, you might define your vector and other *container classes* in terms of pointers to objects of some class:

```
class common {
    // ...
};
```

```
class cvector {
    common** v;
    //...
public:
    cvector(int);
    common*& elem(int);
    common*& operator[](int);
    //...
};
```

Note that since pointers and not the objects themselves are stored in such vectors, an object can be "in" several such vectors at the same time. This is a very useful feature for container classes such as vectors, linked lists, sets, etc. Furthermore, a pointer to a derived class can be assigned to a pointer to its base class, so the cvector above can be used to hold pointers to objects of all classes derived from common. For example:

```
class apple : public common { /* ... */ };
class orange : public common { /* ... */ };
class apple_vector : public cvector {
public:

cvector fruitbowl(100);
//...
apple aa;
orange oo;
//...
fruitbowl[0] = &aa;
fruitbowl[1] = &oo;
```

However, the exact type of an object entered into such a container class is no longer known by the compiler. For example, in the preceding example you know that an element of the vector is a common, but is it an apple or an orange? Typically, that exact type must be recovered later to enable correct use of the object. To do this you must either store some form of type information in the object itself or ensure that only objects of a given type are put in the container. The latter is trivially achieved using a derived class. For example, you could make a vector of apple pointers:

```
class apple_vector : public cvector {
public:
    apple*& elem(int i)
        { return (apple*&) cvector::elem(i); }
    //...
};
```

using the *type-casting* notation *(type)expression* to convert the common*& (a reference to a pointer to a common) returned by cvector::elem to an apple*&. This use of derived classes provides an alternative to generic classes. It is a bit harder to write (unless macros are used so that derived classes are in fact used to implement generic classes; see §7.3.5), but has the advantage that all derived classes share a single copy of the base class functions. For a generic class such as vector(type), a new copy of those functions must be made (by implement()) for each new type used. The alternative, storing type identification in each object, brings us to a style of programming often referred to as *object based*.

1.18   Virtual Functions

Consider writing a program for displaying shapes on a screen. The common attributes of shapes are represented by class shape, specific attributes by specific derived classes:

```
class shape {
    point center;
    color col;
    //...
public:
    void move(point to) { center=to; draw(); }
    point where() { return center; }
    virtual void draw();
    virtual void rotate(int);
    //...
};
```

Functions that can be defined without knowledge of the specific shape (for example, move and where), can be declared as usual. The rest are declared virtual, that is, to be defined in a derived class. For example:

```
class circle: public shape {
    int radius;
public:
    void draw();
    void rotate(int i) {}
    //...
};
```

Now if shape_vec is a vector of shapes, you can write:

```
for (int i = 0; i<no_of_shapes; i++)
    shape_vec[i].rotate(45);
```

to rotate (and redraw) all shapes 45 degrees.

This style is extremely useful in interactive programs when objects of various types are treated in a uniform manner by the basic software. In a sense, the typical operation is for the user to point to some object and say *Who are you? What are you?* or *Do your stuff!* without providing type information. The program can and must figure that out for itself.

Chapter 2

Declarations and Constants

*Perfection is achieved
only on the point of collapse.
– C.N.Parkinson*

This chapter presents the fundamental types (`char`, `int`, `float`, etc.) and the fundamental ways of deriving new types (functions, vectors, pointers, etc.) from them. A name is introduced into a program by a declaration specifying its type and perhaps an initial value; the concepts of declaration, definition, scope of names, lifetime of objects, and type are presented. The notations for constants in C++ are described, and so are the methods for defining symbolic constants. The examples simply demonstrate language features. A more extensive and realistic example is used to present C++ expressions and statements in the next chapter. The mechanisms for specifying user-defined types with associated operations are presented in Chapters 4, 5, and 6 and are not mentioned here.

2.1   Declarations

Before a name (identifier) can be used in a C++ program it must be declared; that is, its type must be specified to inform the compiler what kind of entity the name refers to. Here are some examples illustrating the diversity of declarations:

```
char ch;
int count = 1;
```

```
char* name = "Bjarne";
struct complex { float re, im; };
complex cvar;
extern complex sqrt(complex);
extern int error_number;
typedef complex point;
float real(complex* p) { return p->re; };
const double pi = 3.1415926535897932385;
struct user;
```

As can be seen from these examples, a declaration can do more than simply associate a type with a name. Most of these *declarations* are also *definitions*; that is, they also define an entity for the name to refer to. For ch, count, and cvar, that entity is an appropriate amount of memory to be used as a variable – that memory will be allocated. For real, it is the specified function. For the constant pi, it is the value 3.1415926535897932385. For complex, that entity is a new type. For point, it is the type complex, so that point becomes a synonym for complex. Only the declarations

```
extern complex sqrt(complex);
extern int error_number;
struct user;
```

are not also definitions. That is, the entity they refer to must be defined elsewhere. The code (body) for the function sqrt must be specified by some other declaration, the memory for the int variable error_number must be allocated by some other declaration of error_number, and some other declaration of the type user must define what that type looks like. There must always be exactly one definition for each name in a C++ program, but there can be many declarations, and all declarations must agree on the type of the entity referred to, so this fragment has two errors:

```
int count;
int count;                        // error: redefinition
extern int error_number;
extern short error_number; // error: type mismatch
```

and this has none (for the use of extern see §4.2):

```
extern int error_number;
extern int error_number;
```

Some definitions specify a "value" for the entities they define:

```
struct complex { float re, im; };
typedef complex point;
float real(complex* p) { return p->re };
const double pi = 3.1415926535897932385;
```

For types, functions, and constants the "value" is permanent; for nonconstant data types the initial value may be changed later:

```
int count = 1;
char* name = "Bjarne";
// ...
count = 2;
name = "Marian";
```

Of the definitions only

```
char ch;
```

does not specify a value. Any declaration that specifies a value is a definition.

2.1.1 Scope

A declaration introduces a name into a scope; that is, a name can be used only in a specific part of the program text. For a name declared in a function (often called a local name), that scope extends from the point of declaration to the end of the block in which its declaration occurs; for a name not in a function or in a class (often called a global name), the scope extends from the point of declaration to the end of the file in which its declaration occurs. A declaration of a name in a block can hide a declaration in an enclosing block or a global name; that is, a name can be redefined to refer to a different entity within a block. After exit from the block the name resumes its previous meaning. For example:

```
int x;              // global x

f() {
    int x;          // local x hides global x
    x = 1;          // assign to local x
    {
        int x;      // hides first local x
        x = 2;      // assign to second local x
    }
    x = 3;          // assign to first local x
}

int* p = &x;        // take address of global x
```

Hiding names is unavoidable when writing large programs. However, a human reader can easily fail to notice that a name has been hidden and some errors caused by this are very difficult to find, mainly because they are rare. Consequently, name hiding should be minimized. Using names such as i and x for global variables or for local variables in a large function is asking for trouble.

It is possible to use a hidden global name by using the scope resolution operator `::`. For example:

```
int x;

f()
{
    int x = 1;      // hide global x
    ::x = 2;        // assign to global x
}
```

There is no way to use a hidden local name.

The scope of a name starts at its point of declaration; this means that a name can even be used to specify its own initial value. For example:

```
int x;

f()
{
    int x = x;      // perverse
}
```

This is not illegal, just silly, and the compiler will warn that **x** has been "used before set" if you try. It is, however, possible to use a single name to refer to two different objects in a block without using the `::` operator. For example:

```
int x = 11;

f()                 // perverse
{
    int y = x;      // global x
    int x = 22;
    y = x;          // local x
}
```

The variable **y** is initialized to the value of the global **x**, 11, and then assigned the value of the local variable **x**, 22.

Function argument names are considered declared in the outermost block of a function, so

```
f(int x)
{
    int x;          // error
}
```

is an error, because **x** is defined twice in the same scope.

2.1.2 Objects and Lvalues

One can allocate and use "variables" that do not have names, and it is possible to assign to strange looking expressions (for example `*p[a+10]=7`).

Consequently, there is a need for a name for "something in memory". Here is the appropriate quote from the C++ reference manual: "An object is a region of storage; an lvalue is an expression referring to an object" (§r.5). The word *lvalue* was originally coined to mean "something that can be on the left-hand side of an assignment." However, not every lvalue may be used on the left-hand side of an assignment; one can have an lvalue referring to a constant (see §2.4).

2.1.3 Lifetime

Unless the programmer specifies otherwise, an object is created when its definition is encountered and destroyed when its name goes out of scope. Objects with global names are created and initialized once (only) and "live" until the the program terminates. Objects defined by a declaration with the keyword `static` behave in this way too. For example†:

```
int a = 1;

void f()
{
    int b = 1;             // initialized at each call of f()
    static int c = 1;   // initialized once only
    cout << " a = " << a++
         << " b = " << b++
         << " c = " << c++ << "\n";
}

main()
{
    while (a < 4) f();
}
```

produces this output

```
a = 1 b = 1 c = 1
a = 2 b = 1 c = 2
a = 3 b = 1 c = 3
```

A `static` variable that is not explicitly initialized is implicitly initialized to zero (§2.4.5).

Using the `new` and `delete` operators, the programmer can also create objects whose lifetime is controlled directly; see §3.2.4.

---

† The `#include <stream.h>` directive has been left out of the examples in this chapter to save space. It is necessary to complete examples producing output.

2.2 Names

A name (identifier) consists of a sequence of letters and digits. The first character must be a letter. The underscore character _ is considered a letter. C++
imposes no limit on the number of characters in a name, but some parts of an
implementation are not under control of the compiler writer (in particular, the
loader), and they, unfortunately, sometimes do. Some run-time environments
also make it necessary to extend or restrict the set of characters accepted in an
identifier; extensions (for example, allowing the character $ in a name) yield
nonportable programs. A C++ keyword (see §r.2.3) cannot be used as a
name. Examples of names:

```
hello    this_is_a_most_unusually_long_name
DEFINED  foO      bAr      u_name   HorseSense
var0     var1     CLASS    _class   ___
```

Examples of character sequences that cannot be used as identifiers:

```
012      a fool   $sys     class    3var
pay.due  foo-bar  .name    if
```

   Upper- and lowercase letters are distinct, so `Count` and `count` are different names, but it is unwise to choose names that differ only slightly from
each other. Names starting with underscore are traditionally used for special
facilities in the run-time environment, so it is unwise to use such names in
application programs.

   When reading a program, the compiler always looks for the longest string
of characters that could make up a name, so `var10` is a single name, not the
name `var` followed by the number `10`, and `elseif` is a single name, not the
keyword `else` followed by the keyword `if`.

2.3 Types

Every name (identifier) in a C++ program has a type associated with it. This
type determines what operations can be applied to the name (that is, to the
entity referred to by the name) and how such operations are interpreted. For
example:

```
int error_number;
float real(complex* p);
```

Since `error_number` is declared to be an `int`, it can be assigned to, used in
arithmetic expressions, etc. The function `real` on the other hand, can be
called with the address of a `complex` as its argument. It is possible to take
the address of either one. Some names, like `int` and `complex`, are names of
types. A type name is typically used to specify the type of another name in a
declaration. The only other operations on a type name are `sizeof` (for determining the amount of memory required to hold an object of the type) and `new`

(for free-store allocation of objects of the type). For example:

```
main()
{
    int* p = new int;
    cout << "sizeof(int) = " << sizeof(int) "\n";
}
```

A type name can also be use to specify explicit conversion from one type to another (§3.2.4). For example:

```
float f;
char* p;
// ...
long ll = long(p);   // convert p to a long
int i = int(f);      // convert f to an int
```

2.3.1 Fundamental Types

C++ has a set of fundamental types corresponding to the most common fundamental storage units of a computer and the most common fundamental ways of using them:

```
char
short int
int
long int
```

to represent integers of different sizes,

```
float
double
```

to represent floating point numbers,

```
unsigned char
unsigned short int
unsigned int
unsigned long int
```

to represent unsigned integers, logical values, bit vectors, etc. For a more compact notation, `int` can be dropped from multiword combinations without changing the meaning; thus `long` means `long int` and `unsigned` means `unsigned int`. In general, when a type is missing in a declaration, `int` is assumed. For example:

```
const a = 1;
static x;
```

each define an object of type `int`.

The integer type `char` is the most suitable for holding and manipulating characters on a given computer; it is typically an 8-bit byte. Sizes of C++

objects are expressed in terms of multiples of the size of a char, so by definition *sizeof(char)≡1*. Depending on the hardware, a char is a signed or an
unsigned integer. The type unsigned char is of course always unsigned and
using it yields more portable programs, but there can be a significant perfor-
mance penalty for using it instead of plain char.

The reason for providing more than one integer type, more than one
unsigned type, and more than one floating point type is to allow the programmer to take advantage of hardware characteristics. On many machines there
are significant differences in memory requirements, memory access times, and
computation speed between the different varieties of fundamental types.
Knowing a machine, it is usually easy to choose, for example, the appropriate
integer type for a particular variable. Writing truly portable low-level code is
harder. This is all that is guaranteed about sizes of fundamental types:

$$1 \equiv sizeof(char) \leq sizeof(short) \leq sizeof(int) \leq sizeof(long)$$

$$sizeof(float) \leq sizeof(double)$$

However, it is usually reasonable to assume that a char can hold integers in
the range 0..127 (it can always hold a character of the machine's character
set), that a short and an int have at least 16 bits, that an int is of a size
appropriate for integer arithmetic, and that a long has at least 24 bits.
Assuming more is hazardous, and even this rule of thumb does not apply
universally. A table of hardware characteristics for a few machines can be
found in §r.2.6.

The unsigned integer types are ideal for uses that treat storage as a bit
vector. Using an unsigned instead of an int to gain one more bit to
represent positive integers is almost never a good idea. Attempts to ensure
that some values are positive by declaring variables unsigned will typically be
defeated by the implicit conversion rules. For example:

```
unsigned surprise = -1;
```

is legal (but the compiler does warn about it).

2.3.2 Implicit Type Conversion

The fundamental types can be mixed freely in assignments and expressions.
Wherever possible, values are converted so as not to lose information. The
exact rules can be found in §r.6.6.

There are cases in which information may get lost or even distorted.
Assignment of a value of one type to a variable of another type with fewer bits
in its representation is necessarily a potential source of trouble. For example,
assume that the following is executed on a machine with two's complement
representation of integers and 8-bit characters:

```
int i1 = 256+255;
char ch = i1;            // ch == 255
int i2 = ch;             // i2 == ?
```

One bit (the most significant!) is lost in the assignment ch=i1, and ch will hold the bit pattern "all ones" (that is, 8 ones); there is no way that this could become 511 when assigned to i2! But what could be the value of i2? On a DEC VAX where a char is signed, the answer is −1; on an AT&T 3B20 where a char is unsigned, the answer is 255. C++ does not have a run-time mechanism for detecting this kind of problem, and compile-time detection is too difficult in general, so the programmer must be careful.

2.3.3 Derived Types

From the fundamental types (and from user-defined types), other types can be derived by using the declaration operators

```
*          pointer
&          reference
[ ]        vector
( )        function
```

and the structure definition mechanism. For example:

```
int* a;
float v[10];
char* p[20];      // vector of 20 character pointers
void f(int);
struct str { short length; char* p; };
```

The rules for composing types using these operators are explained in detail in §r.8.3-4. The basic idea is that the declaration of a derived type mirrors its use. For example:

```
int v[10];        // declare a vector
i = v[3];         // use an element of the vector

int* p;           // declare of a pointer
i = *p;           // use the object pointed to
```

All problems in understanding the notation for derived types stem from the fact that * and & are prefix operators and [ ] and ( ) are postfix, so that parentheses must be used to express types in which the operator precedences are awkward. For example, since [ ] has higher precedence than *:

```
int* v[10];       // vector of pointers
int (*p)[10];     // pointer to vector
```

Most people simply remember how the most common types look.

It can be tedious to use one declaration for each name one wants to introduce into a program, especially if their types are identical. It is, however, possible to declare several names in a single declaration; instead of a single name, the declaration simply contains a list of comma-separated names. For example, one can declare two integers like this:

```
int x, y;        // int x; int y;
```

When declaring derived types one should note that operators apply to individual names only (and not to any other names in the same declaration). For example:

```
int* p, y;       // int* p;  int y;  NOT int* y;
int x, *p;       // int x;  int* p;
int v[10], *p;   // int v[10];  int* p;
```

The author's opinion is that such constructs make a program less readable and should be avoided.

2.3.4 Void

The type `void` behaves syntactically as a fundamental type. It can, however, be used only as part of a derived type; there are no objects of type `void`. It is used to specify that a function does not return a value or as the base type for pointers to objects of unknown type.

```
void f();        // f does not return a value
void* pv;        // pointer to object of unknown type
```

A pointer of any type can be assigned to a variable of type `void*`. At first this may not seem very useful, since a `void*` cannot be dereferenced, but this restriction is exactly what makes the `void*` type useful. Its primary use is for passing pointers to functions that are not allowed to make assumptions about the type of the object and for returning untyped objects from functions. To use such an object, explicit type conversion must be used. Such functions typically exist at the very lowest level of the system where real hardware resources are manipulated. For example:

```
void* allocate(int size);
void deallocate(void*);

f() {
    int* pi = (int*)allocate(10*sizeof(int));
    char* pc = (char*)allocate(10);
    // ...
    deallocate(pi);
    deallocate(pc);
}
```

2.3.5 Pointers

For most types T, T* is the type pointer to T. That is, a variable of type T* can hold the address of an object of type T. For pointers to vectors and pointers to functions, you unfortunately need a more complicated notation:

```
int* pi;
char** cpp;                 // pointer to pointer to char
int (*vp)[10];              // pointer to vector of 10 ints
int (*fp)(char, char*);     // pointer to function
                            // taking (char,char*) arguments
                            // and returning an int
```

The fundamental operation on a pointer is *dereferencing*, that is, referring to the object pointed to by the pointer. This operation is also called *indirection*. The dereferencing operator is (prefix) unary *. For example:

```
char c1 = 'a';
char* p = &c1;              // p holds the address of c1
char c2 = *p;              // c2 = 'a'
```

The variable pointed to by p is c1 and the value stored in c1 is 'a', so the value of *p assigned to c2 is 'a'.

It is possible to perform some arithmetic operations on pointers. Here, for example, is a function that counts the number of characters in a string (not counting the terminating 0):

```
int strlen(char* p)
{
    int i = 0;
    while (*p++) i++;
    return i;
}
```

Another way of finding the length is first to find the end of the string and then subtract the address of the beginning of the string from the address of the end:

```
int strlen(char* p)
{
    char* q = p;
    while (*q++) ;
    return q-p-1;
}
```

Pointers to functions can be extremely useful; they are discussed in §4.6.7.

2.3.6 Vectors

For a type T, T[size] is the type "vector of size elements of type T." The elements are indexed from 0 to size-1. For example:

```
float v[3];       // a vector of 3 floats: v[0], v[1], v[2]
int a[2][5];      // two vectors of five ints
char* vpc[32];    // vector of 32 character pointers
```

A loop for writing out the integer values of the lowercase letters could be written like this:

```
extern int strlen(char*);

char alpha[] = "abcdefghijklmnopqrstuvwxyz";

main()
{
    int sz = strlen(alpha);

    for (int i=0; i<sz; i++) {
        char ch = alpha[i];
        cout << "'" << chr(ch) << "'"
             << " = " << ch
             << " = 0" << oct(ch)
             << " = 0x" << hex(ch) << "\n";
    }
}
```

The function `chr()` returns the string representation of a small integer; for example, `chr(80)` is `"P"` on a machine using the ASCII character set. The function `oct()` produces an octal representation of its integer argument, and `hex()` produces a hexadecimal representation of its integer argument; `chr()`, `oct()`, and `hex()` are declared in `<stream.h>`. The function `strlen()` was used to count characters in `alpha`; alternatively, the size of `alpha` could have been used (§2.4.4). When using the ASCII character set, the output will look like this:

```
'a' = 97 = 0141 = 0x61
'b' = 98 = 0142 = 0x62
'c' = 99 = 0143 = 0x63
...
```

Note that it is not necessary to specify the size of the vector `alpha`; the compiler counts the number of characters in the character string specified as the initializer. Using a string as the initializer for a vector of characters is a convenient, but unfortunately also a unique, use of strings. There is no similar assignment of a string to a vector. For example,

```
char v[9];
v = "a string";           // error
```

is an error since assignment is not defined for vectors.

Obviously strings are only appropriate for initializing vectors of characters; for other types, a more elaborate notation must be used. This notation can also be used for character vectors. For example:

```
int  v1[] = { 1, 2, 3, 4 };
int  v2[] = { 'a', 'b', 'c', 'd' };

char v3[] = { 1, 2, 3, 4 };
char v4[] = { 'a', 'b', 'c', 'd' };
```

Note that **v4** is a vector of four (not five) characters; it is not terminated by a zero, as convention and all library routines require. This notation is also commonly restricted to static objects.

Multidimensional arrays are represented as vectors of vectors, and using comma notation as used for array bounds in some other languages gives compile-time errors because comma (,) is a sequencing operator (see §3.2.2). For example, try this

```
int bad[5,2];            // error
```

and this

```
int v[5][2];
int bad = v[4,1];        // error
int good = v[4][1];      // correct
```

A declaration

```
char v[2][5];
```

declares a vector with two elements, each of which is a vector of type char[5]. In the following example, the first of those vectors is initialized with the first five letters and the second to the first five digits.

```
char v[2][5] = {
    'a', 'b', 'c', 'd', 'e',
    '0', '1', '2', '3', '4'
};

main() {
    for (int i = 0; i<2; i++) {
        for (int j = 0; j<5; j++)
            cout << "v[" << i << "][" << j
                 << "]=" << chr(v[i][j]) << "   ";
        cout << "\n";
    }
}
```

It will produce:

```
v[0][0]=a  v[0][1]=b  v[0][2]=c  v[0][3]=d  v[0][4]=e
v[1][0]=0  v[1][1]=1  v[1][2]=2  v[1][3]=3  v[1][4]=4
```

2.3.7 Pointers and Vectors

In C++, pointers and vectors are very closely related. The name of a vector can also be used as a pointer to its first element, so the alphabet example could be written like this:

```
char alpha[] = "abcdefghijklmnopqrstuvwxyz";
char* p = alpha;
char ch;

while (ch = *p++)
    cout << chr(ch) << " = " << ch
        << " = 0" << oct(ch) << "\n";
```

The declaration of p could also be written

```
char* p = &alpha[0];
```

This equivalence is extensively used in function calls, in which a vector argument is always passed as a pointer to the first element of the vector; thus, in this example,

```
extern int strlen(char*);
char v[] = "Annemarie";
char* p = v;
strlen(p);
strlen(v);
```

the same value is passed to strlen in both calls. The snag is that it is impossible to avoid this; that is, there is no way of declaring a function so that the vector v is copied when the function is called (§4.6.3).

The result of applying the arithmetic operators +, -, ++, or -- to pointers depends on the type of the object pointed to. When an arithmetic operator is applied to a pointer p of type T*, p is assumed to point to an element of a vector of objects of type T; p+1 means next element of that vector and p-1 the previous element. This implies that the value of p+1 will be sizeof(T) larger than the value of p. For example, executing

```
main()
{
    char cv[10];
    int iv[10];

    char* pc = cv;
    int* pi = iv;

    cout << "char* " << long(pc+1)-long(pc) << "\n";
    cout << "int*  " << long(pi+1)-long(pi) << "\n";
}
```

produced

```
char* 1
int*  4
```

since characters occupy one byte each and integers occupy four bytes each on my machine. The pointer values were converted to the type `long` before the subtraction using explicit type conversion (§3.2.5). They were converted to `long` and not to the "obvious" type `int` because there are machines on which a pointer will not fit into an `int` (that is, `sizeof(int)<sizeof(char*)`).

Subtraction of pointers is only defined when both pointers point to elements of the same vector (although the language has no way of ensuring that is the case). When subtracting one pointer from another, the result is the number of vector elements between the two pointers (an integer). One can add an integer to a pointer or subtract an integer from a pointer; in both cases, the result is a pointer value. If that value does not point to an element of the same vector as the original pointer, the result of using that value is undefined. For example:

```
int v1[10];
int v2[10];

int i = &v1[5]-&v1[3];          // 2
    i = &v1[5]-&v2[3];          // result undefined

int* p = v2+2;                  // p == &v2[2]
     p = v2-2;                  // *p undefined
```

2.3.8 Structures

A vector is an aggregate of elements of the same type; a `struct` is an aggregate of elements of (nearly) arbitrary types. For example:

```
struct address {
    char* name;          // "Jim Dandy"
    long  number;        // 61
    char* street;        // "South St"
    char* town;          // "New Providence"
    char  state[2];      // 'N' 'J'
    int   zip;           // 7974
};
```

defines a new type called `address` consisting of the items you need to send mail to someone (`address` is not general enough to handle all mailing addresses, but sufficient as an example). Note the semicolon at the end; it is one of the very few places in C++ where it is necessary to have a semicolon after a curly brace, so people are prone to forget it.

Variables of the type `address` can be declared exactly as other variables, and the individual members can be accessed using the . (dot) operator. For example:

```
        address jd;
        jd.name = "Jim Dandy";
        jd.number = 61;
```

The notation used for initializing vectors can also be used for variables of structure types. For example:

```
        address jd = {
            "Jim Dandy",
            61, "South St",
            "New Providence", {'N','J'}, 7974
        };
```

Using a constructor (§5.2.4) is usually better, however. Note that jd.state could not be initialized by the string "NJ". Strings are terminated by the character '\0' so "NJ" has three characters, that is, one more than will fit into jd.state.

Structure objects are often accessed through pointers using the -> operator. For example:

```
        void print_addr(address* p)
        {
            cout << p->name << "\n"
                 << p->number << " " << p->street << "\n"
                 << p->town << "\n"
                 << chr(p->state[0]) << chr(p->state[1])
                 << " " << p->zip << "\n";
        }
```

Objects of structure types can be assigned, passed as function arguments, and returned as the result from a function. For example:

```
        address current;

        address set_current(address next)
        {
            address prev = current;
            current = next;
            return prev;
        }
```

Other plausible operations such as comparison (== and !=) are not defined. However, the user can define such operators; see Chapter 6.

It is not possible to compute the size of an object of a structure type simply as the sum of its members. The reason for this is that many machines require objects of certain types to be allocated only on some architecture-dependent boundaries (a typical example: an integer must be allocated on a word boundary) or simply handle such objects much more efficiently if they are. This leads to "holes" in the structures. For example, (on my machine) sizeof(address) is 24 and not 22 as one might have expected.

Note that the name of a type becomes available for use immediately after it has been encountered, and not just after the complete declaration has been seen. For example:

```
struct link {
    link* previous;
    link* successor;
};
```

It is not possible to declare new objects of a structure type until the complete declaration has been seen, so

```
struct no_good {
    no_good member;
};
```

is an error (the compiler is not able to determine the size of no_good). To allow two (or more) structure types to refer to each other, it is possible simply to declare a name to be the name of a structure type. For example:

```
struct list;     // to be defined later

struct link {
    link* pre;
    link* suc;
    list* member_of;
};

struct list {
    link* head;
};
```

Without the first declaration of list, the declaration of link would have caused a syntax error.

2.3.9 Type Equivalency

Two structure types are different even when they have the same members. For example:

```
struct s1 { int a; };
struct s2 { int a; };
```

are two different types, so

```
s1 x;
s2 y = x;        // error: type mismatch
```

Structure types are also different from fundamental types, so

```
s1 x;
int i = x;       // error: type mismatch
```

There is, however, a mechanism for declaring a new name for a type without introducing a new type. A declaration prefixed by the keyword `typedef` declares not a new variable of the given type, but a new name for the type. For example:

```
typedef char* Pchar;
Pchar p1, p2;
char* p3 = p1;
```

This can be a convenient shorthand.

2.3.10 References

A *reference* is an alternative name for an object. The primary use of references are in specifying operations for user-defined types; they are discussed in Chapter 6. They can also be useful as function arguments. The notation X& means *reference to* X. For example:

```
int i = 1;
int& r = i;       // r and i now refer to the same int
int x = r         // x = 1
r = 2;            // i = 2;
```

A reference must be initialized (there must be something for it to be a name for). Note that initialization of a reference is something quite different from assignment to it.

Despite appearances, no operator operates on a reference. For example,

```
int ii = 0;
int& rr = ii;
rr++;             // ii is incremented to 1
```

is legal, but `rr++` does not increment the reference `rr`; rather, `++` is applied to an `int` that happens to be `ii`. Consequently, the value of a reference cannot be changed after initialization; it always refers to the objects it was initialized to denote. To get a pointer to the object denoted by a reference `rr`, one can write `&rr`.

The obvious implementation of a reference is a (constant) pointer that is dereferenced each time it is used. This makes initialization of a reference trivial when the initializer is an lvalue (an object you can take the address of; see §r.5). However, the initializer for a T& need not be an lvalue or even of type T. In such cases:

[1] First, type conversion is applied if necessary (see §r.6.6-8, §r.8.5.6);

[2] Then, the resulting value is placed in a temporary variable; and

[3] Finally, the address of this is used as the value of the initializer.

Consider the declaration

```
double& dr = 1;
```

The interpretation of this is:

```
double* drp;       // reference represented as a pointer
double temp;
temp = double( 1 );
drp = &temp;
```

A reference can be used to implement a function that is supposed to change the value of its argument.

```
int x = 1;
void incr(int& aa) { aa++; }
incr(x);                          // x = 2
```

The semantics of argument passing are defined to be those of initialization, so when called, incr's argument aa became another name for x. However, to keep a program readable it is in most cases best to avoid functions that modify their arguments. It is often preferable to return a value from the function explicitly or to require a pointer argument:

```
int x = 1;
int next(int p) { return p+1; }
x = next(x);                      // x = 2

void inc(int* p) { (*p)++; }
inc(&x);                          // x = 3
```

References can also be used to define functions that can be used on both the left- and on the right-hand side of an assignment. Again, many of the most interesting uses of this are found in the design of nontrivial user-defined types. As an example, let us define a simple associative array. First we define struct pair like this:

```
struct pair {
    char* name;
    int val;
};
```

The basic idea is that a string has an integer value associated with it. It is easy to define a function, find(), that maintains a data structure consisting of one pair for each different string that has been presented to it. To shorten the presentation, a very simple (and inefficient) implementation is used:

```
const large = 1024;
static pair vec[large+1];

pair* find(char* p)
/*
    maintain a set of "pair"s:
    search for p, return its "pair" if found
    otherwise return an unused "pair"
*/
```

```
    {
        for (int i=0; vec[i].name; i++)
            if (strcmp(p,vec[i].name)==0) return &vec[i];

        if (i == large) return &vec[large-1];

        return &vec[i];
    }
```

This function can be used by the function value() that implements an array
of integers indexed by character strings (rather than the other way around):

```
    int& value(char* p)
    {
        pair* res = find(p);
        if (res->name == 0) { // hitherto unseen: initialize
            res->name = new char[strlen(p)+1];
            strcpy(res->name,p);
            res->val = 0;       // initial value: 0
        }
        return res->val;
    }
```

For a given argument string, value() finds the corresponding integer object
(*not* the value of the corresponding integer); it then returns a reference to it.
This could be used like this:

```
    const MAX = 256; // larger than the largest word

    main()
    // count the number of occurrences of each word on input
    {
        char buf[MAX];

        while (cin>>buf) value(buf)++;

        for (int i=0; vec[i].name; i++)
            cout << vec[i].name << ": " << vec[i].val << "\n";
    }
```

Each time around the loop reads one word from the standard input string cin
into buf (see Chapter 8), and then updates the counter associated with it by
find(). Finally, the resulting table of different words in the input, each with
its number of occurrences, is printed. For example, given the input

```
    aa bb bb aa aa bb aa aa
```

this program will produce:

```
    aa: 5
    bb: 3
```

It is easy to refine this into a proper associative array type by using a class with the selection operator [ ] overloaded (§6.7).

2.3.11 Registers

On many machine architectures, (small) objects can be accessed notably faster when placed in a register. Ideally, the compiler will determine the optimal strategy for using any registers available on the machine for which a program is compiled. However, that task is nontrivial, so it is sometimes worthwhile for a programmer to give the compiler a hint. This is done by declaring an object `register`. For example:

```
register int i;
register point cursor;
register char* p;
```

Register declarations should only be used when efficiency really is important. Declaring every variable `register` will clutter the program text, and may even increase the code size and the runtime (it typically takes instructions to get an object in and out of a register).

It is not possible to take the address of a name declared `register`, nor can a register be global.

2.4   Constants

C++ provides a notation for values of the fundamental types: character constants, integer constants, and floating point constants. In addition, zero (0) can be used as a constant of any pointer type, and character strings are constants of type `char[]`. It is also possible to specify symbolic constants. A symbolic constant is a name whose value cannot be changed in its scope. In C++, there are three kinds of symbolic constants: (1) any value of any type can be given a name and used as a constant by adding the keyword `const` to its definition; (2) a set of integer constants can be defined as an enumeration; and (3) any vector or function name is a constant.

2.4.1 Integer Constants

Integer constants come in four guises: decimal, octal, hexadecimal, and character constants. Decimal constants are the most commonly used and look as you would expect them to:

```
       0      1234     976     12345678901234567890
```

The type of a decimal constant is `int` provided it fits into an `int`, otherwise it is `long`. The compiler ought to warn about constants that are too long to represent on the machine.

A constant starting with zero followed by x (`0x`) is a hexadecimal (base 16) number, and a constant starting with zero followed by a digit is an octal (base 8) number. Examples of octal constants:

        0   02   077   0123

their decimal equivalents are 0, 2, 63, and 83. These constants look like this in hexadecimal notation

        0x0   0x2   0x3f   0x53

The letters a, b, c, d, e, and f, or their uppercase equivalents, are used to represent 10, 11, 12, 13, 14, and 15, respectively. Octal and hexadecimal notations are most useful for expressing bit patterns; using these notations to express genuine numbers can lead to surprises. For example, on a machine on which an int is represented as a 2's complement 16-bit integer 0xffff is the negative decimal number –1; had more bits been used to represent an integer, it would have been 65535.

2.4.2 Floating Point Constants

A floating point constant is of type double. Again the compiler ought to warn about floating point constants that are too large to be represented. Here are some floating point constants:

        1.23   .23   0.23   1.   1.0   1.2e10   1.23e-15

Note that a space cannot occur in the middle of a floating point constant. For example, 65.43 e-21 is not a floating point constant but four separate lexical tokens

        65.43   e   –   21

and will cause a syntax error.

    If you want a floating point constant of type float, you can define one like this (§2.4.6):

        const float pi8 = 3.14159265;

2.4.3 Character Constants

Even though C++ does not have a separate character data type, but rather an integer type that can hold a character, it does have a special and convenient notation for characters. A character constant is a character enclosed single quotes; for example 'a' and '0'. Such character constants are really symbolic constants for the integer value of the characters in the character set of the machine on which the C++ program is to run (which is not necessarily the same character set as is used on the computer on which the program is compiled). So, if you are running on a machine using the ASCII character set, the value of '0' is 48; but if your machine uses EBCDIC, it is 240. Using

character constants rather than decimal notation makes programs more portable. A few characters also have standard names that use the backslash \ as
an escape character:

```
'\b'    backspace
'\f'    formfeed
'\n'    newline
'\r'    carriage return
'\t'    horizontal tab
'\v'    vertical tab
'\\'    backslash
'\''    single quote
'\"'    double quote
'\0'    null, the integer value 0
```

These are single characters despite their appearance. It is also possible to
represent a character as a one-, two-, or three-digit octal number (\ followed
by octal digits), or as a one-, two-, or three-digit hexadecimal number (\x followed by hexadecimal digits). For example:

```
'\6'            '\x6'           6           ASCII ack
'\60'           '\x30'          48          ASCII '0'
'\137'          '\x05f'         95          ASCII '_'
```

This makes it possible to represent every character in the machine's character
set, and in particular to embed such characters in character strings (see the
next section). Using any numeric notation for characters makes a program
nonportable across machines with different character sets.

2.4.4 Strings

A string constant is a character sequence enclosed in double quotes:

```
"this is a string"
```

Every string constant contains one more character than it appears to have; they
are all terminated by the null character '\0', with the value 0. For example:

```
sizeof("asdf")==5;
```

The type of a string is "vector of the appropriate number of characters", so
"asdf" is of type char[5]. The empty string is written "" (and has the type
char[1]). Note that for every string s, strlen(s)==sizeof(s)-1
because strlen() does not count the terminating 0.

The backslash convention for representing nongraphic characters can also be
used within a string. This makes it possible to represent the double quote and
the escape character backslash \ within a string. The most common such character by far is the newline character, '\n'. For example:

```
cout<<"beep at end of message\007\n";
```

where 7 is the value of the ASCII character `bel`.

It is not possible to have a "real" newline in a string:

```
"this is not a string
but a syntax error"
```

However, a backslash immediately followed by a newline may occur in a string; both will be ignored. For example:

```
cout << "this is \
ok"
```

will print

```
this is ok
```

An escaped newline in a string does not cause a newline to be inserted in the string; it is simply a notational convenience.

It is possible to have the null character in a string, but most programs will not suspect that there are characters after it. For example, the string `"asdf\000hjkl"` will be treated as `"asdf"` by standard functions such as `strcpy()` and `strlen()`.

When embedding a numeric constant in a string using the octal or hexadecimal notation, it is wise always to use three digits for the number. The notation is hard enough to read without having to worry about whether the character after a constant is a digit or not. Consider these examples:

```
char v1[] = "a\x0fah\0129";    // 'a' '\xfa' 'h' '\12' '9'
char v2[] = "a\xfah\129";      // 'a' '\xfa' 'h' '\12' '9'
char v3[] = "a\xfad\127";      // 'a' '\xfad' '\127'
```

Note that a two-digit hexadecimal notation is not sufficient on machines with 9-bit bytes.

2.4.5 Zero

Zero (0) can be used as a constant of any integer, floating point, or pointer type. No object is allocated with the address 0. The type of zero will be determined by context. It will typically (but not necessarily) be represented by the bit pattern *all-zeros* of the appropriate size.

2.4.6 Const

The keyword `const` can be added to the declaration of an object to make that object a constant rather than a variable. For example:

```
const int model = 145;
const int v[] = { 1, 2, 3, 4 };
```

Since it cannot be assigned to, a constant must be initialized. Declaring something const ensures that its value will not change within its scope:

```
model = 165;              // error
model++;                  // error
```

Note that const modifies a type; that is, it restricts the ways in which an object can be used, rather than specifying how the constant is to be allocated. It is, for example, perfectly reasonable, and sometimes useful, to declare a function that returns a const:

```
const char* peek(int i)
{
    return private[i];
}
```

A function such as this could be used to allow someone to read a string that should not be overwritten (by that someone).

However, a compiler can take advantage of an object being a constant in several ways (depending on how smart it is, of course). The most obvious is that typically no store needs to be allocated for a constant since the compiler knows its value. Furthermore, the initializer for a constant is often (but not always) a constant expression; if so, it can be evaluated at compile time. However, it is typically necessary to allocate store for a vector of constants since the compiler cannot in general figure out which elements of the vector are referred to in expressions. On many machines, however, efficiency improvements can be achieved even in this case by placing vectors of constants in read-only storage.

When using a pointer, two objects are involved; the pointer itself and the object pointed to. "Prefixing" a declaration of a pointer with const makes the object, but not the pointer, a constant. For example:

```
const char* pc = "asdf";        // pointer to constant
pc[3] = 'a';                     // error
pc = "ghjk";                     // ok
```

To declare a pointer itself, rather than the object pointed to, to be a constant, the operator *const is used. For example:

```
char *const cp = "asdf";         // constant pointer
cp[3] = 'a';                     // ok
cp = "ghjk";                     // error
```

To make both objects constant both must be declared const. For example:

```
const char *const cpc = "asdf";  // const pointer to const
cpc[3] = 'a';                    // error
cpc = "ghjk";                    // error
```

An object that is a constant when accessed through one pointer may be variable when accessed in other ways. This is particularly useful for function arguments. By declaring a pointer argument `const`, the function is prohibited from modifying the object pointed to. For example:

```
char* strcpy(char* p, const char* q); // cannot modify *q
```

One may assign the address of a variable to a pointer to constant since no harm can come from that. However, the address of a constant cannot be assigned to an unrestricted pointer since this would allow the object's value to be changed. For example:

```
int a = 1;
const c = 2;
const* p1 = &c;         // ok
const* p2 = &a;         // ok
int* p3 = &c;           // error
*p3 = 7;                // change the value of c
```

As usual, if the type is missing in a declaration, `int` is chosen as default.

2.4.7 Enumerations

There is an alternative method for defining integer constants that is often more convenient than using `const`. For example:

```
enum { ASM, AUTO, BREAK };
```

defines three integer constants, called enumerators, and assigns values to them. Since enumerator values are by default assigned increasing from 0, this is equivalent to writing

```
const ASM = 0;
const AUTO = 1;
const BREAK = 2;
```

An enumeration can be named. For example:

```
enum keyword { ASM, AUTO, BREAK };
```

The name of the enumeration becomes a synonym for `int`, not a new type. Declaring a variable `keyword` instead of plain `int` can give both the user and the compiler a hint as to the intended use. For example:

```
keyword key;

switch (key) {
case ASM:
    // do something
    break;
case BREAK:
    // do something
    break;
}
```

causes the compiler to issue a warning because only two out of three `keyword` values are handled.

Values can also be explicitly given to enumerators. For example:

```
enum int16 {
    sign=0100000,
    most_significant=040000,
    least_significant=1
};
```

Such values need not be distinct, increasing, or positive.

2.5 Saving Space

When programming nontrivial applications, there invariably comes a time when one wants more memory space than is available or affordable. There are two ways of squeezing more space out of what is available:

[1] Putting more than one small object into a byte; and

[2] Using the same space to hold different objects at different times.

The former can be achieved by using *fields*, the latter by using *unions*. These constructs are described in the following sections. Since their typical use is purely to optimize a program, and they are more often than not nonportable, the programmer should think twice before using them. Often a better approach is to change the way data is managed; for example, to rely more on dynamically allocated store (§3.2.6) and less on pre-allocated static storage.

2.5.1 Fields

It seems extravagant to use a `char` to represent a binary variable, for example an on/off switch, but a `char` is the smallest object that can be independently allocated in C++. It is possible, however, to bundle several such tiny variables together as *fields* in a `struct`. A member is defined to be a field by specifying the number of bits it is to occupy after its name. Unnamed fields are allowed; they do not affect the meaning of the named fields, but can be used to make the layout better in some machine-dependent way:

```
struct sreg {
    unsigned enable : 1;
    unsigned page : 3;
    unsigned : 1;              // unused
    unsigned mode : 2;
    unsigned : 4;              // unused
    unsigned access : 1;
    unsigned length : 1;
    unsigned non_resident : 1;
};
```

This happens to be the layout of a DEC PDP11/45 status register 0 (assuming that fields are allocated left-to-right in a word). This example also illustrates the other main use of fields: to name parts of an externally imposed layout. A field must be of integer type and is used like other integers, except that it is not possible to take the address of a field. In an operating system kernel or in a debugger, the type sreg could be used like this:

```
sreg* sr0 = (sreg*)0777572;
//...
if (sr0->access) {                  // access violation
    // clean up the mess
    sr0->access = 0;
}
```

However, using fields to pack several variables into a single byte does not necessarily save space. It saves data space, but the size of the code needed to manipulate these variables increases on most machines. Programs have been known to shrink significantly when binary variables were converted from bit fields to characters! Furthermore, it is typically much faster to access a char or a int than to access a field. Fields are simply a convenient shorthand for using logical operators to extract information from and insert information into part of a word.

2.5.2 Unions

Consider designing a symbol table in which an entry holds a name and a value, and the value is either a string or an integer:

```
struct entry {
    char* name;
    char  type;
    char* string_value;    // used if type=='s'
    int   int_value;       // used if type=='i'
};

void print_entry(entry* p)
{
    switch (p->type) {
    case 's':
        cout << p->string_value;
        break;
    case 'i':
        cout << p->int_value;
        break;
    default:
        cerr << "type corrupted\n";
        break;
    }
}
```

Since `string_value` and `int_value` can never be used at the same time, space is clearly lost. It can be easily recovered by specifying that both should be members of a union, like this:

```
struct entry {
    char* name;
    char  type;
    union {
        char* string_value;      // used if type=='s'
        int   int_value;         // used if type=='i'
    };
};
```

This leaves all code using an `entry` unchanged, but ensures that when an `entry` is allocated, `string_value` and `int_value` have the same address. This implies that all the members of a union together only take up as much space as the largest member.

Using a union so that a value is always read using the member it was written with is a pure optimization. However, in large programs, this is not easy to ensure that a union is used in this way only, and subtle errors can be introduced through misuse. It is possible to encapsulate a union so that the correspondence between a type field and the types of the union members can be guaranteed to be correct (§5.4.6).

Unions are sometimes used for "type conversion" (this is mainly done by programmers trained in languages without type conversion facilities, where cheating is necessary). For example, on a VAX this "converts" an `int` to an `int*` simply by assuming bitwise equivalence:

```
struct fudge {
    union {
        int  i;
        int* p;
    };
};

fudge a;
a.i = 4096;
int* p = a.p;    // bad usage
```

However, this is not really a conversion at all; on some machines an `int` and a `int*` do not occupy the same amount of space, and on others no integer can have an odd address. Such use of a union is not portable, and there is an explicit and portable way of specifying type conversion (§3.2.5).

Unions are occasionally used deliberately to avoid type conversion. One might, for example, use a `fudge` to find the representation of the pointer 0:

```
fudge.p = 0;
int i = fudge.i;    // i need not be 0
```

It is also possible to give a union a name; that is, to make it a type in its own right. For example, `fudge` could be declared like this:

```
union fudge {
    int   i;
    int*  p;
};
```

and (mis)used exactly as before. Named unions do, however, also have legitimate uses; see §5.4.6.

2.6 Exercises

1. (∗1) Get the "Hello, world" program (§1.1.1) to run.
2. (∗1) For each of the declarations in §2.1, do the following: If the declaration is not a definition, write a definition for it. If the declaration is a definition, write a declaration for it that is not also a definition.
3. (∗1) Write declarations for the following: a pointer to a character; a vector of 10 integers; a reference to a vector of 10 integers; a pointer to a vector of character strings; a pointer to a pointer to a character; a constant integer; a pointer to a constant integer; and a constant pointer to an integer. Initialize each one.
4. (∗1.5) Write a program that prints the sizes of the fundamental and pointer types. Use the `sizeof` operator.
5. (∗1.5) Write a program that prints out the letters `'a'..'z'` and the digits `'0'..'9'` and their integer values. Do the same for other printable characters. Do the same, but use hexadecimal notation.
6. (∗1) Print out the bit pattern used to represent the pointer 0 on your system. Hint: §2.5.2.
7. (∗1.5) Write a function that prints the exponent and mantissa of a `double` argument.
8. (∗2) What, on your system, are the largest and the smallest value of the following types: `char`, `short`, `int`, `long`, `float`, `double`, `unsigned`, `char*`, `int*`, and `void*`? Are there further restrictions on the values? For example, may an `int*` have an odd value? What is the alignment of objects of those types? For example, may an `int` have an odd address?
9. (∗1) What is the longest local name you can use in a C++ program on your system? What is the longest external name you can use in a C++ program on your system? Are there any restrictions on the characters you can use in a name?
10. (∗2) Define one like this:

```
const one = 1;
```

Try to change the value of `one` to 2. Define `num` as

```
const num[] = { 1, 2 };
```

Try to change the value of num[1] to 2.

11. (*1) Write a function that swaps (exchanges the values of) two integers. Use int* as the argument type. Write another swap function using int& as the argument type.

12. (*1) What is the size of the vector str in the following example:

```
char str[] = "a short string";
```

What is the length of the string "a short string"?

13. (*1.5) Define a table of the names of months of the year and the number of days in them. Write out that table. Do this twice: once using a vector for the names and a vector for the number of days, and once using a vector of structures, each structure holding the name of a month and the number of days in it.

14. (*1) Use typedef to define types: unsigned char, constant unsigned char, pointer to integer, pointer to pointer to char, pointer to vectors of characters, vector of 7 integer pointers, pointer to a vector of 7 integer pointers, and vector of 8 vectors of 7 integer pointers.

Chapter 3

Expressions and Statements

On the other hand,
we cannot ignore efficiency.
— Jon Bentley

C++ has a small, but flexible, set of statement types for controlling the flow of control through a program and a rich set of operators for manipulating data. A single complete example introduces the most commonly used facilities. After that, expressions are summarized, and explicit type conversion and the use of free store are presented in some detail. Then statements are summarized, and finally, indentation style and comments are discussed.

3.1 A Desk Calculator

Statements and expressions are introduced by presenting a desk calculator program that provides the four standard arithmetic operations as infix operators on floating point numbers. The user can also define variables. For example, given the input

```
r=2.5
area=pi*r*r
```

(pi is predefined) the calculator program will write:

```
2.5
19.635
```

where 2.5 is the result of the first line of input and 19.635 the result of the second.

The calculator consists of four main parts: a parser, an input function, a symbol table, and a driver. Actually, it is a miniature compiler with the parser doing the syntactic analysis, the input function handling input and lexical analysis, the symbol table holding permanent information, and the driver handling initialization, output, and errors. There are many features that one could add to this calculator to make it more useful, but the code is long enough as it is (200 lines), and most features would just add code without providing additional insight into the use of C++.

3.1.1 The Parser

Here is a grammar for the language accepted by the calculator:

```
program:
    END                         // END is end-of-input
    expr_list END

expr_list:
    expression PRINT            // PRINT is '\n' or ';'
    expression PRINT expr_list

expression:
    expression + term
    expression - term
    term

term:
    term / primary
    term * primary
    primary

primary:
    NUMBER                      // C++ floating point
    NAME                        // C++ name except '_'
    NAME = expression
    - primary
    ( expression )
```

In other words, a program is a sequence of lines; each line consists of one or more expressions separated by semicolons. The basic units of an expression are numbers, names, and the operators *, /, +, - (both unary and binary), and =. Names need not be declared before use.

The style of syntax analysis used is usually called *recursive descent*; it is a popular and straightforward top-down technique. In a language such as C++, in which function calls are relatively cheap, it is also an efficient technique. For each production in the grammar, there is a function that calls other functions. Terminal symbols (for example, END, NUMBER, +, and -) are recognized by the lexical analyzer, get_token(), and nonterminal symbols are recognized by the syntax analyzer functions, `expr()`, `term()`, and `prim()`. As soon as both operands of a (sub)expression are known, it is evaluated; in a real compiler code is generated at this point.

The parser uses a function `get_token()` to get input. The value of the last call of `get_token()` can be found in the variable `curr_tok`. The value of `curr_tok` is of the enumeration `token_value`:

```
enum token_value {
    NAME,          NUMBER,        END,
    PLUS='+',      MINUS='-',     MUL='*',       DIV='/',
    PRINT=';',     ASSIGN='=',    LP='(',        RP=')'
};
token_value curr_tok;
```

Each parser function assumes that `get_token()` has been called so that `curr_tok` holds the next token to be analyzed. This allows the parser to look one token ahead and obliges every parser function always to read one token more than is used by the production it was called to handle. Each parser function evaluates "its" expression and returns the value. The function `expr()` handles addition and subtraction; it consists of a single loop that looks for terms to add or subtract:

```
double expr()                      // add and subtract
{
    double left = term();

    for(;;)                        // ``forever''
        switch (curr_tok) {
        case PLUS:
            get_token();           // eat '+'
            left += term();
            break;
        case MINUS:
            get_token();           // eat '-'
            left -= term();
            break;
        default:
            return left;
        }
}
```

This function really does not do very much itself. In a manner rather typical of higher-level functions in a large program, it calls other functions to do the work. Note that an expression such as 2-3+4 is evaluated as (2-3)+4, as specified in the grammar.

The curious notation `for(;;)` is the standard way to specify an infinite loop; you could pronounce it "forever." It is a degenerate form of a **for** statement ; while(1) is an alternative. The `switch` statement is executed repeatedly until no + or - is found, and then the `return` statement in the default case is executed.

The operators `+=` and `-=` are used to handle the addition and subtraction; `left=left+term()` and `left=left-term()` could have been used without changing the meaning of the program. However, `left+=term()` and `left-=term()` are not only shorter, but also express the intended operation directly. For a binary operator @, an expression `x@=y` means `x=x@y`, except that `x` is evaluated once only; this applies to the binary operators

$$+ \quad - \quad * \quad / \quad \% \quad \& \quad ! \quad \verb|^| \quad << \quad >>$$

so that the following assignment operators are possible

$$= \quad += \quad -= \quad *= \quad /= \quad \%= \quad \&= \quad != \quad \verb|^|= \quad <<= \quad >>=$$

Each is a separate lexical token, so `a + = 1;` is a syntax error because of the space between the + and the =. (% is the modulo, or remainder, operator; &, !, and ^ are the bitwise logical operators AND, OR, and exclusive OR; << and >> are the left shift and right shift operators.) The functions `term()` and `get_token()` must be declared before `expr()`.

Chapter 4 discusses how to organize a program as a set of files. With one exception, the declarations for this desk calculator example can be ordered so that everything is declared exactly once and before it is used. The exception is `expr()`, which calls `term()`, which calls `prim()`, which in turn calls `expr()`. This loop must be broken somehow; a declaration

```
double expr();   // cannot do without
```

before the definition of `prim()` will do nicely.

Function `term()` handles multiplication and division in the same way:

```
double term()                        // multiply and divide
{
    double left = prim();

    for (;;)
        switch (curr_tok) {
        case MUL:
            get_token();         // eat '*'
            left *= prim();
            break;
        case DIV:
            get_token();         // eat '/'
            double d = prim();
            if (d == 0) return error("divide by 0");
            left /= d;
            break;
        default:
            return left;
        }
}
```

Testing to ensure that one does not divide by zero is necessary since the result of doing so is undefined and usually disastrous. The function error(char*) is described later. The variable d is introduced into the program where it is needed, and it is initialized immediately. In many languages, a declaration can occur only at the head of a block. This restriction can lead to quite nasty contortions of programming style and/or to unnecessary errors. Most often, an uninitialized local variable is simply an indication of bad style; the exceptions are variables that are to be initialized by input operations and variables of vector or structure type that cannot be conveniently initialized by single assignments†. Note that = is the assignment operator, and == is a comparison operator.

The function prim handling a *primary* is of much the same kind, except that because we are getting lower in the call hierarchy a bit of real work is being done and no loop is necessary:

```
double prim()              // handle primaries
{
    switch (curr_tok) {
    case NUMBER:           // floating point constant
        get_token();
        return number_value;
    case NAME:
        if (get_token() == ASSIGN) {
            name* n = insert(name_string);
            get_token();
            n->value = expr();
            return n->value;
        }
        return look(name_string)->value;
    case MINUS:            // unary minus
        get_token();
        return -prim();
    case LP:
        get_token();
        double e = expr();
        if (curr_tok != RP) return error(") expected");
        get_token();
        return e;
    case END:
        return 1;
    default:
        return error("primary expected");
    }
}
```

---

† In a slightly better language these exceptions would also be handled.

When a NUMBER (that is, a floating point constant) is seen, its value is returned. The input routine get_token( ) places the value in the global variable number_value. Use of a global variable in a program often indicates that the structure is not quite clean, that some sort of optimization has been applied. So it is here; ideally, a lexical token typically consists of two parts: a value specifying the kind of token (a token_value in this program) and (when needed) the value of the token. Here, there is only a single simple variable curr_tok, so that the global variable number_value is needed to hold the value of the last NUMBER read. This works only because the calculator always uses one number in the computation before reading another from input.

In the same way that the value of the last NUMBER seen is kept in number_value, the character string representation of the last NAME seen is kept in name_string. Before doing anything to a name, the calculator must first look ahead to see if it is being assigned to or simply used. In both cases the symbol table must be consulted. The table itself is presented in §3.1.3; here it must be observed that it contains entries of the form:

```
struct name {
    char* string;
    name* next;
    double value;
};
```

where next is used only by the functions maintaining the table:

```
name* look(char*);
name* insert(char*);
```

Both return a pointer to a name corresponding to the character string argument; look( ) complains if the name has not been defined. This means that in the calculator a name can be used without previous declaration, but its first use should be as the left hand of an assignment.

3.1.2 The Input Function

Reading input is often the messiest part of a program. The reason is that if a program must communicate with a person, it must cope with that person's whims, conventions, and seemingly random errors. Trying to force the person to behave in a manner more suitable for the machine is often (rightly) considered offensive. The task of a low-level input routine is to read characters one by one and compose higher level tokens from them. These tokens are then the units of input for higher-level routines. Here, low-level input is done by get_token( ). Hopefully, writing a low-level input routine is not an everyday task; in a good system, there will be standard functions for this.

The rules for input to the calculator were deliberately chosen to be somewhat awkward for the stream functions to handle; slight modifications in the token definitions would have made get_token( ) deceptively simple.

The first problem is that the newline character '\n' is significant to the calculator, but the stream input functions consider it a *whitespace* character. That is, to those functions, '\n' is only significant as a token terminator. To cope with this, whitespace (space, tabs, etc.) must be examined:

```
char ch;

do {             // skip whitespace except '\n'
    if(!cin.get(ch)) return curr_tok = END;
} while (ch!='\n' && isspace(ch));
```

The call cin.get(ch) reads a single character from the standard input stream into ch. The test if (!cin.get(ch)) fails if no character can be read from cin; in this case END is returned to terminate the calculator session. The operator ! (NOT) is used since get() returns a nonzero value in case of success.

The (inline) function isspace() from <ctype.h> provides the standard test for whitespace (§8.4.1); isspace(c) returns a nonzero value if c is a whitespace character, zero otherwise. The test is implemented as a table lookup, so using isspace() is much faster than testing for the individual whitespace characters; the same applies to the functions isalpha(), isdigit(), and isalnum() used in get_token().

After whitespace has been skipped, the next character is used to determine what kind of lexical token is coming. Let us look at some of the cases separately before presenting the complete function. The expression terminators '\n' and ';' are handled like this

```
switch (ch) {
case ';':
case '\n':
    cin >> WS;  // skip whitespace
    return curr_tok=PRINT;
```

Skipping whitespace (again) is not necessary, but doing it avoids repeated calls of get_token(). WS is a standard whitespace object declared in <stream.h>; its only use is to discard whitespace. An error in the input or the end of input will not be detected until the next call of get_token(). Note the way several case labels can be used for a single sequence of statements handling those cases. The token PRINT is returned and put into curr_tok in both cases.

Numbers are handled like this:

```
case '0': case '1': case '2': case '3': case '4':
case '5': case '6': case '7': case '8': case '9':
case '.':
    cin.putback(ch);
    cin >> number_value;
    return curr_tok=NUMBER;
```

Stacking case labels horizontally rather than vertically is generally not a good idea since it is much harder to read, but having one line for each digit is tedious. Since operator `>>` is already defined for reading floating point constants into a `double`, the code is trivial: first the initial character (a digit or a dot) is put back into `cin`, and then the constant can be read into `number_value`.

A name, that is a `NAME` token, is defined as a letter possibly followed by some letters or digits:

```
if (isalpha(ch)) {
    char* p = name_string;
    *p++ = ch;
    while (cin.get(ch) && isalnum(ch)) *p++ = ch;
    cin.putback(ch);
    *p = 0;
    return curr_tok=NAME;
}
```

This builds a zero-terminated string in `name_string`. The functions `isalpha()` and `isalnum()` are provided in `<ctype.h>`; `isalnum(c)` is nonzero if `c` is a letter or a digit, zero otherwise.

Here, finally, is the complete input function:

```
token_value get_token()
{
    char ch;

    do {            // skip whitespace except '\n'
        if(!cin.get(ch)) return curr_tok = END;
    } while (ch!='\n' && isspace(ch));

    switch (ch) {
    case ';':
    case '\n':
        cin >> WS;        // skip whitespace
        return curr_tok=PRINT;
    case '*':
    case '/':
    case '+':
    case '-':
    case '(':
    case ')':
    case '=':
        return curr_tok=ch;
    case '0': case '1': case '2': case '3': case '4':
    case '5': case '6': case '7': case '8': case '9':
    case '.':
        cin.putback(ch);
        cin >> number_value;
        return curr_tok=NUMBER;
```

```
        default:                             // NAME, NAME=, or error
            if (isalpha(ch)) {
                char* p = name_string;
                *p++ = ch;
                while (cin.get(ch) && isalnum(ch)) *p++ = ch;
                cin.putback(ch);
                *p = 0;
                return curr_tok=NAME;
            }
            error("bad token");
            return curr_tok=PRINT;
        }
    }
```

Since the `token_value` of an operator was defined as the integer value of the operator, all the operator cases can be handled trivially.

3.1.3 The Symbol Table

The symbol table is accessed by a single function:

```
    name* look(char* p, int ins =0);
```

Its second argument indicates whether the character string is supposed to have been previously inserted. The initializer `=0` specifies a default argument to be used when `look` is called with only one argument. This gives the notational convenience of having `look("sqrt2")` mean `look("sqrt2",0)`; that is, lookup, not insertion. To get the same notational convenience for insertions, a second function is defined:

```
    inline name* insert(char* s) { return look(s,1); }
```

As mentioned previously, table entries are of this type:

```
    struct name {
        char* string;
        name* next;
        double value;
    };
```

The member `next` is used to link names together in the table.

The table itself is simply a vector of pointers to objects of type `name`:

```
    const TBLSZ = 23;
    name* table[TBLSZ];
```

Since all static objects are by default initialized to zero, this trivial declaration of `table` also ensures proper initialization.

To find an entry for a name in the table, `look()` uses a simple hash code (names with the same hash code are linked together):

```
int ii = 0;                                              // hash
char* pp = p;
while (*pp) ii = ii<<1 ^ *pp++;
if (ii < 0) ii = -ii;
ii %= TBLSZ;
```

That is, each character in the input string p is "added" to ii (the "sum" of
the previous characters) by an exclusive or. A bit in x^y is set if and only if
the corresponding bits in the operands x and y are different. Before xor'ing in
a character, ii is shifted one bit to the left to avoid using only one byte of it.
This can also be expressed like this:

```
ii <<= 1;
ii ^= *pp++;
```

Using ^ is marginally better and faster than using +. The shift is essential for
getting a reasonable hash code in both cases. The statements

```
if (ii < 0) ii = -ii;
ii %= TBLSZ;
```

ensure that ii is in the range 0..TBLSZ-1; % is the modulo (also called
remainder) operator.
   Here is the complete function:

```
extern int strlen(const char*);
extern int strcmp(const char*, const char*);
extern char* strcpy(char*, const char*);

name* look(char* p, int ins =0)
{
    int ii = 0;                                          // hash
    char* pp = p;
    while (*pp) ii = ii<<1 ^ *pp++;
    if (ii < 0) ii = -ii;
    ii %= TBLSZ;

    for (name* n=table[ii]; n; n=n->next)        // search
        if (strcmp(p,n->string) == 0) return n;

    if (ins == 0) error("name not found");

    name* nn = new name;                             // insert
    nn->string = new char[strlen(p)+1];
    strcpy(nn->string,p);
    nn->value = 1;
    nn->next = table[ii];
    table[ii] = nn;
    return nn;
}
```

After the hash code `ii` has been calculated, the name is found by a simple search through the `next` fields. Each `name` is checked using the standard string compare function `strcmp()`. If the string is found, its `name` is returned; otherwise, a new `name` is added.

Adding a `name` involves creating a new `name` object on the free store using the `new` operator (see §3.2.6), initializing it, and adding it to the list of names. The latter is done by putting the new name at the head of the list since this can be done without even testing whether or not there is a list. The character string for the name must also be stored away in free store. The function `strlen()` is used to find how much store is needed, `new` is used to allocate it, and `strcpy()` is used to copy the string to that store.

3.1.4 Error Handling

Since the program is so simple, error handling is not a major concern. The error function simply counts the errors, writes out an error message, and returns:

```
int no_of_errors;

double error(char* s) {
    cerr << "error: " << s << "\n";
    no_of_errors++;
    return 1;
}
```

The reason for returning a value is that errors typically occur in the middle of the evaluation of an expression, so that one should either abort that evaluation entirely or else return a value that is unlikely to cause subsequent errors. The latter is adequate for this simple calculator. Had `get_token()` kept track of the line numbers, `error()` could have informed the user approximately where the error occurred. This would have been useful when the calculator was used noninteractively.

Often, a program must be terminated after an error has occurred because no sensible way of continuing has been devised. This can be done by calling `exit()`, which first cleans up things like output streams (§8.3.2) and then terminates the program with its argument as the return value. A more drastic way of terminating a program is a call of `abort()` that terminates immediately, or immediately after storing information for a debugger (a *core dump*) somewhere; please consult your manual for details.

3.1.5 The Driver

With all the pieces of the program in place, we need only a driver to initialize and start things. In this simple example `main()` can do that:

```
int main()
{
    // insert pre-defined names:
    insert("pi")->value = 3.1415926535897932385;
    insert("e")->value  = 2.7182818284590452354;

    while (cin) {
        get_token();
        if (curr_tok == END) break;
        if (curr_tok == PRINT) continue;
        cout << expr() << "\n";
    }

    return no_of_errors;
}
```

Conventionally, main() returns zero if the program terminates normally and nonzero otherwise, so returning the number of errors accomplishes this nicely. As it happens, the only initialization needed is to insert the predefined names into the symbol table.

The primary task of the main loop is to read expressions and write out the answer. This is achieved by the line:

```
    cout << expr() << "\n";
```

Testing cin each time around the loop ensures that the program terminates if something goes wrong with the input stream, and testing for END ensures that the loop is correctly exited when get_token() encounters end-of-file. A statement exits its nearest enclosing switch statement or loop (that is, a for statement, while statement, or do statement). Testing for PRINT (that is, for '\n' and ';') relieves expr() of the responsibility for handling empty expressions. A continue statement is equivalent to going to the very end of a loop, so that in this case

```
    while (cin) {
        // ...
        if (curr_tok == PRINT) continue;
        cout << expr() << "\n";
    }
```

is equivalent to

```
    while  (cin) {
        // ...
        if (curr_tok == PRINT) goto end_of_loop;
        cout << expr() << "\n";
    end_of_loop: ;
    }
```

Loops are described in greater detail in §r.9.

3.1.6 Command Line Arguments

After the program was written and tested, I noticed that typing expressions to standard input was often a bother since a common use was to evaluate a single expression. Were it possible to present that expression as a command line argument, many keystrokes could be avoided.

As mentioned previously, a program starts by calling main(). When this is done, main() is given two arguments specifying the number of arguments, usually called argc, and a vector of arguments, usually called argv. The arguments are character strings so the type of argv is char*[argc]. The name of the program (as it occurs on the command line) is passed as argv[0], so argc is always at least 1. For example, for the command

        dc 150/1.1934

the arguments have these values:

```
argc        2
argv[0]     "dc"
argv[1]     "150/1.1934"
```

It is not difficult to get hold of a command line argument; the problem is how to use it without reprogramming. In this case, it turns out to be trivial since an input stream can be bound to a character string instead of to a file (§8.5). For example, cin can be made to read characters from a string rather than the standard input:

```
int main(int argc, char* argv[])
{
    switch (argc) {
    case 1:                 // read from standard input
        break;
    case 2:                 // read argument string
        cin = *new istream(strlen(argv[1]),argv[1]);
        break;
    default:
        error("too many arguments");
        return 1;
    }

    // as before
}
```

The program is unchanged except for adding the arguments to main() and using them in the switch statement. It would be easy to modify main() to accept several command line arguments, but this does not appear to be necessary, especially as several expressions can be passed as a single argument:

        dc "rate=1.1934;150/rate;19.75/rate;217/rate"

Quotes are necessary here because ; is the UNIX system command separator.

3.2   Operator Summary

The C++ operators are systematically and completely described in §r.7; please read that section. Here, however, is a summary and some examples. Each operator is followed by one or more names commonly used for it and an example of its use. In these examples a *class_name* is the name of a class, a *member* is a member name, an *object* is an expression yielding a class object, a *pointer* is an expression yielding a pointer, an *expr* is an expression, and an *lvalue* is an expression denoting a nonconstant object. A *type* can be a fully general type name (with *, ( ), etc.) only when it appears in parentheses; elsewhere there are restrictions.

Unary operators and assignment operators are right associative; all others are left associative. That is a=b=c means a=(b=c), a+b+c means (a+b)+c, and *p++ means *(p++), *not* (*p)++.

Operator Summary (part 1)		
: :	scope resolution	*class_name* : : *member*
: :	global	: : *name*
->	member selection	*pointer* -> *member*
[ ]	subscripting	*pointer* [*expr*]
( )	function call	*expr* (*expr_list*)
( )	value construction	*type* (*expr_list*)
sizeof	size of object	sizeof *expr*
sizeof	size of type	sizeof (*type*)
++	post increment	*lvalue* ++
++	pre increment	++ *lvalue*
--	post decrement	*lvalue* --
--	pre decrement	-- *lvalue*
~	complement	~ *expr*
!	not	! *expr*
-	unary minus	- *expr*
+	unary plus	+ *expr*
&	address of	& *lvalue*
*	dereference	* *expr*
new	create (allocate)	new *type*
delete	destroy (de-allocate)	delete *pointer*
delete[ ]	destroy vector	delete[*expr*] *pointer*
( )	cast (type conversion)	(*type*) *expr*
*	multiply	*expr* * *expr*
/	divide	*expr* / *expr*
%	modulo (remainder)	*expr* % *expr*
+	add (plus)	*expr* + *expr*
-	subtract (minus)	*expr* - *expr*

Each box holds operators with the same precedence. An operator has higher precedence than operators in lower boxes. For example: `a+b*c` means `a+(b*c)` because `*` has higher precedence than `+`, and `a+b-c` means `(a+b)-c` because `+` and `-` have the same precedence (and because `+` is left associative).

Operator Summary (part 2)		
`<<`	shift left	*lvalue << expr*
`>>`	shift right	*lvalue >> expr*
`<`	less than	*expr < expr*
`<=`	less than or equal	*expr <= expr*
`>`	greater than	*expr > expr*
`>=`	greater than or equal	*expr >= expr*
`==`	equal	*expr == expr*
`!=`	not equal	*expr != expr*
`&`	bitwise AND	*expr & expr*
`^`	bitwise exclusive OR	*expr ^ expr*
`¦`	bitwise inclusive OR	*expr ¦ expr*
`&&`	logical AND	*expr && expr*
`¦¦`	logical inclusive OR	*expr ¦¦ expr*
`? :`	arithmetic if	*expr ? expr : expr*
`=`	simple assignment	*lvalue = expr*
`*=`	multiply and assign	*lvalue *= expr*
`/=`	divide and assign	*lvalue /= expr*
`%=`	modulo and assign	*lvalue %= expr*
`+=`	add and assign	*lvalue += expr*
`-=`	subtract and assign	*lvalue -= expr*
`<<=`	shift left and assign	*lvalue <<= expr*
`>>=`	shift right and assign	*lvalue >>= expr*
`&=`	AND and assign	*lvalue &= expr*
`¦=`	inclusive OR and assign	*lvalue ¦= expr*
`^=`	exclusive OR and assign	*lvalue ^= expr*
`,`	comma (sequencing)	*expr , expr*

3.2.1 Parentheses

Parentheses are overused in the C++ syntax; they have a confusing number of uses: they are used around arguments in function calls, around the type in a type conversion (casts), in type names to denote functions, and also to resolve precedence conflicts. Fortunately, the latter is not necessary very often since precedence levels and associativity rules are defined to make expressions "work as expected" (that is, reflect the most common usage). For example:

```
if (i<=0 || max<i) // ...
```

has the obvious meaning. However, parentheses should be used whenever a programmer is in doubt about those rules, and some programmers prefer the slightly longer and less elegant

```
if ( (i<=0) || (max<i) ) // ...
```

Use of parentheses becomes more common as the subexpressions become more complicated, but complicated subexpressions are a source of errors, so if you start feeling the need for parentheses, you might consider breaking up the expression by using an extra variable. There are also cases when the operator precedence does not result in the "obvious" interpretation. For example:

```
if (i&mask == 0) // ...
```

does not apply a mask to i and then test if the result is zero. Since == has higher precedence than &, the expression is interpreted as i&(mask==0). In this case parentheses are important:

```
if ((i&mask) == 0) // ...
```

It might also be worth noting that the following does not work the way a naive user might expect:

```
if (0 <= a <= 99) // ...
```

It is legal, but it is interpreted as (0<=a)<=99, where the result of the first comparison is either 0 or 1, but not a (except when a is 1). To test whether a is in the range 0..99 one might use

```
if (0<=a && a<=99) // ...
```

3.2.2 Evaluation Order

The order of evaluation of subexpressions within an expression is undefined. For example:

```
int i = 1;
v[i] = i++;
```

may be evaluated as either v[1]=1 or v[2]=1. Better code can be generated in the absence of restrictions on expression evaluation order. It would be nice if the compiler warned about such ambiguities, but most compilers do not.
    The operators

```
        ,        &&        ||
```

guarantee that their left-hand operand is evaluated before their right-hand

operand. For example, b=(a=2,a+1) assigns 3 to b. Examples of the use of
&& and ¦¦ are presented in §3.3.1. Note that the sequencing operator ,
(comma) is logically different from the comma used to separate arguments in a
function call. Consider:

```
f1(v[i],i++);              // two arguments.
f2( (v[i],i++) );          // one argument.
```

The call of f1 has two arguments, v[i] and i++, and the order of evaluation
of the argument expressions is undefined. Order dependence of argument
expressions is very poor style and nonportable. The call of f2 has one argument, the comma expression (v[i],i++), which is equivalent to i++.

Parentheses cannot be used to force evaluation order. For example,
a*(b/c) may be evaluated as (a*b)/c since * and / have the same precedence. When evaluation order is important, one can introduce an extra
(temporary) variable; for example, (t=b/c,a*t).

3.2.3 Increment and Decrement

The ++ operator is used to express incrementing directly, rather than expressing it indirectly using a combination of an addition and an assignment. By
definition ++*lvalue* means *lvalue*+=1 which again means *lvalue*=*lvalue*+1 provided *lvalue* has no side effects. The expression denoting the object to be
incremented is evaluated once (only). Decrementing is similarly expressed by
the -- operator. The operators ++ and -- can be used both as prefix and as
postfix operators. The value of ++x is the new (that is, incremented) value of
x. For example, y=++x is equivalent to y=(x+=1). The value of x++, however, is the old value of x. For example, y=x++ is equivalent to
y=(t=x,x+=1,t) where t is a variable of the same type as x.

The increment operators are particularly useful for incrementing and decrementing variables in loops. For example, one can copy a zero terminated
string like this:

```
inline void cpy(char* p, const char* q)
{
    while (*p++ = *q++) ;
}
```

Remember that incrementing and decrementing of pointers, like addition and
subtraction of pointers, operate in terms of elements of the vector pointed into
by the pointer; p++ makes p point to the next element. For a pointer p of type
T* the following holds by definition:

```
long(p+1) == long(p)+sizeof(T);
```

3.2.4 Bitwise Logical Operators

The bitwise logical operators

&   ¦   ^   ~   >>   <<

are applied to integers; that is, objects of type char, short, int, long, and their unsigned counterparts, and the results produced are integers too.

A typical use of bitwise logical operators is to implement the notion of a small set (a bit vector). In this case, each bit of an unsigned integer represents one member of the set, and the number of bits limits the number of members. The binary operator & is interpreted as intersection, ¦ as union, and ^ as difference. An enumeration can be used to name the members of such a set. Here is a small example borrowed from the implementation (*not* the user interface) of <stream.h>:

```
enum state_value { _good=0, _eof=1, _fail=2, _bad=4 };
```

Defining _good is not necessary; I just wanted a proper name for the state in which there were no problems. The state of a stream can be reset like this:

```
cout.state = _good;
```

One can test whether a stream has been corrupted or an operation has failed like this:

```
if (cout.state&(_bad¦_fail)) // no good
```

The extra parentheses are necessary because & has higher precedence than ¦.

A function that reaches the end of input can report it like this:

```
cin.state ¦= _eof;
```

The ¦= operator is used because the stream might have been corrupted already (that is, state==_bad) so that

```
cin.state = _eof
```

would have cleared that condition. One could find the way the states of two streams differ like this:

```
state_value diff = cin.state^cout.state;
```

For the type stream_state, such a difference is not very useful, but for other similar types it is most useful. For example, consider comparing a bit vector that represents the set of interrupts being handled with another that represents the set of interrupts waiting to be handled.

Note that using fields (§2.5.1) is really a convenient shorthand for shifting and masking to extract bit fields from a word. This can, of course, also be done using the bitwise logical operators. For example, one could extract the middle 16 bits of a 32-bit int like this:

```
unsigned short middle(int a) { return (a>>8)&0xffff; }
```

Do not confuse the bitwise logical operators with the logical operators:

```
&&          ||          !
```

The latter return either a 0 or a 1, and they are primarily useful for writing the test in an if, while, or for statement (§3.3.1). For example, !0 (not zero) is the value 1, whereas ~0 (complement of zero) is the bit pattern all-ones, which typically is the value –1.

3.2.5 Type Conversion

Occasionally it is necessary to convert a value of some type explicitly to a value of another. An explicit type conversion produces a value of one type given a value of another. For example:

```
float r = float(1);
```

converts the integer value 1 to the floating point value 1.0 before the assignment. The result of a type conversion is not an lvalue, so it may not be assigned to (unless the type is a reference type).

There are two notations for explicit type conversion: the traditional C *cast* notation (double)a and the functional notation double(a). The functional notation cannot be used for types that do not have a simple name. For example, to convert a value to a pointer type one must either use the cast notation

```
char* p = (char*)0777;
```

or define a new type name:

```
typedef char* Pchar;
char* p = Pchar(0777);
```

In my opinion the functional notation is preferable for nontrivial examples. Consider these two equivalent examples:

```
Pname n2 = Pbase(n1->tp)->b_name;    // functional notation
Pname n3 = ((Pbase)n2->tp)->b_name; // cast notation
```

Since the -> operator has higher precedence than a cast has, the last expression is interpreted as

```
((Pbase)(n2->tp))->b_name
```

By using explicit type conversion on pointer types it is possible to pretend that an object has any type at all. For example,

```
any_type* p = (any_type*)&some_object;
```

will allow some_object to be manipulated as an any_type through p.

When a type conversion is not necessary it should be avoided. Programs using lots of explicit type conversions are harder to understand than programs that do not. Such programs are, however, easier to understand than programs that simply do not use types to represent higher-level concepts (for example, a program that operates on a device register using shifting and masking on integers rather than defining the appropriate `struct` and operating on that; see §2.5.2). Furthermore, the correctness of an explicit type conversion often depends critically on the programmer's understanding of the ways objects of different types are handled in the language and very often also on details of the implementation. For example:

```
int i = 1;
char* pc = "asdf";
int* pi = &i;

i = (int)pc;
pc = (char*)i;   // beware: pc might change value
                 // on some machines
                 // sizeof(int)<sizeof(char*)
pi = (int*)pc;
pc = (char*)pi;  // beware: pc might change value
                 // on some machines a char*
                 // is represented differently from an int*
```

On many machines, no harm will be done, but on others the results are disastrous. At best, such code is nonportable. It is usually safe to assume that pointers to different structures have the same representation. Furthermore, any pointer can be assigned (without explicit type conversion) to a `void*`, and a `void*` can be explicitly converted to a pointer of any type.

In C++, explicit type conversion is unnecessary in many cases when C (and other languages) needs it. In many programs, explicit type conversion can be completely avoided, and in many other programs its use can be localized to a few routines.

3.2.6 Free Store

A named object is either static or automatic (see §2.1.3). A static object is allocated when the program is started and exists throughout the execution of the program. An automatic object is allocated each time its block is entered and exists only until the block is left. It is, however, often useful to create a new object that exists until it is no longer needed. In particular, it is often useful to create an object that can be used after returning from the function in which it is created. The operator `new` creates such objects, and the operator `delete` can be used to destroy them later. Objects allocated by `new` are said to be *on the free store*. Such objects are typically tree nodes or linked list elements that are part of a larger data structure whose size cannot be known at compile time. Consider how one could write a compiler in the style used for the desk calculator. The syntax analysis functions might build a tree representation of the expressions for use by the code generator. For example:

```
struct enode {
    token_value oper;
    enode* left;
    enode* right;
};

enode* expr()
{
    enode* left = term();

    for (;;)
        switch(curr_tok) {
        case PLUS:
        case MINUS:
            get_token();
            enode* n = new enode;
            n->oper = curr_tok;
            n->left = left;
            n->right = term();
            left = n;
            break;
        default:
            return left;
        }
}
```

A code generator might use the resulting tree like this:

```
void generate(enode* n)
{
    switch (n->oper) {
    case PLUS:
        // do something appropriate
        delete n;
    }
}
```

An object created by new exists until it is explicitly destroyed by delete; then the space it occupied can be reused by new. There is no "garbage collector" that looks out for unreferenced objects and makes them available to new for reuse. The delete operator may be applied only to a pointer returned by new or to zero. Applying delete to zero has no effect.

Vectors of objects can also be created using new. For example:

```
char* save_string(char* p)
{
    char* s = new char[strlen(p)+1];
    strcpy(s,p);
    return s;
}
```

Note that to de-allocate space allocated by new, delete must be able to determine the size of the object allocated. For example:

```
int main(int argc, char* argv[])
{
    if (argc < 2) exit(1);
    char* p = save_string(arg[1]);
    delete p;
}
```

This implies that an object allocated using the standard implementation of new will occupy slightly more space than a static object (typically one word more).

It is also possible to specify the size of a vector explicitly in a delete operation. For example:

```
int main(int argc, char* argv[])
{
    if (argc < 2) exit(1);
    int size = strlen(argv[1])+1;
    char* p = save_string(argv[1]);
    delete[size] p;
}
```

The vector size provided by the user is ignored except for some user-defined types (§5.5.5).

The free store operators are implemented by the functions (§r.7.2.3):

```
void* operator new(long);
void operator delete(void*);
```

The standard implementation of new does not initialize the object returned.

What happens when new can find no store to allocate? Since even virtual memory is finite, this is bound to happen sometime; a request such as

```
char* p = new char[100000000];
```

will typically cause some kind of trouble. When new fails, it calls the function pointed to by the pointer _new_handler (pointers to functions are discussed in §4.6.9). You can set that pointer directly or use the set_new_handler() function. For example:

```
#include <stream.h>

void out_of_store()
{
    cerr << "operator new failed: out of store\n";
    exit(1);
}

typedef void (*PF)();    // pointer to function type

extern PF set_new_handler(PF);

main()
{
    set_new_handler(&out_of_store);
    char* p = new char[100000000];
    cout << "done, p = " << long(p) << "\n";
}
```

will typically never get to write done, but will instead produce

```
operator new failed: out of store
```

A _new_handler might do something more clever than simply terminating the program. If you know how new and delete work, for example, because you provided your own operator new() and operator delete(), the handler might attempt to find some memory for new to return. In other words, a user might provide a garbage collector, thus rendering use of delete optional. Doing this is most definitely not the task for a beginner, though.

For historical reasons, new simply returns the pointer 0 if it cannot find enough store and no _new_handler has been specified. For example:

```
#include <stream.h>

main()
{
    char* p = new char[100000000];
    cout << "done, p = " << long(p) << "\n";
}
```

will produce

```
done, p = 0
```

You have been warned! Note that by providing a _new_handler, one takes care of the check for memory exhaustion for every use of new in the program (except when a user has provided separate routines for handling allocation of objects of specific user-defined types; see §5.5.6).

3.3 Statement Summary

C++ statements are systematically and completely described in §r.9; please read that section. Here, however, is a summary and some examples.

Statement Syntax

statement:
    declaration
    { *statement-list*$_{opt}$ }
    expression$_{opt}$;

    `if` (*expression*) *statement*
    `if` (*expression*) *statement* `else` *statement*
    `switch` (*expression*) *statement*

    `while` (*expression*) *statement*
    `do` *statement* `while` (*expression*) ;
    `for` (*statement expression*$_{opt}$; *expression*$_{opt}$) *statement*

    `case` *constant-expression* : *statement*
    `default` : *statement*
    `break` ;
    `continue` ;

    `return` *expression*$_{opt}$;

    `goto` *identifier* ;
    identifier : *statement*

statement-list:
    statement
    statement statement-list

Note that a declaration is a statement and that there is no assignment statement or procedure call statement; assignment and function call are handled as expressions.

3.3.1 Tests

A value can be tested by either an `if` statement or a `switch` statement:

    `if` (*expression*) *statement*
    `if` (*expression*) *statement* `else` *statement*
    `switch` (*expression*) *statement*

There is no separate boolean type in C++. The comparison operators

```
    ==          !=          <          <=          >          >=
```

return the integer 1 if the comparison is true and 0 otherwise. It is not uncommon to see TRUE defined as 1 and FALSE defined as 0.

In an if statement, the first (or only) statement is executed if the expression is nonzero, and the second statement (if it is specified) is executed otherwise. This implies that any integer expression can be used as a condition. In particular, if a is an integer

```
    if (a) // ...
```

is equivalent to

```
    if (a != 0) // ...
```

The logical operators

```
    &&          ||          !
```

are most commonly used in conditions. The operators && and || will not evaluate their second argument unless it is necessary. For example:

```
    if (p && 1<p->count) // ...
```

first tests that p is nonzero, and only if it is tests 1<p->count.

Some simple if statements can conveniently be replaced by *arithmetic if* expressions. For example:

```
    if (a <= b)
        max = b;
    else
        max = a;
```

is better expressed like this:

```
    max = (a<=b) ? b : a;
```

The parentheses around the condition are not necessary, but I find the code easier to read when they are used.

Some simple switch statements can alternatively be written as a set of if statements. For example:

```
    switch (val) {
    case 1:
        f();
        break;
    case 2;
        g();
        break;
    default:
        h();
        break;
    }
```

could alternatively be expressed as

```
if (val == 1)
    f( );
else if (val == 2)
    g( );
else
    h( );
```

The meaning is the same, but the first (`switch`) version is preferred because the nature of the operation (testing a value against a set of constants) is explicit in that case. This makes the `switch` statement easier to read for nontrivial examples.

Beware that a case of a switch must be terminated somehow unless you want to carry on executing the next case. For example:

```
switch (val) {                          // beware
case 1:
    cout << "case 1\n";
case 2:
    cout << "case 2\n";
default:
    cout << "default: case not found\n";
}
```

with `val==1` prints

```
case 1
case 2
default: case not found
```

to the great surprise of the uninitiated. A **break** is the most common way of terminating a case, but a **return** is often useful, and even a `goto` can sometimes be used. For example:

```
switch (val) {                          // beware
case 0:
    cout << "case 0\n";
case1:
case 1:
    cout << "case 1\n";
    return;
case 2:
    cout << "case 2\n";
    goto case1;
default:
    cout << "default: case not found\n";
    return;
}
```

Called with `val==2`, this produces

```
case 2
case 1
```

Note that a *case label* is not a suitable label for use in a `goto` statement:

```
goto case 1;     // syntax error
```

3.3.2 Goto

C++ possesses the infamous `goto`.

```
goto identifier ;
identifier : statement
```

It has few uses in general high-level programming, but it can be very useful when a C++ program is generated by a program rather than written directly by a person; for example, gotos can be used in a parser generated from a grammar by a parser generator. The `goto` can also be important in the rare cases when optimal efficiency is essential, for example, in the inner loop of some real-time application.

One of the few sensible uses of the `goto` is to break out from a nested loop or switch (a `break` only breaks out of the innermost enclosing loop or switch). For example:

```
for (int i = 0; i<n; i++)
    for (int j = 0; j<m; j++)
        if (nm[i][j] == a) goto found;
// not found
// ...

found:
// nm[i][j] == a
```

There is also a `continue` statement, that in effect goes to the end of a loop statement, as explained in §3.1.5.

3.4   Comments and Indentation

Judicious use of comments and consistent use of indentation can make the task of reading and understanding a program much more pleasant. There are several different consistent styles of indentation used. The author sees no fundamental reason to prefer one over another (though, like most others, I have my preferences). The same applies to styles of comments.

Comments can be misused in ways that seriously affect the readability of a program. The compiler does not understand the contents of a comment, so it

has no way of ensuring that a comment
  [1] is meaningful;
  [2] describes the program; and
  [3] is up to date.
Most programs contain comments that are incomprehensible, ambiguous, and
just plain wrong. Bad comments can be worse than no comments.

If something can be stated *in the language itself*, it should be, and not just
mentioned in a comment. This remark is aimed at comments such as

```
// variable "v" must be initialized.

// variable "v" must be used only by function "f()".

// call function "init()" before calling
// any other function in this file.

// call function "cleanup()" at the end of your program.

// don't use function "weird()".

// function "f()" takes two arguments.
```

Such comments can often be rendered unnecessary by proper use of C++. For
example, one might utilize the linkage rules (§4.2) and the visibility, initialization, and cleanup rules for classes (see §5.5.2) to make the preceding examples
redundant.

Once something has been stated clearly in the language, it should not be
mentioned a second time in a comment. For example:

```
a = b+c;        // a becomes b+c
count++;        // increment the counter
```

Such comments are worse than simply redundant: they increase the amount of
text the reader has to look at, they often obscure the structure of the program,
and they may be wrong.

The author's preference is for
  [1] A comment for each source file stating what the declarations in it have
       in common, references to manuals, general hints for maintenance, etc.;
  [2] A comment for each nontrivial function stating its purpose, the algo-
       rithm used (unless it is obvious), and maybe something about the
       assumptions it makes about its environment;
  [3] A few comments in places where the code is nonobvious and/or non-
       portable; and
  [4] Very little else.
For example:

```
//  tbl.c: Implementation of the symbol table.
```

```
/*
      Gaussian elimination with partial pivoting.
      See Ralston: "A first course ..." pg 411.
*/

//   swap() assumes the stack layout of an AT&T 3B20.

/***********************************

      Copyright (c) 1984 AT&T, Inc.
      All rights reserved

***********************************/
```

A well-chosen and well-written set of comments is an essential part of a good program. Writing good comments can be as difficult as writing the program itself.

Note also that if `//` comments are used exclusively in a function, then any part of that function can be commented out using `/* */` style comments, and vice versa.

3.5 Exercises

1. (*1) Rewrite the following for statement as an equivalent while statement:

   ```
   for (i=0; i<max_length; i++)
       if (input_line[i] == '?') quest_count++;
   ```

   Rewrite it to use a pointer as the controlled variable; that is, so that the the test is of the form `*p=='?'`.

2. (*1) Fully parenthesize the following expressions:

   ```
   a = b + c * d << 2 & 8
   a & 077 != 3
   a == b || a == c && c < 5
   c = x != 0
   0 <= i < 7
   f(1,2)+3
   a = - 1 + + b -- - 5
   a = b == c ++
   a = b = c = 0
   a[4][2] *= * b ? c : * d * 2
   a-b,c=d
   ```

3. (*2) Find 5 different C++ constructs for which the meaning is undefined.
4. (*2) Find 10 different examples of nonportable C++ code.
5. (*1) What happens if you divide by zero on your system? What happens in case of overflow and underflow?

6. (*1) Fully parenthesize the following expressions:

```
*p++
*--p
++a--
(int*)p->m
*p.m
*a[i]
```

7. (*2) Write functions: `strlen()` that returns the length of a string, `strcpy()` that copies a string into another, and `strcmp()` that compares two strings. Consider what the argument types and return types ought to be, then compare with the standard versions as declared in `<string.h>` and specified in your manual.

8. (*1) See how your compiler reacts to these errors:

```
a := b+1;
if (a = 3) // ...
if (a&077 == 0) // ...
```

Devise more simple errors and see how the compiler reacts.

9. (*2) Write a function `cat()` that takes two string arguments and returns a string that is the concatenation of the arguments. Use `new` to find store for the result. Write a function `rev()` that takes a string argument and reverses the characters in it. That is, after `rev(p)` the last character of `p` will be the first, etc.

10. (*2) What does the following example do?

```
void send(register* to, register* from, register count)
// Duff's device. Helpful comment deliberately deleted.
{
        register n=(count+7)/8;
        switch (count%8) {
                case 0: do {    *to++ = *from++;
                case 7:         *to++ = *from++;
                case 6:         *to++ = *from++;
                case 5:         *to++ = *from++;
                case 4:         *to++ = *from++;
                case 3:         *to++ = *from++;
                case 2:         *to++ = *from++;
                case 1:         *to++ = *from++;
                        } while (--n>0);
        }
}
```

Why would anyone write something like that?

11. (*2) Write a function `atoi()` that takes a string containing digits and returns the corresponding `int`. For example, `atoi("123")` is `123`. Modify `atoi()` to handle C++ octal and hexadecimal notation in addition to plain decimal numbers. Modify `atoi()` to handle the C++ character

constant notation. Write a function `itoa()` that creates a string representation of an integer argument.

12. (*2) Re-write `get_token()` (§3.1.2) to read a line at a time into a buffer and then compose tokens by reading the characters in the buffer.

13. (*2) Add functions such as `sqrt()`, `log()`, and `sin()` to the desk calculator from §3.1. Hint: predefine the names and call the functions through a vector of pointers to functions. Don't forget to check the arguments in a function call.

14. (*3) Allow a user to define functions in the desk calculator. Hint: Define a function as a sequence of operations just as a user would have typed them. Such a sequence can be stored either as a character string or as a list of tokens. Then read and execute those operations when the function is called. If you want a user-defined function to take arguments, you will have to invent a notation for that.

15. (*1.5) Convert the desk calculator to use a `symbol` structure instead of using the static variables `name_string` and `number_value`:

```
struct symbol {
    token_value tok;
    union {
        double number_value;
        char*  name_string;
    };
};
```

16. (*2.5) Write a program that strips comments out of a C++ program. That is, read from `cin` and remove both `//` comments and `/* */` comments and write the result to `cout`. Do not worry about making the layout of the output look nice (that would be another, and much harder, exercise). Do not worry about incorrect programs. Beware of `//`, `/*`, and `*/` in comments, strings, and character constants.

17. (*2) Look at some programs to get an idea of the variety of indentation and commenting styles actually used.

Chapter 4

Functions and Files

To iterate is human,
to recurse divine.
– anon

All nontrivial programs are made up of several separately compiled units (conventionally, simply called files). This chapter describes how separately compiled functions can call each other, how separately compiled functions can share data, and how types used in different files in a program can be kept consistent. Functions are discussed in some detail; this includes argument passing, default arguments, function name overloading, pointers to functions, and, of course, declaration and definition of functions. Finally, macros are presented.

4.1 Introduction

Having a complete program in one file is usually impossible since the code for the standard libraries and operating system is elsewhere. Furthermore, having all of the user's own code in a single file is typically both impractical and inconvenient. The way a program is organized into files can help the reader understand the overall structure of a program and enable the compiler to enforce that structure. Since the unit of compilation is a file, all of a file must be recompiled whenever a change (however small) has been made to it. For even a moderately sized program, the amount of time spent recompiling can be significantly reduced by partitioning the program into suitably sized files.

Consider the calculator example. It was presented as a single source file.

If you typed it in, you undoubtedly had some minor trouble getting the declarations in the right order and at least one "spurious" declaration had to be used to allow the compiler to handle the mutually recursive functions `expr()`, `term()`, and `prim()`. The text stated that the program had four parts (a lexical analyzer, a parser, a symbol table, and a driver), but this was in no way reflected in the code itself. Actually, the calculator was not written like that. That is simply not the way to do it; even if all considerations of programming methodology, maintenance, and compilation efficiency were disregarded for this "throw away" program, the author would still partition this 200-line program into several files simply to make the task of programming more pleasant.

A program consisting of many separately compiled parts must be consistent in its use of names and types in exactly the same way as a program consisting of a single source file. In principle, this can be ensured by the linker. The linker is the program that binds together the separately compiled parts. A linker is sometimes (confusingly) called a loader; the UNIX linker is called `ld`. However, the linkers available on most systems provide little support for such consistency checking.

The programmer can compensate for the lack of support from the linker by supplying extra type information (declarations). A program can then be kept consistent by ensuring that the declarations presented in separate compilations are consistent. Your system will have tools to help ensure this. C++ was designed to encourage such explicit linkage†.

4.2 Linkage

Unless otherwise stated, a name that is not local to a function or a class must refer to the same type, value, function, or object in every separately compiled part of a program. That is, there can only be one nonlocal type, value, function, or object in a program with that name. For example, consider two files:

```
// file1.c:
    int a = 1;
    int f() { /* do something */ }

// file2.c:
    extern int a;
    int f();
    void g() { a = f(); }
```

The a and f() used by g() in file2.c are the ones defined in file1.c. The keyword extern indicates that the declaration of a in file2.c is (just)

---

† C was designed to allow implicit linkage in most cases. The use of C has grown dramatically, however, so that the cases in which implicit linkage can be used are now a small minority.

a declaration and not a definition. Had a been initialized, extern would simply be ignored since a declaration with an initializer is always a definition. An object must be defined exactly once in a program. It may be declared many times, but the types must agree exactly. For example:

```
// file1.c:
    int a = 1;
    int b = 1;
    extern int c;

// file2.c:
    int a;
    extern double b;
    extern int c;
```

There are three errors here: a is defined twice (int a; is a definition meaning int a = 0;), b is declared twice with different types, and c is declared twice but not defined. These kinds of errors (linkage errors) cannot be detected by a compiler that looks at only one file at a time. They are, however, detected by the linker.

The following program is not C++ (even though it is C):

```
// file1.c:
    int a;
    int f() { return a; }

// file2.c:
    int a;
    int g() { return f(); }
```

First, file2.c is not C++ because f() has not been declared, so the compiler will complain. Second, (after file2.c is fixed) the program will not link because a is defined twice.

A name can be made local to a file by declaring it static. For example:

```
// file1.c:
    static int a = 6;
    static int f() { /* ... */ }

// file2.c:
    static int a = 7;
    static int f() { /* ... */ }
```

Since each a and f is declared static, the resulting program is correct. Each file has its own a and its own f().

When variables and functions are explicitly declared static, a program fragment is easier to understand (you don't have to look elsewhere). Using static for functions may also have a beneficial effect on the amount of function call overhead by giving an optimizing compiler an easier job.

Consider these two files:

```
// file1.c:
    const a = 7;
    inline int f() { /* ... */ }
    struct s { int a,b; };

// file2.c:
    const a = 7;
    inline int f() { /* ... */ }
    struct s { int a,b; };
```

If the "exactly one definition" rule is applied to constants, inline functions, and type definitions in the same way it is applied to functions and variables, file1.c and file2.c cannot be part of the same C++ program. But if so, how could two files use the same types and constants? The short answer is that types, constants, etc., can be defined as many times as necessary provided they are identically defined. The full answer is somewhat more complicated (as explained in the next section).

4.3   Header Files

The types in all declarations of the same object must be consistent. One way of achieving this would be to provide type-checking facilities in the linker, but most linkers are 1950's designs and cannot be changed for practical reasons†. Another approach is to ensure that the source code, as submitted to the compiler, is either consistent or contains clues that enable the compiler to detect inconsistencies. One imperfect but simple method of achieving consistency for declarations in different files is to include *header files* containing interface information in source files containing executable code and/or data definitions.

The #include mechanism is an extremely simple text manipulation facility for gathering source program fragments together into a single unit (file) for compilation. The directive

```
    #include "to_be_included"
```

replaces the line in which the #include appears with the contents of the file to_be_included. The content should be C++ source text since the compiler will proceed to read it. Often, the inclusion is handled by a separate program, called the C preprocessor, invoked by CC to transform the source file presented by the programmer into a file without include directives before compilation proper is started. Alternatively, the compiler front-end handles these directives as they appear in the source text. If the programmer wants to see the effect of

---

† It is easy to change one linker, but having done that and written a program that depends on the improvements, how do you port that program to other sites?

the include directives, the command

```
CC -E file.c
```

can be used to preprocess `file.c` in the same way as CC would before starting the compiler proper. To include files from the standard include directory, the angle brackets < and > are used instead of quotes. For example:

```
#include <stream.h>     // from standard include directory
#define "myheader.h"    // from current directory
```

Using `<>` has the advantage that the actual name of the standard include directories are not built into the program (often /usr/include/CC is searched first followed by /usr/include). A space is, unfortunately, significant in an include directive:

```
#include < stream.h >    // will not find <stream.h>
```

It may seem extravagant to recompile a file each time it is included somewhere, but the time needed to compile such a file is typically not much different from the time needed to read some precompiled form of it. The reason is that the program text is quite a compact representation of the program, and that the files included typically contain only declarations and not code needing extensive analysis by the compiler.

The following rule of thumb for what may and may not be placed in a header file is not a language requirement, but simply a suggestion of a reasonable way of using the `#include` mechanism.

A header file may contain:

Type definitions	`struct point { int x, y; };`
Function declarations	`extern int strlen(const char*);`
Inline function definitions	`inline char get() { return *p++; }`
Data declarations	`extern int a;`
Constant definitions	`const float pi = 3.141593;`
Enumerations	`enum bool { false, true };`
Include directives	`#include <signal.h>`
Macro definitions	`#define Case break;case`
Comments	`/* check for end of file */`

But never

Ordinary function definitions	`char get() { return *p++; }`
Data definitions	`int a;`
Constant aggregate definitions	`const tbl[] = { /* ... */ };`

On a UNIX system, header files are conventionally suffixed by `.h`. Files containing function or data definitions must be suffixed by `.c`. They are therefore often referred to as ".h files" and ".c files," respectively. Macros are described in §4.7. Note that macros are far less useful in C++ than they are in C because C++ has language constructs such as `const` for defining constants and `inline` for eliminating function call overhead.

The reason for allowing the definition of simple constants, but not the definition of constant aggregates, in header files, is pragmatic. In principle, there is only a problem in allowing replication of definitions of variables (even function definitions could be replicated). However, it is too difficult for an old-fashioned linker to check the identity of nontrivial constants and to remove unnecessary duplicates. Furthermore, the simple cases are far more common and therefore more important for generating good code.

4.3.1 Single Header File

The simplest solution to the problem of partitioning a program into several files is to put the functions and data definitions in a suitable number of source files and declare the types needed for them to communicate in a single header file that all the other files include. For the calculator program, one could use four `.c` files: `lex.c`, `syn.c`, `table.c`, and `main.c`, and a header file `dc.h` containing declarations of every name used in more than one `.c` file:

```
// dc.h: common declarations for the calculator

#include <stream.h>

enum token_value {
    NAME,          NUMBER,        END,
    PLUS='+',      MINUS='-',     MUL='*',        DIV='/',
    PRINT=';',     ASSIGN='=',    LP='(',         RP=')'
};

extern int no_of_errors;
extern double error(char* s);
extern token_value get_token();
extern token_value curr_tok;
extern double number_value;
extern char name_string[256];

extern double expr();
extern double term();
extern double prim();

struct name {
    char* string;
    name* next;
    double value;
};

extern name* look(char* p, int ins = 0);
inline name* insert(char* s) { return look(s,1); }
```

Leaving out the actual code, `lex.c` will look something like this:

```
// lex.c: input and lexical analysis

#include "dc.h"
#include <ctype.h>

token_value curr_tok;
double number_value;
char name_string[256];

token_value get_token() { /* ... */ }
```

Note that using header files in this manner ensures that every declaration of a user-defined object in a header file will at some point be included in the file in which it is defined. For example, when compiling `lex.c` the compiler will be presented with:

```
extern token_value get_token();
// ...
token_value get_token() { /* ... */ }
```

This ensures that the compiler will detect any inconsistencies in the types specified for a name. For example, had `get_token()` been declared to return a `token_value`, but defined to return an `int`, the compilation of `lex.c` would have failed with a type-mismatch error.

File `syn.c` will look like this:

```
// syn.c: syntax analysis and evaluation

#include "dc.h"

double prim() { /* ... */ }
double term() { /* ... */ }
double expr() { /* ... */ }
```

File `table.c` will look like this:

```
// table.c: symbol table and lookup

#include "dc.h"

extern char* strcmp(const char*, const char*);
extern char* strcpy(char*, const char*);
extern int strlen(const char*);

const TBLSZ = 23;
name* table[TBLSZ];

name* look(char* p, int ins) { /* ... */ }
```

Note that `table.c` itself declares the standard string manipulation functions, so there are no consistency checks on those declarations. It is nearly always better to include a header file than to declare a name `extern` in a `.c` file. This may involve including "too much", but that usually does not seriously affect the time needed for the compilation and will typically save time for the programmer. As an example of this, note how `strlen()` is redeclared again in `main.c` (below). This is a waste of keystrokes and a potential cause of trouble since the compiler cannot check the consistency of those two declarations. Naturally, this problem could have been avoided had every `extern` declaration been placed in `dc.h`, as was intended. This "sloppiness" was left in the program because it is very common in C programs, is very tempting to the programmer, and more often than not leads to errors that are hard to detect and programs that are hard to maintain. You have been warned!

Finally, file `main.c` will look like this:

```
// main.c: initialization, main loop, and error handling

#include "dc.h"

int no_of_errors;

double error(char* s) { /* ... */ }

extern int strlen(const char*);

main(int argc, char* argv[]) { /* ... */ }
```

There is an important case in which the size of header files becomes a serious nuisance. A set of header files and a library can be used to extend the language with a set of general and application-specific types (see Chapters 5-8). In such cases, it is not unusual to find thousands of lines of header files read at the start of every compilation. The contents of those files are usually "frozen" and change only very infrequently. A technique for starting the compiler *primed* with the contents of those header files can be most useful; in a sense one is creating a special purpose language with its own compiler. No standard procedure for creating such a primed compiler has been established.

4.3.2 Multiple Header Files

The single-header style of program partitioning is most useful when the program is small and its parts are not intended to be used separately. Then, it is not serious that it is not possible to determine which declarations are placed in the header file for what reason. Comments can be a help. An alternative is to let each part of a program have its own header file defining the facilities it provides. Each `.c` file then has a corresponding `.h` file, and each `.c` file includes its own `.h` file (specifying what it provides) and maybe also some other `.h` files (specifying what it needs).

Considering this organization for the calculator, we note that `error()` is used by just about every function in the program, and itself uses only `<stream.h>`. This is typical for error functions, and implies that `error()` should be separate from `main()`:

```
// error.h: error handling

extern int no_errors;

extern double error(char* s);

// error.c

#include <stream.h>
#include "error.h"

int no_of_errors;

double error(char* s) { /* ... */ }
```

In this style of use of header files, a `.h` file and its associated `.c` file can be seen as a module in which the `.h` file specifies an interface and the `.c` file specifies an implementation.

The symbol table is independent of the rest of the calculator except for the use of the error function. This can now be made explicit:

```
// table.h: symbol table declarations

struct name {
    char* string;
    name* next;
    double value;
};

extern name* look(char* p, int ins = 0);
inline name* insert(char* s) { return look(s,1); }

// table.c: symbol table definitions

#include "error.h"
#include <string.h>
#include "table.h"

const TBLSZ = 23;
name* table[TBLSZ];

name* look(char* p, int ins) { /* ... */ }
```

Note that the declarations of string manipulating functions are now included from `<string.h>`. This removes yet another potential source of errors.

```
// lex.h: input and lexical analysis declarations

enum token_value {
    NAME,          NUMBER,        END,
    PLUS='+',      MINUS='-',     MUL='*',        DIV='/',
    PRINT=';',     ASSIGN='=',    LP='(',         RP=')'
};

extern token_value curr_tok;
extern double number_value;
extern char name_string[256];

extern token_value get_token();
```

This interface to the lexical analyzer is quite messy. The lack of a proper token type shows itself in the need to present a user of `get_token()` with the actual lexical buffers `number_value` and `name_string`.

```
// lex.c: input and lexical analysis definitions

#include <stream.h>
#include <ctype.h>
#include "error.h"
#include "lex.h"

token_value curr_tok;
double number_value;
char name_string[256];

token_value get_token() { /* ... */ }
```

The interface to the syntax analyzer is particularly clean:

```
// syn.h: declarations for syntax analysis and evaluation

extern double expr();
extern double term();
extern double prim();

// syn.c: definitions for syntax analysis and evaluation

#include "error.h"
#include "lex.h"
#include "syn.h"

double prim() { /* ... */ }
double term() { /* ... */ }
double expr() { /* ... */ }
```

The main program is, as usual, trivial:

```
// main.c: the main program

#include <stream.h>
#include "error.h"
#include "lex.h"
#include "syn.h"
#include "table.h"
#include <string.h>

main(int argc, char* argv[]) { /* ... */ }
```

How many header files to use for a program is a function of many factors. Many of these factors have more to do with the way files are handled on your system than with C++. For example, if your editor does not have facilities for looking at several files at the same time, using many header files becomes less attractive. Similarly, if opening and reading 10 files of 50 lines each is noticeably more time consuming than reading a single file of 500 lines, you might think twice before using the multiple header file style for a small project. A word of caution: a set of 10 header files plus the standard header files is usually manageable. However, if you partition the declarations of a large program into the logically minimal-sized header files (putting each structure declaration in its own file, etc.), you can easily get an unmanageable mess of hundreds of files.

4.3.3 Data Hiding

Using header files, a user can define explicit interfaces to ensure consistent use of types in a program. However, a user can bypass the interface provided by a header file by inserting `extern` declarations into `.c` files.

Note that the following style of linkage is *not* recommended:

```
// file1.c:      // "extern" not used
   int a = 7;
   const c = 8;
   void f(long) { /* ... */ }

// file2.c:      // "extern" in .c file
   extern int a;
   extern const c;
   extern f(int);
   int g() { return f(a+c); }
```

Since the `extern` declarations in `file2.c` are not included with the definitions in `file1.c`, the compiler cannot check the consistency of this program. Consequently, unless the loader is much smarter than average, the two errors in this program will be left for the programmer to find.

A user can protect a file against such undisciplined linkage by declaring names that are not intended for general use static so that they have file scope and are hidden from other parts of a program. For example:

```
// table.c: symbol table definitions

#include "error.h"
#include <string.h>
#include "table.h"

const TBLSZ = 23;
static name* table[TBLSZ];

name* look(char* p, int ins) { /* ... */ }
```

This will ensure that all access to the table really does go through look(). It is not necessary to "hide" the constant TBLSZ.

4.4   Files as Modules

In the preceding section, a .c and a .h file together define a part of a program. The .h file is the interface used by other parts of a program; the .c file specifies the implementation. Such an entity is often called a module. Only names that a user needs to know are made available, and the rest are hidden. This property is often called *data hiding*, even though data is only one of the things that can be hidden. This kind of module provides great flexibility. For example, an implementation can consist of one or more .c files, and several different interfaces can be provided in the form of .h files. Information that a user need not know about is neatly hidden away in the .c files. If it is considered important that a user should not know exactly what the .c files contain, they need not be made available in source form. The equivalent compiler output files (.o files) are sufficient.

It is sometimes a problem that this flexibility is achieved without a formal structure. The language itself does not recognize such a *module* as an entity, and there is no way for the compiler to distinguish between the .h files that define names to be used by other modules (exported) from the .h files used to declare names from other modules (imported).

At other times, it can be a problem that a module defines a set of objects, not a new type. For example, the table module defines one table; if you want two tables, there is no trivial way of providing the other using this idea of modules; Chapter 5 presents a solution to this problem.

Every statically allocated object is initialized to zero by default and other (constant) values can be specified by the programmer. This is only a very primitive form of initialization. Fortunately, using classes, one can specify code to be executed for initialization before any use is made of the module and/or code to be run to clean up after the last use of the module; see §5.5.2.

4.5   How to Make a Library

Phrases such as "put in a library" and "found in some library" are used often (in this book and elsewhere), but what does that mean for a C++ program? Unfortunately, the answer depends on the operating system used; but this section explains how to make and use a library on an 8th edition UNIX system. Other systems provide similar facilities.

A library is basically a set of .o files obtained by compiling a corresponding set of .c files. There typically are one or more .h files containing the declarations necessary to use those .o files. As an example, consider having to provide (in a convenient way) a set of mathematical functions for some unspecified set of users. The header file could look like this:

```
extern double sqrt(double);      // subset of <math.h>
extern double sin(double);
extern double cos(double);
extern double exp(double);
extern double log(double);
```

and the definitions of these functions would be stored in files sqrt.c, sin.c, cos.c, exp.c, and log.c, respectively.

A library called math.a can be made like this

```
$ CC -c sqrt.c sin.c cos.c expr.c log.c
$ ar cr math.a sqrt.o sin.o cos.o expr.o log.o
$ ranlib math.a
```

The source files are first compiled giving the equivalent object files. The ar command is then used to make an archive called math.a. Finally, that archive is indexed for faster access. If your system does not have a ranlib command, you probably do not need it; please look in your manual under ar for details. The library can be used like this:

```
$ CC myprog.c math.a
```

Now, what advantage is there in using math.a instead of simply using the .o files directly? For example:

```
$ CC myprog.c sqrt.o sin.o cos.o expr.o log.o
```

For most programs, finding the right set of .o files is distinctly nontrivial. In the example above, they were all included, but if functions in myprog.c call only the functions sqrt() and cos() then it appears that:

```
$ CC myprog.c sqrt.o cos.o
```

would be sufficient. It is not because cos.c uses sin.c.

The linker that the CC command calls to handle a .a file (in this case, math.a) knows how to extract only the necessary .o files from the set that was used to create the .a file.

In other words, using a library, one can include many definitions using a single name (including definitions of functions and variables used by internal functions and never seen by the user), yet at the same time ensure that only the minimal number of definitions is included in the resulting program.

4.6 Functions

The typical way of getting something done in a C++ program is to call a function to do it. Defining a function is the way to specify how an operation is to be done. A function cannot be called unless it is declared.

4.6.1 Function Declarations

A function declaration gives the name of the function, the type of the value returned (if any) by the function, and the number and types of the arguments that must be supplied in a call of the function. For example,

```
extern double sqrt(double);
extern elem* next_elem();
extern char* strcpy(char* to, const char* from);
extern void exit(int);
```

The semantics of argument passing are identical to the semantics of initialization. Argument types are checked and implicit argument type conversion takes place when necessary. For example, given the preceding declarations

```
double sr2 = sqrt(2);
```

will correctly call the function sqrt( ) with the floating point value 2.0. The value of this checking and type conversion is enormous.

A function declaration may contain argument names. This can be a help to the reader, but the compiler simply ignores such names.

4.6.2 Function Definitions

Every function that is called in a program must be defined somewhere (once only). A function definition is a function declaration in which the body of the function is presented. For example:

```
extern void swap(int*, int*);    // a declaration

void swap(int* p, int* q)        // a definition
{
    int t = *p;
    *p = *q;
    *q = t;
}
```

A function may be declared inline to avoid function call overhead (§1.12), and arguments may be declared register to provide faster access to them (§2.3.11). Both features can be misused, and they should be avoided wherever there are any doubts about their usefulness.

4.6.3 Argument Passing

When a function is called store is set aside for its formal arguments and each formal argument is initialized by its corresponding actual argument. The semantics of argument passing are identical to the semantics of initialization. In particular, the type of an actual argument is checked against the type of the corresponding formal argument and all standard and user-defined type conversions are performed. There are special rules for passing vectors (§4.6.5), a facility for passing unchecked arguments (§4.6.8), and a facility for specifying default arguments (§4.6.6). Consider:

```
void f(int val, int& ref)
{
    val++;
    ref++;
}
```

When f() is called, val++ increments a local copy of the first actual argument whereas ref++ increments the second actual argument. For example,

```
int i = 1;
int j = 1;
f(i,j);
```

will increment j but not i. The first argument, i, is passed *by value*, the second argument, j, is passed *by reference*. As was mentioned in §2.3.10, using functions that modify call-by-reference arguments can make programs hard to read, and should generally be avoided (but see §6.5 and §8.4). It can, however, be noticeably more efficient to pass a large object by reference than to pass it by value. In that case, the argument might be declared const to indicate that the reference is used for efficiency reasons only and not to enable the called function to change the value of the object:

```
void f(const large& arg)
{
    // the value of "arg" cannot be changed
}
```

Similarly, declaring a pointer argument const tells readers that the value of an object pointed to by that argument is not changed by the function. For example:

```
extern int strlen(const char*);          // from <string.h>
extern char* strcpy(char* to, const char* from);
extern int strcmp(const char*, const char*);
```

The importance of this practice increases with the size of a program.

Note that the semantics of argument passing are different from the semantics of assignment. This is important for `const` arguments, reference arguments, and for arguments of some user-defined types (§6.6).

4.6.4 Value Return

A value can (and should) be returned from a function that is not declared `void`. A return value is specified by a return statement. For example:

```
int fac(int n) { return (n>1) ? n*fac(n-1) : 1; }
```

There can be more than one return statement in a function:

```
int fac(int n)
{
    if (n > 1)
        return n*fac(n-1);
    else
        return 1;
}
```

Like the semantics of argument passing, the semantics of function value return are identical to the semantics of initialization. A return statement is considered to initialize a variable of the returned type. The type of a return expression is checked against the type of the returned type and all standard and user-defined type conversions are performed. For example:

```
double f()
{
    // ...
    return 1;    // implicitly converted to double(1)
}
```

Each time a function is called a new copy of its arguments and automatic variables is created. The store is reused after the function returns, so it is unwise to return a pointer to a local variable. The contents of the location pointed to will change unpredictably:

```
int* f() {
    int local = 1;
    // ...
    return &local;      // don't do this
}
```

This error is less common than the equivalent error using references:

```
int& f() {
    int local = 1;
    // ...
    return local;       // don't do this
}
```

Fortunately the compiler warns about such return values. Here is another example:

```
int& f() { return 1; }  // don't do this
```

4.6.5 Vector Arguments

If a vector is used as a function argument, a pointer to its first element is passed. For example:

```
int strlen(const char*);

void f()
{
    char v[] = "a vector";
    strlen(v);
    strlen("Nicholas");
};
```

In other words, an argument of type T[ ] will be converted to a T* when passed as an argument. This implies that an assignment to an element of a vector argument changes the value of an element of the argument vector. In other words, vectors differ from other types in that a vector is not (and cannot be) passed by value.

The size of a vector is not available to the called function. This can be a nuisance, but there are several ways of circumventing this problem. Strings are zero-terminated, so their size can be computed easily. For other vectors a second argument specifying the size can be passed, or a type containing a pointer and a length indicator can be defined and passed instead of a plain vector (see also §1.11). For example:

```
void compute1(int* vec_ptr, int vec_size); // one way

struct vec {                               // another way
    int* ptr;
    int size;
};

void compute2(vec v);
```

Multidimensional arrays are trickier, but often vectors of pointers can be used instead, and they need no special treatment. For example:

```
char* day[] = {
    "mon", "tue", "wed", "thu", "fri", "sat", "sun"
};
```

However, consider defining a function manipulating a two-dimensional matrix. If the dimensions are known at compile time, there is no problem:

```
void print_m34(int m[3][4])
{
    for (int i = 0; i<3; i++) {
        for (int j = 0; j<4; j++)
            cout << " " << m[i][j];
        cout << "\n";
    }
}
```

The matrix is, of course, still passed as a pointer, and the dimensions are used simply for notational convenience.

The first dimension of an array is irrelevant to the problem of finding the location of an element (§2.3.6). It can therefore be passed as an argument:

```
void print_mi4(int m[][4], int dim1)
{
    for (int i = 0; i<dim1; i++) {
        for (int j = 0; j<4; j++)
            cout << " " << m[i][j];
        cout << "\n";
    }
}
```

The difficult case is when both dimensions need to be passed. The "obvious solution" simply does not work:

```
void print_mij(int m[][], int dim1, int dim2) // error
{
    for (int i = 0; i<dim1; i++) {
        for (int j = 0; j<dim2; j++)
            cout << " " << m[i][j];               // surprise!
        cout << "\n";
    }
}
```

First, the argument declaration m[][] is illegal since the second dimension of a multidimensional array must be known to find the location of an element. Secondly, the expression m[i][j] is (correctly) interpreted as *(*(m+i)+j), but that is unlikely to be what the programmer intended. A correct solution is:

```
void print_mij(int** m, int dim1, int dim2)
{
    for (int i = 0; i<dim1; i++) {
        for (int j = 0; j<dim2; j++)
            cout << " " << ((int*)m)[i*dim2+j]; // obscure
        cout << "\n";
    }
}
```

The expression used for accessing the members is equivalent to the one the compiler generates when it knows the last dimension. An extra variable could be introduced to make the code slightly less obscure:

```
int* v = (int*)m;
// ...
v[i*dim2+j]
```

4.6.6 Default Arguments

A function often needs more arguments in the most general case than are needed in the simplest, and often most common, case. For example, the stream library has a function hex() that produces a string containing the hexadecimal representation of an integer. A second integer argument is used to specify the number of characters available for representing the first argument. If the number of characters is too small to represent the integer, truncation occurs; if it is too large, the string is padded with spaces. Often, the programmer does not care about the number of characters needed to represent the integer as long as there are enough, so a zero as the second argument is defined to mean "use just the right number of characters." To avoid littering the program with calls such as hex(i,0), the function is declared like this:

```
extern char* hex(long, int =0);
```

The initializer for the second argument is a *default argument*. That is, if only one argument is present in a call, the default is used as the second. For example:

```
cout << "**" << hex(31) << hex(32,3) << "**";
```

is interpreted as

```
cout << "**" << hex(31,0) << hex(32,3) << "**";
```

and will print:

```
**1f 20**
```

A default argument is type checked at the time of the function declaration and evaluated at the time of the call. It is possible to provide default arguments for trailing arguments only, so

```
int f(int, int =0, char* =0);   // ok
int g(int =0, int =0, char*);   // error
int h(int =0, int, char* =0);   // error
```

Note that the space between the * and the = is significant in this context (*= is an assignment operator):

```
int nasty(char*=0);             // syntax error
```

4.6.7 Overloaded Function Names

Most often, it is a good idea to give different functions different names, but when some functions perform the same task on objects of different types, it can be more convenient to give them the same name. Using the same name for different operations on different types is called *overloading*. The technique is already used for the basic operations in C++: there is only one name for addition, +, but it can be used to add values of integer, floating-point, and pointer types. This idea is easily extended to handle operations defined by the programmer, that is, functions. To protect the programmer against accidental reuse of a name, a name can be used for more than one function only if it is first declared to be overloaded. For example:

```
overload print;
void print(int);
void print(char*);
```

As far as the compiler is concerned, the only thing functions of the same name have in common is that name. Presumably, they are in some sense similar, but the language does not constrain or aid the programmer. Thus, overloaded function names are primarily a notational convenience. This convenience is significant for functions with conventional names such as sqrt, print, and open. When a name is semantically significant, as with operators such as +, *, and << (§6.2) and in the case of constructors (§5.2.4 and §6.3.1), this convenience becomes essential. When an overloaded function f is called, the compiler must figure out which of the functions with the name f is to be invoked. This is done by comparing the types of the actual arguments with the types of the formal arguments of all the functions called f. Finding which function to call is done in three separate steps:

[1] Look for an exact match and use that function if found;
[2] Look for a match using built-in conversions and use any function found; and
[3] Look for a match using user-defined conversions (§6.3), and if there is a unique set of conversions, use the function found.

For example:

```
overload print(double), print(int);

void f()
{
    print(1);
    print(1.0);
}
```

The exact-match rule ensures that f will print 1 as an integer and 1.0 as a floating-point number. A zero, char, or short is an exact match for an int argument. Similarly, a float is an exact match for a double.

For arguments to functions with overloaded names, the C++ standard conversion rules (§r.6.6) do not fully apply. The conversions that may destroy information are not performed, leaving int to long, int to double, zero to long, zero to double, and the pointer conversions: zero to pointer, pointer to void*, and pointer to derived class to pointer to base class (§7.2.4).

Here is an example in which conversion is necessary:

```
overload print(double), print(long);

void f(int a)
{
    print(a);
}
```

Here a may be printed as either a double or a long. The ambiguity can be resolved by use of explicit type conversion (either print(long(a)) or print(double(a))).

Given these rules, one can ensure that the simplest algorithm (function) will be used when the efficiency or precision of computations differ significantly for the types involved. For example:

```
overload pow;
int pow(int, int);
double pow(double, double);       // from <math.h>
complex pow(double, complex);     // from <complex.h>
complex pow(complex, int);
complex pow(complex, double);
complex pow(complex, complex);
```

The process of finding a match ignores unsigned and const.

4.6.8 Unspecified Number of Arguments

For some functions, it is not possible to specify the number and type of all arguments expected in a call. Such a function is declared by terminating the list of argument declarations with the ellipsis (. . .) which means "and maybe some more arguments." For example:

```
int printf(char* ...);
```

This specifies that a call of printf must have at least one argument, a char*, but may or may not have others. For example:

```
printf("Hello, world\n");
printf("My name is %s %s\n", first_name, second_name);
printf("%d + %d = %d\n",2,3,5);
```

Such a function must rely on information not available to the compiler when interpreting its argument list. In the case of printf(), the first argument is a format string containing special character sequences that allow `printf()` to handle other arguments correctly; `%s` means "expect a `char*` argument" and `%d` means "expect an `int` argument." However, the compiler does not know that, so it cannot ensure that the expected arguments are really there, or that an argument is of the proper type. For example:

```
printf("My name is %s %s\n",2);
```

will compile and (at best) cause some strange looking output.

Clearly, if an argument has not been declared, the compiler does not have the information needed to perform the standard type checking and type conversion for it. In this case, a `char` or a `short` is passed as an `int`, and a `float` is passed as a `double`. This is not necessarily what the user expects.

The extreme use of the ellipsis, as in `wild(...)`, turns off argument checking completely, leaving the programmer open to a host of problems well known to C programmers. A well-designed program needs at most a few functions for which the argument types are not completely specified. Overloaded functions and functions using default arguments can be used to take care of type checking in most cases when one would otherwise consider leaving argument types unspecified. Only when both the number of arguments *and* the type of arguments vary is the ellipsis necessary. The most common use of the ellipsis is to specify an interface to C library functions that were defined when the alternatives were not available:

```
extern int fprintf(FILE*, char* ...);   // from <stdio.h>
extern int execl(char* ...);            // from <sysent.h>
extern int abort(...);                  // from <libc.h>
```

A standard set of macros available for accessing the unspecified arguments in such functions can be found in `<stdargs.h>`. Consider writing an error function that takes one integer argument indicating the severity of the error followed by an arbitrary number of strings. The idea is to compose the error message by passing each word as a separate string argument:

```
void error(int ...);

main(int argc, char* argv[])
{
    switch (argc) {
    case 1:
        error(0,argv[0],0);
        break;
    case 2:
        error(0,argv[0],argv[1],0);
        break;
    default:
        error(1,argv[0],"with",dec(argc-1),"arguments",0);
    }
}
```

The error function could be defined like this:

```
#include <stdargs.h>

void error(int n ...)
/*
    "n" followed by a zero-terminated list of char*s
*/
{
    va_list ap;
    va_start(ap,n);        // arg startup

    for (;;) {
        char* p = va_arg(ap,char*);
        if (p == 0) break;
        cerr << p << " ";
    }

    va_end(ap);            // arg cleanup

    cerr << "\n";
    if (n) exit(n);
}
```

First a `va_list` is defined and initialized by a call of `va_start()`. The macro `va_start` takes the name of the `va_list` and the name of the last formal argument as arguments. The macro `va_arg()` is used to pick the unnamed arguments in order. In each call the programmer must supply a type; `va_arg()` assumes that an actual argument of that type has been passed, but it typically has no way of ensuring that. Before returning from a function in which `va_start()` has been used, `va_end()` must be called. The reason is that `va_start()` may modify the stack in such a way that a return cannot successfully be done; `va_end()` undoes any such modifications.

4.6.9 Pointer to Function

There are only two things one can do to a function: call it and take its address. The pointer obtained by taking the address of a function can then be used to call the function. For example:

```
void error(char* p) { /* ... */ }

void (*efct)(char*);               // pointer to function

void f()
{
    efct = &error;                 // efct points to error
    (*efct)("error");              // call error through efct
}
```

To call a function through a pointer, for example, `efct`, one must first dereference the pointer, `*efct`. Since the function call operator `( )` has higher precedence than the dereference operator `*` has, one cannot just write `*efct("error")`; that means `*(efct("error"))`, which is a type error. The same applies to the declaration syntax (see also §7.3.4).

Note that pointers to functions have argument types declared just like the functions themselves. In pointer assignments, the complete function type must match exactly. For example:

```
void (*pf)(char*);          // pointer to void(char*)
void f1(char*);             // void(char*);
int  f2(char*);             // int(char*);
void f3(int*);              // void(int*);

void f()
{
    pf = &f1;               // ok
    pf = &f2;               // error: bad return type
    pf = &f3;               // error: bad argument type

    (*pf)("asdf");          // ok
    (*pf)(1);               // error: bad argument type

    int i = (*pf)("qwer");  // error: void assigned to int
}
```

The rules for argument passing are the same for calls directly to a function and for calls to a function through a pointer.

It is often convenient to define a name for a pointer-to-function type to avoid using the somewhat nonobvious syntax all the time. For example:

```
typedef int (*SIG_TYP)();           // from <signal.h>
typedef void (*SIG_ARG_TYP)();
SIG_TYP signal(int, SIG_ARG_TYP);
```

A vector of pointers to functions is often useful. For example, the menu system for my mouse-based† editor is implemented using vectors of pointers to functions to represent operations. The system cannot be described in detail here, but this is the general idea:

```
typedef void (*PF)();

PF edit_ops[] = { // edit operations
    cut, paste, snarf, search
};

PF file_ops[] = { // file management
    open, reshape, close, write
};
```

Then define and initialize the pointers that define actions selected from a menu associated with the mouse buttons:

```
PF* button2 = edit_ops;
PF* button3 = file_ops;
```

In a complete implementation, more information is needed to define each menu item. For example, a string specifying the text to be displayed must be stored somewhere. As the system is used, the meaning of mouse buttons changes frequently with the context. Such changes are performed (partly) by changing the value of the button pointers. When a user selects a menu item, such as item 3 for button 2, the associated operation is executed:

```
(*button2[3])();
```

One way to gain appreciation of the expressive power of pointers to functions is to try to write such code without them. A menu can be modified at runtime by inserting new functions into the operator table. It is also easy to construct new menus at runtime.

Pointers to functions can be used to provide polymorphic routines, that is, routines that can be applied to objects of many different types:

```
typedef int (*CFT)(char*,char*);

int sort(char* base, unsigned n, int sz, CFT cmp)
/*
    Sort the "n" elements of vector "base"
    into increasing order
    using the comparison function pointed to by "cmp".
    The elements are of size "sz".

    Very inefficient algorithm: bubble sort
*/
{
    for (int i=0; i<n-1; i++)
        for (int j=n-1; i<j; j--) {
            char* pj = base+j*sz;       // b[j]
            char* pj1 = pj-sz;          // b[j-1]
            if ((*cmp)(pj,pj1) < 0)
                // swap b[j] and b[j-1]
                for (int k=0; k<sz; k++) {
                    char temp = pj[k];
                    pj[k] = pj1[k];
                    pj1[k] = temp;
                }
        }
}
```

---

† A mouse is a pointing device with at least one button. Mine is red, round, and has three buttons.

The sort routine does not know the type of the objects it sorts, only the number of elements (the vector size), the size of each element, and the function to call to perform a comparison. The type of sort() was chosen to be the same as the type of the standard C library sort routine, qsort(). Real programs use qsort(). Since sort() does not return a value, it should have been declared void, but the type void had not been introduced into C when qsort() was defined. Similarly, it would have been more honest to use void* instead of char* as the argument type. Such a sort function could be used to sort a table such as this:

```
struct user {
    char* name;
    char* id;
    int dept;
};

typedef user* Puser;

user heads[] = {
    "McIlroy M.D.",      "doug", 11271,
    "Aho A.V.",          "ava",  11272,
    "Weinberger P.J.",   "pjw",  11273,
    "Schryer N.L.",      "nls",  11274,
    "Schryer N.L.",      "nls",  11275,
    "Kernighan B.W.",    "bwk",  11276
};

void print_id(Puser v, int n)
{
    for (int i=0; i<n; i++)
        cout << v[i].name << "\t"
             << v[i].id << "\t"
             << v[i].dept << "\n";
}
```

To be able to sort, one must first define appropriate comparison functions. A comparison function must return a negative value if its first argument is less than the second, zero if they are equal, and a positive number otherwise:

```
int cmp1(char* p, char* q)      // Compare name strings
{
    return strcmp(Puser(p)->name, Puser(q)->name);
}

int cmp2(char* p, char* q)      // Compare dept numbers
{
    return Puser(p)->dept - Puser(q)->dept;
}
```

This program sorts and prints:

```
main ()
{
    sort((char*)heads,6,sizeof(user),cmp1);
    print_id(heads,6);      // in alphabetical order
    cout << "\n";
    sort((char*)heads,6,sizeof(user),cmp2);
    print_id(heads,6);      // in department number order
}
```

It is possible to take the address of an `inline` function, and also to take the address of an overloaded function (§r.8.9).

4.7 Macros

Macros are defined §r.11. They are very important in C, but have far fewer uses in C++. The first rule about them is: don't use them if you do not have to. It has been observed that almost every macro demonstrates a flaw in either the programming language or in the program. If you want to use macros, please read the reference manual for your own implementation of the C preprocessor very carefully first.

A simple macro is defined like this:

```
#define name rest of line
```

When `name` is encountered as a token, it is replaced by `rest of line`. For example,

```
named = name
```

will be expanded into

```
named = rest of line
```

A macro can also be defined to take arguments. For example:

```
#define mac(a,b) argument1: a argument2: b
```

When `mac` is used, two argument strings must be presented. They will replace a and b when `mac()` is expanded. For example,

```
expanded = mac(foo bar, yuk yuk)
```

will be expanded into

```
expanded = argument1: foo bar argument2: yuk yuk
```

Macros manipulate strings and know little about C++ syntax and nothing about C++ types or scope rules. Only the expanded form of a macro is seen by the compiler, so an error in a macro will be reported when the macro is expanded, not when it is defined. This leads to very obscure error messages.

Here are some plausible macros:

```
#define Case break;case
#define nl <<"\n"
#define forever for(;;)
#define MIN(a,b) (((a)<(b))?(a):(b))
```

Here are some completely unnecessary macros:

```
#define PI 3.141593
#define BEGIN {
#define END }
```

Here are some examples of dangerous macros:

```
#define SQUARE(a) a*a
#define INCR_xx (xx)++
#define DISP = 4
```

To see why they are dangerous, try expanding this:

```
int xx = 0;              // global counter

void f() {
    int xx = 0;          // local variable
    xx = SQUARE(xx+2);   // xx = xx+2*xx+2;
    INCR_xx;             // increments local xx
    if (a-DISP==b) {     // a-= 4==b
        // ...
    }
}
```

If you must use a macro, use the scope resolution operator `::` when referring to global names (§2.1.1), and enclose occurrences of a macro argument
name in parentheses whenever possible (see MIN above).

Note the different effects of expanding these two macros:

```
#define m1(a) something(a)    // thoughtful comment
#define m2(a) something(a)    /* thoughtful comment */
```

For example,

```
int a = m1(1)+2;
int b = m2(1)+2;
```

expands into

```
int a = something(1)     // thoughtful comment+2;
int b = something(1)     /* thoughtful comment */+2;
```

Using macros, you can design your own private language; it will most likely
be incomprehensible to others. Furthermore, the C preprocessor is a very simple macro processor. When you try to do something nontrivial, you are likely
to find it either impossible or unnecessarily hard to do (but see §7.3.5).

4.8 Exercises

1. (∗1) Write declarations for the following: a function taking arguments of type pointer to character and reference to integer and returning no value; a pointer to such a function; a function taking such a pointer as an argument; and a function returning such a pointer. Write the definition of a function that takes such a pointer as argument and returns its argument as the return value. Hint: Use `typedef`.

2. (∗1) What does the following mean? What would it be good for?

```
typedef int (rifii&) (int, int);
```

3. (∗1.5) Write a program like "Hello, world" that takes a name as a command line argument and writes "Hello, *name*". Modify this program to take any number of names as arguments and say hello to each.

4. (∗1.5) Write a program that reads an arbitrary number of files whose names are given as command line arguments and writes them one after another on `cout`. Since this program concatenates its arguments to produce its output you might call it `cat`.

5. (∗2) Convert a small C program to C++. Modify the header files to declare all functions called and to declare the type of every argument. Replace `#defines` when possible with `enum`, `const` or `inline`. Remove `extern` declarations from `.c` files and convert to C++ function definition syntax. Replace calls of `malloc()` and `free()` with `new` and `delete`. Remove unnecessary casts.

6. (∗2) Implement `sort()` (§4.6.7) using a more efficient sorting algorithm.

7. (∗2) Look at the definition of `struct tnode` in §r.8.5. Write a function for entering new words into a tree of `tnodes`. Write a function to write out a tree of `tnodes`. Write a function to write out a tree of `tnodes` with the words in alphabetical order. Modify `tnode` so that it stores (only) a pointer to an arbitrarily long word stored on free store using `new`. Modify the functions to use the new definition of `tnode`.

8. (∗2) Write a "module" that implements a stack. The `.h` file should declare functions `push()`, `pop()`, and any other suitable functions (only). A `.c` file defines the functions and the data necessary to hold the stack.

9. (∗2) Know your standard header files. List the files in `/usr/include` and `/usr/include/CC` (or wherever the standard header files are kept on your system). Read any that look interesting.

10. (∗2) Write a function to invert a two dimensional array.

11. (∗2) Write an encryption program that reads from `cin` and writes the encoded characters to `cout`. You might use this simple encryption scheme: The encrypted form of a character c is c^`key[i]`, where `key` is a string passed as a command line argument. The program uses the characters in `key` in a cyclic manner until all the input has been read. Re-encrypting encoded text with the same key produces the original text. If no key (or a

null string) is passed, then no encryption is done.

12. (*3) Write a program to help decipher messages encrypted with the method described above without knowing the key. Hint: David Kahn: *The Code-breakers*, Macmillan, 1967, New York, pp 207-213.

13. (*3) Write an `error` function that takes a `printf`-style format string containing `%s`, `%c`, and `%d` directives and an arbitrary number of arguments. Don't use `printf()`. Look at §8.2.4 if you don't know the meaning of `%s` etc. Use `<stdargs.h>`.

14. (*1) How would you choose names for pointer to function types defined using `typedef`.

15. (*2) Look at some programs to get an idea of the diversity of styles of names actually used. How are upper-case letters used? How is the underscore used? When are short names such as `i` and `x` used?

16. (*1) What is wrong with these macro definitions?

```
#define PI = 3.141593;
#define MAX(a,b) a>b?a:b
#define fac(a) (a)*fac((a)-1)
```

17. (*3) Write a macro processor that defines and expands simple macros (like the C preprocessor does). Read from `cin` and write to `cout`. At first don't try to handle macros with arguments. Hint: The desk calculator (§3.1) contains a symbol table and a lexical analyzer that you could modify.

Classes

*Those types are not "abstract";
they are as real as* int *and* float.
— Doug McIlroy

This chapter describes C++'s facilities for defining new types for which access to data is restricted to a specific set of access functions. The ways in which a data structure can be protected, initialized, accessed, and finally cleaned up are explained. Examples include simple classes for symbol table management, stack manipulation, set manipulation, and implementation of a discriminating (that is, "safe") union. The following two chapters will complete the description of C++'s facilities for creating new types and provide more interesting examples.

5.1 Introduction and Overview

The aim of the C++ class concept, as described in this and the following two chapters, is to provide the programmer with a tool for creating new types that can be used as conveniently as the built-in types. Ideally, a user-defined type should not differ from built-in types in the way it is used, only in the way it is created.

A type is the concrete representation of an idea (concept). For example, the C++ type float with its operations +, -, *, etc., provides a restricted, but concrete, version of the mathematical concept of a real number. The reason for designing a new type is to provide a concrete and specific definition of a concept that has no direct and obvious counterpart among the built-in types.

For example, one might provide a type `trunk_module` in a program dealing with telephony or a type `list_of_paragraphs` for a text processing program. A program that provides types that closely match the concepts of the application is typically easier to understand and easier to modify than a program that does not. A well chosen set of user-defined types makes a program more concise; it also enables the compiler to detect illegal uses of objects that otherwise would not be detected until the program is tested.

The fundamental idea in defining a new type is to separate the incidental details of the implementation (for example, the layout of the data used to store an object of the type) from the properties essential to the correct use of it (for example, the complete list of functions that can access the data). Such a separation can be expressed by channeling all use of the data structure and internal housekeeping routines through a specific interface.

This chapter consists of four fairly separate parts:

§5.2 Classes and Members. This section introduces the basic notion of a user-defined type called a `class`. Access to objects of a class can be restricted to a set of functions declared as part of the class; such functions are called member functions. Objects of a class are created and initialized by member functions specifically declared for that purpose; such functions are called constructors. A member function can be specifically declared to "clean up" each object of a class when it is destroyed; such a function is called a destructor.

§5.3 Interfaces and Implementations. This section presents two examples of how a class can be designed, implemented, and used.

§5.4 Friends and Unions. This section presents many additional details about classes. It shows how access to private parts of a class can be granted to a function that is not a member of that class. Such a function is called a `friend`. This section also shows how to define a discriminating union.

§5.5 Constructors and Destructors. An object can be created as an automatic, a static, or as an object on the free store. An object can also be a member of some aggregate (a vector or class type), which in turn can be allocated in one of those three ways. The use of constructors and destructors is explained in some detail.

5.2   Classes and Members

A `class` is a user-defined type. This section introduces the basic facilities for defining a class, creating objects of a class, manipulating such objects, and finally cleaning up such objects after use.

5.2.1 Member Functions

Consider implementing the concept of a date using a `struct` to define the representation of a `date` and a set of functions for manipulating variables of this type:

```
struct date { int month, day, year; };
date today;
void set_date(date*, int, int, int);
void next_date(date*);
void print_date(date*);
// ...
```

There are no explicit connections between the functions and the data type. Such a connection can be established by declaring the functions as members:

```
struct date {
    int month, day, year;

    void set(int, int, int);
    void get(int*, int*, int*);
    void next();
    void print();
};
```

Functions declared this way are called member functions and can be invoked only for a specific variable of the appropriate type using the standard syntax for structure member access. For example:

```
date today;
date my_birthday;

void f()
{
    my_birthday.set(30,12,1950);
    today.set(18,1,1985);

    my_birthday.print();
    today.next();
}
```

Since different structures can have member functions with the same name, one must specify the structure name when defining a member function:

```
void date::next()
{
    if ( ++day > 28 ) {
        // do the hard part
    }
}
```

In a member function, member names can be used without explicit reference to an object. In that case, the name refers to that member of the object for which the function was invoked.

5.2.2 Classes

The declaration of `date` in the previous subsection provides a set of functions for manipulating a `date`, but it does not specify that those functions should be the only ones to access objects of type `date`. This restriction can be expressed by using a `class` instead of a `struct`:

```
class date {
    int month, day, year;
public:
    void set(int, int, int);
    void get(int*, int*, int*);
    void next();
    void print();
};
```

The `public` label separates the class body into two parts. The names in the first, *private*, part can be used only by member functions. The second, *public*, part constitutes the interface to objects of the class. A `struct` is simply a `class` with all members public, so the member functions are defined and used exactly as before. For example:

```
void date::print()      // print using US notation
{
    cout << month << "/" << day << "/" << year ;
}
```

However, nonmember functions are barred from using the private members of class `date`. For example:

```
void backdate()
{
    today.day--;        // error
}
```

There are several benefits to be obtained from restricting access to a data structure to an explicitly declared list of functions. Any error causing a `date` to take on an illegal value (for example, December 36, 1985) must be caused by code in a member function, so the first stage of debugging, localization, is completed before the program is even run. This is a special case of the general observation that any change to the behavior of the type `date` can and must be effected by changes to its members. Another advantage is that a potential user of such a type need only examine the definition of the member functions to learn to use it.

The protection of private data relies on restriction of the use of the class member names. It can therefore be circumvented by address manipulation and explicit type conversion, but this, of course, is cheating.

5.2.3 Self-reference

In a member function, one can refer directly to members of the object for which the member function is invoked. For example:

```
class x {
    int m;
public:
    int readm() { return m; }
};

x aa;
x bb;

void f()
{
    int a = aa.readm();
    int b = bb.readm();
    // ...
}
```

In the first call of the member `readm()`, m refers to `aa.m` and in the second it refers to `bb.m`.

A pointer to the object for which a member function is invoked constitutes a hidden argument to the function. The implicit argument can be explicitly referred to as `this`. In every function of a class `x`, the pointer `this` is implicitly declared as

```
x* this;
```

and initialized to point to the object for which the member function is invoked. Since `this` is a keyword it cannot be explicitly declared. Class `x` could equivalently be declared like this:

```
class x {
    int m;
public:
    int readm() { return this->m; }
};
```

Using `this` when referring to members is unnecessary; the major use of `this` is for writing member functions that manipulate pointers directly. A typical example of this is a function that inserts a link on a doubly linked list:

```
class dlink {
    dlink* pre; // previous
    dlink* suc; // next
public:
    void append(dlink*);
    // ...
};

void dlink::append(dlink* p)
{
    p->suc = suc;        // that is, p->suc = this->suc
    p->pre = this;       // explicit use of "this"
    suc->pre = p;        // that is, this->suc->pre = p
    suc = p;             // that is, this->suc = p
}

dlink* list_head;

void f(dlink* a, dlink* b)
{
    // ...
    list_head->append(a);
    list_head->append(b);
}
```

Links of this general nature are the basis for the list classes described in Chapter 7. To append a link to a list, the objects pointed to by this, pre, and suc must be updated. They are all of type dlink, so the member function dlink::append() can access them. The unit of protection in C++ is a class, not an individual object of a class.

5.2.4 Initialization

The use of functions such as set_date() to provide initialization for class objects is inelegant and error prone. Since it is nowhere stated that an object must be initialized, a programmer can forget to do so, or (often with equally disastrous results) do so twice. A better approach is to allow the programmer to declare a function with the explicit purpose of initializing objects. Because such a function constructs values of a given type, it is called a constructor. A constructor is recognized by having the same name as the class itself. For example:

```
class date {
    // ...
    date(int, int, int);
};
```

When a class has a constructor, all objects of that class will be initialized. If
the constructor requires arguments, they must be supplied:

```
date today = date(23,6,1983);
date xmas(25,12,0);         // abbreviated form
date my_birthday;           // illegal, initializer missing
```

It is often nice to provide several ways of initializing a class object. This
can be done by providing several constructors. For example:

```
class date {
    int month, day, year;
public:
    // ...
    date(int, int, int); // day month year
    date(char*);         // date in string representation
    date(int);           // day, today's month and year
    date();              // default date: today
};
```

Constructors obey the same rules for argument types as do other overloaded
functions (§4.6.7). As long as the constructors differ sufficiently in their argument types the compiler can select the correct one for each use:

```
date today(4);
date july4("July 4, 1983");
date guy("5 Nov");
date now;                    // default initialized
```

Note that member functions can be overloaded without explicit use of the
overload keyword. Since the complete list of member functions appears in
the class declaration and often is short, there is no compelling reason to
require use of the word **overload** to protect against accidental reuse of a
name.

The proliferation of constructors in the **date** example is typical. When
designing a class there is always the temptation to provide "everything,"
because it seems easier to provide a feature just in case somebody wants it or
because it looks nice than to decide on what is really needed. The latter takes
more thought, but typically leads to smaller and more comprehensible programs. One way of reducing the number of related functions is to use default
arguments. In the **date**, each argument can be given a default value interpreted as "pick the default: **today**."

```
class date {
    int month, day, year;
public:
    // ...
    date(int d =0, int m =0, int y =0);
    date(char*);    // date in string representation
};
```

```
date::date(int d, int m, int y)
{
    day = d ? d : today.day;
    month = m ? m : today.month;
    year = y ? y : today.year;
    // check that the date is valid
    // ...
}
```

When using an argument value to indicate "pick the default," the value chosen must be outside the set of possible values for the argument. For day and month this is clearly so, but for year zero may not be an obvious choice. Fortunately there is no year zero on the European calendar; 1AD (year==1) comes immediately after 1BC (year==-1), but this would probably be too subtle for a real program.

An object of a class with no constructors can be initialized by assigning another object of that class to it. This can also be done where constructors have been declared. For example:

```
date d = today; // initialization by assignment
```

In essence, there is a default constructor defined as bitwise copy of objects of the same class. If that default is not wanted for a class X, it can be redefined by a constructor named X(X&). This will be discussed further in §6.6.

5.2.5 Cleanup

More often than not, a user-defined type has a constructor to ensure proper initialization. Many types also need the inverse operation, a *destructor*, to ensure proper cleanup of objects of the type. The name of the destructor for class X is ~X() ("the complement of the constructor"). In particular, many classes use some memory from the free store (see §3.2.6) that is allocated by a constructor and de-allocated by a destructor. For example, here is a conventional stack type that has been completely stripped of error handling to make it shorter:

```
class char_stack {
    int size;
    char* top;
    char* s;
public:
    char_stack(int sz) { top=s=new char[size=sz]; }
    ~char_stack()      { delete s; }    // destructor
    void push(char c)  { *top++ = c; }
    char pop()         { return *--top; }
};
```

When a char_stack goes out of scope, the destructor will be called:

```
void f()
{
    char_stack s1(100);
    char_stack s2(200);
    s1.push('a');
    s2.push(s1.pop());
    char ch = s2.pop();
    cout << chr(ch) << "\n";
}
```

When f() is called, the char_stack constructor will be called for s1 to allocate a vector of 100 characters and for s2 to allocate a vector of 200 characters; at the return from f(), these two vectors will be freed again.

5.2.6 Inline

When programming using classes, it is very common to use many small functions. In essence, a function is provided where a traditionally structured program would simply have some typical way of using a data structure; what was a convention becomes a standard recognized by the compiler. This can lead to horrible inefficiencies because the cost of calling a function (though not at all high compared with other languages) is still much higher than the couple of memory references needed for the body of a trivial function.

The inline function facility was designed to handle this problem. A member function defined (not just declared) in the class declaration is taken to be inline. This means, for example, that the code generated for the functions using char_stacks presented previously does not contain any function calls except the ones used to implement the output operations! In other words, there is no minimum run-time cost to take into account when designing a class; even the tiniest operation can be provided efficiently. This observation invalidates the most commonly stated reason for using public data members.

A member function can also be declared inline outside the class declaration. For example:

```
class char_stack {
    int size;
    char* top;
    char* s;
public:
    char pop();
    // ...
};

inline char char_stack::pop()
{
    return *--top;
}
```

5.3   Interfaces and Implementations

What makes a good class? Something that has a small and well-defined set of operations. Something that can be seen as a "black box" manipulated exclusively through that set of operations. Something whose actual representation could conceivably be modified without affecting the way that set of operations is used. Something one might want more than one of.

Containers of all sorts provide obvious examples: tables, sets, lists, vectors, dictionaries, etc. Such a class will have an insert operation, typically it will also have operations for checking whether a specific member has been inserted, maybe it will have operations for sorting the members, maybe it will have operations for examining all members in some order, and finally it may also have an operation for removing a member. Container classes typically have constructors and destructors.

Data hiding and a well-defined interface can also be obtained through a module concept (see, for example, §4.4: files as modules). However, a class is a type; to use it, one must create objects of that class, and one can create as many such objects as are needed. A module is itself an object; to use it, one need only initialize it, and there is exactly one such object.

5.3.1   Alternative Implementations

As long as the declaration of the public part of a class and the declaration of the member functions remain unchanged, the implementation of a class can be changed without affecting its users. As an example of this, consider a symbol table like the one used for the desk calculator example in Chapter 3. It is a table of names:

```
struct name {
    char* string;
    name* next;
    double value;
};
```

Here is a version of a class `table`:

```
// file table.h:

class table {
    name* tbl;
public:
    table()   { tbl = 0; }

    name* look(char*, int = 0);
    name* insert(char* s) { return look(s,1); }
};
```

This table differs from the table defined in Chapter 3 in that it is a proper type. One can declare more than one `table`, one can have a pointer to a table, etc. For example:

```
#include "table.h"

table globals;
table keywords;
table* locals;

main() {
        locals = new table;
        // ...
}
```

Here is an implementation of `table::look()` using a linear search through the linked list of names in the table:

```
#include <string.h>

name* table::look(char* p, int ins)
{
    for (name* n = tbl; n; n=n->next)
        if (strcmp(p,n->string) == 0) return n;

    if (ins == 0) error("name not found");

    name* nn = new name;
    nn->string = new char[strlen(p)+1];
    strcpy(nn->string,p);
    nn->value = 1;
    nn->next = tbl;
    tbl = nn;
    return nn;
}
```

Now consider improving class `table` to use hashed lookup as used in the desk calculator example. Doing so is made more difficult by the constraint that code written using the version of class `table` just defined should still be valid without modification:

```
class table {
    name** tbl;
    int size;
public:
    table(int sz = 15);
    ~table();

    name* look(char*, int =0);
    name* insert(char* s) { return look(s,1); }
};
```

The data structure and the constructor were changed to reflect the need for

a specific size of a table when hashing is used. Providing the constructor with
a default argument ensures that old code that did not specify a table size is still
correct. Default arguments are very useful in situations when one must change
a class without affecting old code. The constructor and destructor now handle
the creation and deletion of hash tables:

```
table::table(int sz)
{
    if (sz < 0) error("negative table size");
    tbl = new name*[size = sz];
    for (int i = 0; i<sz; i++) tbl[i] = 0;
}

table::~table()
{
    for (int i = 0; i<size; i++)
        for (name* n = tbl[i]; n; n=n->next) {
            delete n->string;
            delete n;
        }
    delete tbl;
}
```

A simpler and cleaner version of table::~table() can be obtained by
declaring a destructor for class name. The lookup function is nearly identical
to the one used in the desk calculator example (§3.1.3):

```
#include <string.h>

name* table::look(char* p, int ins)
{
    int ii = 0;
    char* pp = p;
    while (*pp) ii = ii<<1 ^ *pp++;
    if (ii < 0) ii = -ii;
    ii %= size;

    for (name* n=tbl[ii]; n; n=n->next)
        if (strcmp(p,n->string) == 0) return n;

    if (ins == 0) error("name not found");

    name* nn = new name;
    nn->string = new char[strlen(p)+1];
    strcpy(nn->string,p);
    nn->value = 1;
    nn->next = tbl[ii];
    tbl[ii] = nn;
    return nn;
}
```

Clearly, the member functions of a class must be recompiled whenever a change is made to the class declaration. Ideally, such a change would not affect users of the class at all. Unfortunately, this is not so. To allocate a variable of a class type, the compiler needs to know the size of an object of the class. If the size of such objects is changed, files that contain uses of the class must be recompiled. Software that determines the (minimal) set of files that need recompiling after a change to a class declaration can be (and has been) written, but is not yet in widespread use.

Why, you may ask, was C++ designed in such a way that recompilation of users of a class is necessary after a change to the private part? And why indeed need the private part be present in the class declaration at all? In other words, since users of a class are not allowed to access the private members, why must their declarations be present in the header files the user is supposed to read? The answer is *efficiency*. On many systems, both the compilation process and the sequence of operations implementing a function call are simpler when the size of automatic objects (objects on the stack) is known at compile time.

This problem could be avoided by representing every class object as a pointer to the "real" object. Since all such pointers would have the same size, and the allocation of the "real" objects could be defined in a file where the private part is available, this would solve the problem. However, this solution imposes an extra memory reference when accessing class members, and worse, involves at least one invocation of the free store allocation and de-allocation routines for each call of a function with an automatic class object. It would also make the implementation of inline member functions that access private data infeasible. Furthermore, such a change would make it impossible to link C++ and C program fragments together (because a C compiler would treat a struct differently from a C++ compiler). This was deemed unsuitable for C++.

5.3.2 A Complete Class

Programming without data hiding (using structures) requires less forethought than programming with it (using classes). One can define a structure without too much thought about how it is supposed to be used, but when defining a class, one tends to focus on providing a complete set of operations for the new type; this is an important shift in emphasis. The time spent designing a new type is typically recovered many times over in the development and testing of a program.

Here is an example of a complete type, intset, providing the concept "set of integers":

```
class intset {
    int cursize, maxsize;
    int *x;
public:
    intset(int m, int n);          // at most m ints in 1..n
    ~intset();

    int member(int t);             // is "t" a member?
    void insert(int t);            // add "t" to set

    void iterate(int& i)           { i = 0; }
    int ok(int& i)                 { return i<cursize; }
    int next(int& i)               { return x[i++]; }
};
```

To test this class we can create and then print a set of random integers. Such a
set might constitute a drawing of a lottery. This simple set could also be used
to check a sequence of integers for duplicates, but for most applications the set
type would have to be a bit more elaborate. As always, errors are possible:

```
#include <stream.h>

void error(char *s)
{
    cerr << "set: " << s << "\n";
    exit(1);
}
```

Class intset is used by a main() expecting two integer arguments. The
first argument specifies the number of random numbers to be generated. The
second argument specifies the range the random integers will be expected in:

```
main(int argc, char *argv[])
{
    if (argc != 3) error("two arguments expected");
    int count = 0;
    int m = atoi(argv[1]);         // number of set members
    int n = atoi(argv[2]);         // in the range 1..n
    intset s(m,n);

    while (count<m) {
        int t = randint(n);
        if (s.member(t)==0) {
            s.insert(t);
            count++;
        }
    }

    print_in_order(&s);
}
```

The reason that the argument count, argc, has to be 3 for a program requiring two arguments is that the name of the program is always passed as argv[0]. The function

```
extern int atoi(char*);
```

is a standard library function for converting the string representation of an integer into its internal (binary) form. The random numbers are generated using the standard function rand():

```
extern int rand();          // Not too random: beware

int randint(int u)          // in the range 1..u
{
    int r = rand();
    if (r < 0) r = -r;
    return 1 + r%u ;
}
```

The implementation details of a class should be of little interest to a user, but here are the member functions anyway. The constructor allocates an integer vector of the specified maximum set size and the destructor de-allocates it:

```
intset::intset(int m, int n)     // at most m ints in 1..n
{
    if (m<1 !! n<m) error("illegal intset size");
    cursize = 0;
    maxsize = m;
    x = new int[maxsize];
}

intset::~intset()
{
    delete x;
}
```

Integers are inserted so that they are kept in increasing order in the set:

```
void intset::insert(int t)
{
    if (++cursize > maxsize) error("too many elements");
    int i = cursize-1;
    x[i] = t;

    while (i>0 && x[i-1]>x[i]) {
        int t = x[i];                // swap x[i] and [i-1]
        x[i] = x[i-1];
        x[i-1] = t;
        i--;
    }
}
```

A simple binary search is used to find a member:

```
int intset::member(int t)          //  binary search
{
    int l = 0;
    int u = cursize-1;

    while (l <= u) {
        int m = (l+u)/2;
        if (t < x[m])
            u = m-1;
        else if (t > x[m])
            l = m+1;
        else
            return 1;    // found
    }
    return 0;                // not found
}
```

Finally, since the representation of an `intset` is hidden to a user, we must provide a set of operations that allow a user to iterate through the set in some order. A set is not intrinsically ordered, so we cannot simply provide a way of accessing the vector (tomorrow, I might reimplement `intset` as a linked list).

Three functions are provided: `iterate()` for initializing an iteration, `ok()` for checking if there is a next member, and `next()` for getting the next member:

```
class intset {
    // ...
    void iterate(int& i)        { i = 0; }
    int ok(int& i)              { return i<cursize; }
    int next(int& i)            { return x[i++]; }
};
```

To allow these three operations to cooperate and to remember how far the iteration has progressed, the user must supply an integer argument. Since the elements are kept in a sorted list, their implementation is trivial. Now the `print_in_order` function can be defined:

```
void print_in_order(intset* set)
{
    int var;
    set->iterate(var);
    while (set->ok(var)) cout <<  set->next(var) << "\n";
}
```

An alternative way of providing an iterator is presented in §6.8.

5.4 Friends and Unions

This section describes some more features relating to classes. It presents a way of granting a nonmember function access to private members. It describes how member name conflicts can be resolved, how class declarations can be nested, and how undesirable nesting can be avoided. It also discusses how objects of a class can share data members and how pointers to members can be used. Finally there is an example showing how one can design a discriminating (safe) union.

5.4.1 Friends

Assume that you have defined two classes, vector and matrix. Each hides its representation and provides a complete set of operations for manipulating objects of its type. Now define a function multiplying a matrix by a vector. For simplicity, assume that a vector has four elements, indexed 0..3, and that a matrix has four vectors, indexed 0..3. Assume also, that elements of a vector are accessed through a function elem() that checks the index, and that matrix has a similar function. One approach is to define a global function multiply() like this:

```
vector multiply(matrix& m, vector& v);
{
    vector r;
    for (int i = 0; i<3; i++) { // r[i] = m[i] * v;
        r.elem(i) = 0;
        for (int j = 0; j<3; j++)
            r.elem(i) += m.elem(i,j) * v.elem(j);
    }
    return r;
}
```

This is in some way the "natural" way of doing it, but it is very inefficient. Each time multiply() is called, elem() is called 4*(1+4*3) times.

Now, if we made multiply() a member of class vector, we could dispense with the checking of indices when accessing a vector element, and if we made multiply() a member of class matrix, we could dispense with the checking of indices when accessing a matrix element. However, a function cannot be a member of two classes. What is needed is a language construct that grants a function access to the private part of a class. A nonmember function that is allowed access to the private part of a class is called a friend of the class. A function is made a friend of a class by a friend declaration in that class. For example:

```
class matrix;

class vector {
    float v[4];
    // ...
    friend vector multiply(matrix&, vector&);
};

class matrix {
    vector v[4];
    // ...
    friend vector multiply(matrix&, vector&);
};
```

There is nothing special about a friend function apart from the right to access the private part of a class. In particular, a friend function does not have a this pointer (unless it is a member function in its own right). A friend declaration is a real declaration. It introduces the name of the function into the outermost scope of a program and is checked against other declarations of that name. A friend declaration can be placed in either the private or the public part of a class declaration; it does not matter where.

The multiply function can now be written using the elements of the vectors and the matrix directly:

```
vector multiply(matrix& m, vector& v)
{
    vector r;
    for (int i = 0; i<3; i++) { // r[i] = m[i] * v;
        r.v[i] = 0;
        for (int j = 0; j<3; j++)
            r.v[i] += m.v[i][j] * v.v[j];
    }
    return r;
}
```

There are ways of handling this particular efficiency problem without using the friend mechanism (one might define a vector multiply operation and define multiply() using that). However, there are many problems that are most easily solved given the ability to grant a function that is not a member of a class access to the private part of that class. Chapter 6 contains many examples of the use of friend. The relative merits of friends and member functions will be discussed later.

A member function of one class can be the friend of another. For example:

```
class x {
    // ...
    void f();
};
```

```
class y {
    // ...
    friend void x::f();
};
```

It is not unusual for all functions of one class to be friends of another. There is even a shorthand for this:

```
class x {
    friend class y;
    // ...
};
```

This friend declaration makes all of y's member functions friends of x.

5.4.2 Member Name Qualification

Occasionally, it is useful to distinguish explicitly between class member names and other names. The scope resolution operator : : can be used:

```
class x {
    int m;
public:
    int readm()      { return x::m; }
    void setm(int m) { x::m = m; }
};
```

In x::setm() the argument name m hides the member m, so that the member could only be referred to using its qualified name, x::m. The left-hand operand of :: must be the name of a class.

A name prefixed by (just) :: must be a global name. This is particularly useful to enable popular names such as read, put, and open to be used for member function names without losing the ability to refer to the nonmember version. For example:

```
class my_file {
    // ...
public:
    int open(char*, char*);
};

int my_file::open(char* name, char* spec)
{
    // ...
    if (::open(name,flag)) { // use the UNIX(2) open()
        // ...
    }
    // ...
}
```

5.4.3 Nested Classes

Class declarations can be nested. For example:

```
class set {
    struct setmem {
        int mem;
        setmem* next;
        setmem(int m, setmem* n) { mem=m; next=n; }
    };
    setmem* first;
public:
    set() { first=0; }
    insert(int m) { first = new setmem(m,first); }
    // ...
};
```

Unless the nested class is very simple, such declarations are messy. Furthermore, nesting of classes is at most a notational convenience, since a nested class is *not* hidden in the scope of its lexically enclosing class:

```
class set {
    struct setmem {
        int mem;
        setmem* next;
        setmem(int m, setmem* n);
    };
    // ...
};

setmem::setmem(int m, setmem* n) { mem=m; next=n; }
setmem m1(1,0);
```

Constructs such as `set::setmem::setmem()` are neither necessary nor legal. The only way of hiding a class name is by using the files-as-modules technique (§4.4). Most nontrivial classes are better declared separately:

```
class setmem {
friend class set;          // access by members of set only
    int mem;
    setmem* next;
    setmem(int m, setmem* n) { mem=m; next=n; }
};

class set {
    setmem* first;
public:
    set() { first=0; }
    insert(int m) { first = new setmem(m,first); }
    // ...
};
```

5.4.4 Static members

A class is a type, not a data object, and each object of the class has its own copy of the data members of the class. However, some types are most elegantly implemented if all objects of that type share some data. Preferably, such shared data is declared as part of the class. For example, to manage tasks in an operating system or a simulation, a list of all tasks is often useful:

```
class task {
    // ...
    task* next;
    static task* task_chain;
    void schedule(int);
    void wait(event);
    // ...
};
```

Declaring the member `task_chain` as `static` ensures that there will be only one copy of it, not one copy per task object. It is still in the scope of class `task`, however, and can be accessed from "the outside" only if it was declared public. In that case, its name must be qualified by its class name:

```
task::task_chain
```

In a member function, it can be referred to as plain `task_chain`. The use of `static` class members can reduce the need for global variables considerably.

5.4.5 Pointers to Members

It is possible to take the address of a member of a class. Taking the address of a member function is often useful since the techniques and reasons for using pointers to functions presented in §4.6.9 apply equally to member functions. However, there is currently a defect in the language: it is not possible to express the type of the pointer obtained from this operation. Consequently one must cheat by taking advantage of a quirk in the current implementation. The example below is *not* guaranteed to work, and use of this trick should be localized so that a program can be converted to use the proper language construct when it becomes available. The trick is to take advantage of the fact that `this` is currently implemented as the (hidden) first argument to a member function.

```
#include <stream.h>

struct cl
{
    char* val;
    void  print(int x) { cout << val << x << "\n"; };
    cl(char* v) { val = v; }
};
```

```
// ``fake'' type for member functions:
typedef void (*PROC)(void*, int);

main()
{
    cl z1("z1 ");
    cl z2("z2 ");
    PROC pf1 = PROC(&z1.print);
    PROC pf2 = PROC(&z2.print);
    z1.print(1);
    (*pf1)(&z1,2);
    z2.print(3);
    (*pf2)(&z2,4);
}
```

In many cases, virtual functions (see Chapter 7) can be used where one would otherwise use pointers to functions†.

5.4.6 Structures and Unions

By definition, a `struct` is simply a class with all members public, that is

```
struct s { ...
```

is simply a shorthand for

```
class s { public: ...
```

Structures are used when data hiding is inappropriate.

A named union is defined as a `struct` where every member has the same address (see §r.8.5.13). If one knows that only one member of a structure will have a useful value at any one time, a union can save space. For example, one could define a union for holding lexical tokens in a C compiler:

```
union tok_val {
    char* p;            // string
    char v[8];          // identifier (max 8 char)
    long i;             // integer values
    double d;           // floating point values
};
```

---

† Later versions of C++ support a concept of *pointer to member*; `cl::*` means "pointer to member of cl". For example:

```
typedef void (cl::*PROC)(int);
PROC pf1 = &cl::print;          // no cast needed
PROC pf2 = &cl::print;
```

The operators . and -> are used for calls through a pointer to member function. For example:

```
(z1.*pf1)(2);
((&z2)->*pf2)(4);
```

The problem is that the compiler cannot in general know which member is in use at any one time, so proper type checking is not possible. For example:

```
void strange(int i)
{
    tok_val x;
    if (i)
        x.p = "2";
    else
        x.d = 2;
    sqrt(x.d);              // error if i != 0
}
```

Furthermore, a union defined like this cannot be initialized. For example:

```
tok_val curr_val = 12;   // error: int assigned to tok_val
```

is illegal. Constructors can be used to handle this:

```
union tok_val {
    char* p;               // string
    char v[8];             // identifier (max 8 char)
    long i;                // integer values
    double d;              // floating point values

    tok_val(char*);        // must decide between p and v
    tok_val(int ii)        { i = ii; }
    tok_val(double dd)     { d = dd; }
};
```

This handles cases when the member types can be resolved by the rules for function name overloading (see §4.6.7 and §6.3.3). For example:

```
void f()
{
    tok_val a = 10;        // a.i = 10
    tok_val b = 10.0;      // b.d = 10.0
}
```

When this is not possible (for types such as char* and char[8], int and char, etc.), the proper member can only be found by examining the initializer at run time or by providing an extra argument. For example:

```
tok_val::tok_val(char* pp)
{
    if (strlen(pp) <= 8)
        strncpy(v,pp,8); // short string
    else
        p = pp;            // long string
}
```

Such cases are, in general, better avoided.

Using constructors does not prevent accidental misuse of a tok_val by assigning a value of one type and then retrieving it as another type. This problem can be solved by embedding the union in a class that keeps track of which type of value is stored:

```
class tok_val {
    char tag;
    union {
        char* p;
        char v[8];
        long i;
        double d;
    };
    int check(char t, char* s)
        { if (tag!=t) { error(s); return 0; } return 1; }
public:
    tok_val(char* pp);
    tok_val(long ii)   { i=ii; tag='I'; }
    tok_val(double dd) { d=dd; tag='D'; }

    long& ival()       { check('I',"ival"); return i; }
    double& fval()     { check('D',"fval"); return d; }
    char*& sval()      { check('S',"sval"); return p; }
    char*  id()        { check('N',"id");   return v; }
};
```

The constructor taking a string argument uses the standard function `strncpy()` to copy short strings; `strncpy()` resembles `strcpy()`, but takes a third argument indicating the number of characters to be copied:

```
tok_val::tok_val(char* pp)
{
    if (strlen(pp) <= 8) {        // short string
        tag = 'N';
        strncpy(v,pp,8);          // copy 8 characters
    }
    else {                        // long string
        tag = 'S';
        p = pp;                   // just store the pointer
    }
}
```

The `tok_val` type can be used like this:

```
void f()
{
    tok_val t1("short");         // assign to v
    tok_val t2("long string");   // assign to p
    char s[8];
    strncpy(s,t1.id(),8);        // ok
    strncpy(s,t2.id(),8);        // check() will fail
}
```

5.5 Constructors and Destructors

When a class has a constructor, it is called whenever an object of that class is created. When a class has a destructor, it is called whenever an object of that class is destroyed. Objects can be created as

[1] An automatic object: created each time its declaration is encountered in the execution of the program and destroyed each time the block in which it occurs is left;

[2] A static object: created once at the start of the program and destroyed once at the termination of the program;

[3] A free store object: created using the new operator and destroyed using the delete operator; and

[4] A member object: as a member of another class or as a vector element.

An object can also be constructed by explicit use of a constructor in an expression (see §6.4), in which case it is an automatic object. In the following subsections it is assumed that objects are of a class with a constructor and a destructor. The class table from §5.3 is used as an example.

5.5.1 Caveat

If x and y are objects of class c1, x=y by default means a bitwise copy of y into x (see §2.3.8). Having assignment interpreted this way can cause a surprising (and usually undesired) effect when used on objects of a class for which a constructor and a destructor have been defined. For example:

```
class char_stack {
    int size;
    char* top;
    char* s;
public:
    char_stack(int sz) { top=s=new char[size=sz]; }
    ~char_stack()       { delete s; }     // destructor
    void push(char c)  { *top++ = c; }
    char pop()         { return *--top; }
};

void h()
{
    char_stack s1(100);
    char_stack s2 = s1; // trouble
    char_stack s3(99);
    s3 = s2;            // trouble
}
```

Here the constructor char_stack::char_stack() is called twice: for s1 and s3. It is not called for s2 since that variable was initialized by assignment. However, the destructor char_stack::~char_stack() is called three times: for s1, s2, and s3! Furthermore, the default interpretation of assignment is bitwise copy, so s1, s2, and s3 will at the end of h( ) each contain a pointer to the vector of characters allocated on the free store when s1 was created. No pointer to the vector of characters allocated when s3 was created will remain. Such anomalies can be avoided: see Chapter 6.

5.5.2 Static Store

Consider this:

```
table tbl1(100);

void f() {
    static table tbl2(200);
}

main()
{
    f();
}
```

Here, the constructor table::table() as defined in §5.3.1 will be called twice: once for tbl1 and once for tbl2. The destructor table::~table() will also be called twice: to destroy tbl1 and tbl2 after exit from main(). Constructors for global static objects in a file are executed in the order in which the declarations occur; destructors are called in the reverse order. It is undefined whether the constructor for a local static object is called if the function in which it is declared is not. If a constructor for a local static object is called, it is called after the constructors for the global static objects lexically preceding it have been called.

Arguments for constructors for static objects must be constant expressions:

```
void g(int a)
{
    static table t(a);   // error
}
```

Traditionally, the execution of main() has been seen as the execution of the program. This was never so, not even in C, but only by allocating a static object of a class with a constructor and/or a destructor does the programmer have an obvious and simple way of specifying code to be executed before and/or after the call of main.

Calling constructors and destructors for static objects serves an extremely important function in C++. It is the way to ensure proper initialization and cleanup of data structures in libraries. Consider <stream.h>. Where did cin, cout, and cerr come from? Where did they get initialized? And, most importantly, since the output streams keep internal buffers of characters, how do these buffers get flushed? The simple and obvious answer is that the work is done by the appropriate constructors and destructors before and after the execution of main(). There are alternatives to using constructors and destructors for initializing and cleaning up library facilities. They are all either very specialized or very ugly.

If a program is terminated using the function exit(), the destructors for static objects will be called, but if the program is terminated using abort(), they are not. Note that this implies that exit() does not terminate a program immediately. Calling exit() in a destructor may cause an infinite recursion.

Sometimes when you design a library, it is necessary, or simply convenient, to invent a type with a constructor and a destructor with the sole purpose of initialization and cleanup. Such a type would be used once only: to allocate a static object so that the constructor and the destructor are called.

5.5.3 Free Store

Consider this:

```
main() {
    table* p = new table( 100 );
    'table* q = new table( 200 );
    delete p;
    delete p;                 // probably an error
}
```

The constructor table::table() will be called twice, and so is the destructor table::~table(). It is worth noting that C++ offers no guarantee that a destructor is ever called for an object created using new. The preceding program never deleted q, but deleted p twice! Depending on the type of p and q, the programmer may or may not consider this an error. Not deleting an object is typically not an error, only a waste of space. Deleting p twice is typically a serious error. A typical result of applying delete to the same pointer twice is an infinite loop in the free store management routine, but the behavior in this case is not specified by the language definition and depends on the implementation.

The user can define a new implementation of the new and delete operators (see §3.2.6). It is also possible to specify the way a constructor or destructor interacts with the new and delete operators (see §5.5.6).

5.5.4 Class Objects as Members

Consider

```
class classdef {
    table members;
    int no_of_members;
    // ...
    classdef(int size);
    ~classdef();
};
```

The intention is clearly that a `classdef` should contain a table of members of size `size`, and the problem is to get the constructor `table::table()` called with the argument `size`. It can be done like this

```
classdef::classdef(int size)
: members(size)
{
    no_of_members = size;
    // ...
}
```

The arguments for a member constructor (here `table::table()`) are placed in the definition (not in a declaration) of the constructor of the class containing it (here `classdef::classdef()`). The member constructor is then called before the body of the constructor specifying its argument list.

If there are more members needing argument lists for constructors, they can be specified similarly. For example:

```
class classdef {
    table members;
    table friends;
    int no_of_members;
    // ...
    classdef(int size);
    ~classdef();
};
```

The argument lists for the members are separated by commas (not by colons), and the initializer lists for members can be presented in any order:

```
classdef::classdef(int size)
: friends(size), members(size)
{
    no_of_members = size;
    // ...
}
```

The order in which the constructors are called is not specified, so argument lists with side effects are not recommended:

```
classdef::classdef(int size)
: friends(size=size/2), members(size)    // bad style
{
    no_of_members = size;
    // ...
}
```

If a constructor for a member needs no arguments, then no argument list needs to be specified. For example, since `table::table` was defined with a default argument 15, the following is correct:

```
classdef::classdef(int size)
: members(size)
{
    no_of_members = size;
    // ...
}
```

and the size of the `friends` table will be 15.

When a class object containing class objects (for example, a `classdef`) is destroyed, the body of that object's own destructor is executed first and then the members' destructors are executed.

Consider the traditional alternative to having class objects as members: to have pointer members and initialize them in a constructor:

```
class classdef {
    table* members;
    table* friends;
    int no_of_members;
    // ...
    classdef(int size);
    ~classdef();
};

classdef::classdef(int size)
{
    members = new table(size);
    friends = new table;        // default table size
    no_of_members = size;
    // ...
}
```

Since the tables were created using new they must be destroyed using `delete`:

```
classdef::~classdef()
{
    // ...
    delete members;
    delete friends;
}
```

Separately created objects like this can be useful, but note that `members` and `friends` point to separate objects that require an allocation and a de-allocation operation each. Furthermore, a pointer plus an object on the free store takes up more space than a member object.

5.5.5 Vectors of Class Objects

To declare a vector of objects of a class with a constructor, that class must have a constructor that can be called without an argument list. Even default arguments cannot be used. For example,

```
        table tblvec[10];
```

is an error because `table::table()` requires an integer argument. There is no way for specifying arguments for a constructor in a vector declaration. To allow the declaration of vectors of tables, the declaration of class `table` (§5.3.1) could be modified like this:

```
        class table {
            // ...
            void init(int sz);   // like the old constructor
        public:
            table(int sz)        // as before, but no default
                { init(sz); }
            table()              // the default
                { init(15); }
            // ...
        };
```

The destructor must be called for each element of a vector when that vector is destroyed. This is done implicitly for vectors that are not allocated using new. However, this cannot be done implicitly for vectors on the free store because the compiler cannot distinguish the pointer to a single object from a pointer to the first element of a vector of objects. For example:

```
        void f()
        {
            table* t1 = new table;
            table* t2 = new table[10];
            delete t1;  // one table
            delete t2;  // trouble: 10 tables
        }
```

In this case the programmer must supply the vector size:

```
        void g(int sz)
        {
            table* t1 = new table;
            table* t2 = new table[sz];
            delete t1;
            delete[sz] t2;
        }
```

But why could the compiler not deduce the number of elements from the amount of storage allocated? Because the free store allocator is not part of the language and might have been supplied by the programmer.

5.5.6 Small Objects

When using many small objects allocated on the free store, you might find your program consuming considerable time allocating and de-allocating such objects. One solution is to provide a better general purpose allocator, and another is for the designer of a class to take over free store management for objects of that particular class by defining appropriate constructors and destructors.

Consider class `name` used in the `table` examples. It could be defined like this:

```
struct name {
    char* string;
    name* next;
    double value;

    name(char*, double, name*);
    ~name();
};
```

The programmer can take advantage of the fact that allocating and de-allocating objects of a known type can be handled far more efficiently (in time and space) than with a general implementation of `new` and `delete`. The general idea is to preallocate "chunks" of `name` objects, and link them together to reduce allocation and de-allocation to simple linked list operations. The variable `nfree` is the head of a list of unused names.

```
const NALL = 128;
name* nfree;
```

The allocator used by the `new` operator stores the size of an object with the object in order for the `delete` operator to function correctly. This space overhead is easily avoided by a type-specific allocator. For example, the following allocator uses 16 bytes to store a `name` on my machine, whereas the standard free store allocator needs 20. Here is how that can be done:

```
name::name(char* s, double v, name* n)
{
    register name* p = nfree;          // first allocate

    if (p)
        nfree = p->next;
    else {                             // allocate & link
        name* q = (name*)new char[ NALL*sizeof(name) ];
        for (p=nfree=&q[NALL-1]; q<p; p--) p->next = p-1;
        (p+1)->next = 0;
    }

    this = p;
    string = s;                        // then initialize
    value = v;
    next = n;
}
```

The assignment to this informs the compiler that the programmer has taken control and that the default mechanism for allocating storage should not be used. The constructor name::name() handles the case in which a name is allocated by new only, but for many types this is always the case; §5.5.8 explains how to write a constructor to handle both free store and other types of allocation.

Note that the space could not simply be allocated like this:

```
name* q = new name[NALL];
```

since this would cause infinite recursion when new called name::name().

De-allocation is typically trivial:

```
name::~name()
{
    next = nfree;
    nfree = this;
    this = 0;
}
```

Assigning 0 to this in a destructor ensures that the standard de-allocator is not used.

5.5.7 Caveat

When assigning to this in a constructor, the value of this is undefined until that assignment. A reference to a member before that assignment is therefore undefined and likely to cause disaster. The current compiler does not try to ensure that an assignment to this occurs on every execution path:

```
mytype::mytype(int i)
{
    if (i) this = mytype_alloc();
    // assignment to members
};
```

will compile and no object will be allocated when i==0.

It is possible for a constructor to determine whether it was called by new or not. If it is called by new, the pointer this has the value zero at entry, otherwise this points to space already allocated for the object (for example on the stack). It is therefore easy to write a constructor that allocates store if (and only if) it was invoked through new. For example:

```
mytype::mytype(int i)
{
    if (this == 0) this = mytype_alloc();
    // assignment to members
};
```

There is no equivalent feature enabling a destructor to decide if its object was created using new, nor is there a feature enabling it to decide whether it was invoked by delete or by an object going out of scope. If knowing this is important, the user can store the relevant information somewhere for the destructor to read. Alternatively, the user can ensure that objects of that class are only allocated appropriately. If the former problem is handled, the latter is uninteresting.

If the implementer of a class is also its only user, it is reasonable to simplify a class based on assumptions about its use. When a class is designed for wider use, such assumptions are often better avoided.

5.5.8 Variable Sized Objects

By taking control of allocation and de-allocation, a user can also construct objects whose size is not determined at compile time. The preceding examples implemented the container classes vector, stack, intset, and table as fixed sized access structures containing pointers to the actual storage. This implies that two allocation operations are necessary to create such objects on the free store and that every access to stored information will involve an extra indirection. For example:

```
class char_stack {
    int size;
    char* top;
    char* s;
public:
    char_stack(int sz) { top=s=new char[size=sz]; }
    ~char_stack()      { delete s; }    // destructor
    void push(char c)  { *top++ = c; }
    char pop()         { return *--top; }
};
```

If every object of a class is allocated on the free store, this is not necessary. Here is an alternative:

```
class char_stack {
    int size;
    char* top;
    char s[1];
public:
    char_stack(int sz);
    void push(char c)  { *top++ = c; }
    char pop()         { return *--top; }
};
```

```
char_stack::char_stack(int sz)
{
    if (this) error("stack not on free store");
    if (sz < 1) error("stack size < 1");
    this = (char_stack*)new char[sizeof(char_stack)+sz-1];
    size = sz;
    top = s;
}
```

Note that a destructor is no longer necessary, since `delete` can free the space used by a `char_stack` without any help from the programmer.

5.6   Exercises

1. (∗1) Modify the desk calculator from Chapter 3 to use class `table`.
2. (∗1) Design `tnode` (§r.8.5) as a class with constructors, destructors, etc. Define a tree of `tnodes` as a class with constructors, destructors, etc.
3. (∗1) Modify class `intset` (§5.3.2) into a set of strings.
4. (∗1) Modify class `intset` into a set of nodes where `node` is a structure you define.
5. (∗3) Define a class for analyzing, storing, evaluating, and printing simple arithmetic expressions consisting of integer constants and the operators +, -, ∗, and /. The public interface should look like this:

```
class expr {
    // ...
public:
    expr(char*);
    int eval();
    void print();
};
```

The string argument for the constructor `expr::expr()` is the expression. The function `expr::eval()` returns the value of the expression, and `expr::print()` prints a representation of the expression on `cout`. A program might look like this:

```
expr x("123/4+123*4-3");
cout << "x = " << x.eval() << "\n";
x.print();
```

Define class `expr` twice: once using a linked list of nodes as the representation, and once using a character string as the representation. Experiment with different ways of printing the expression: fully parenthesized, postfix notation, assembly code, etc.

6. (∗1) Define a class `char_queue` so that the public interface does not depend of the representation. Implement `char_queue` (1) as a linked list

and (2) as a vector. Do not worry about concurrency.

7. (∗2) Define a class `histogram` that keeps count of numbers in some intervals specified as arguments to `histogram`'s constructor. Provide functions to print out the histogram. Handle out of range values. Hint: `<task.h>`.

8. (∗2) Define some classes for providing random numbers of certain distributions. Each class has a constructor specifying parameters for the distribution and a function `draw` that returns the "next" value. Hint: `<task.h>`. See also class `intset`.

9. (∗2) Re-write the `date` example (§5.2.2), the `char_stack` example (§5.2.5), and the `intset` example (§5.3.2) without using member functions (not even constructors and destructors). Use `class` and `friend` only. Test each of the new versions. Compare them with the versions using member functions.

10. (∗3) Design a symbol table class and a symbol table entry class for some language. Have a look at a compiler for that language to see what the symbol table really looks like.

11. (∗2) Modify the expression class from Exercise 5 to handle variables and the assignment operator `=`. Use the symbol table class from Exercise 10.

12. (∗1) Given the program:

```
#include <stream.h>

main()
{
    cout << "Hello, world\n";
}
```

modify it to produce the output

```
Initialize
Hello, world
Clean up
```

Do not change `main( )` in any way.

Chapter 6

Operator Overloading

Here be Dragons!
– ancient map

This chapter describes the mechanism for operator overloading provided in C++. A programmer can define a meaning for operators when applied to objects of a specific class; in addition to arithmetic, logical, and relational operators, call ( ) and subscripting [ ] can be defined, and both assignment and initialization can be redefined. Explicit and implicit type conversion between user-defined and basic types can be defined. It is shown how to define a class for which an object cannot be copied or destroyed except by specific user-defined functions.

6.1   Introduction

Programs often manipulate objects that are concrete representations of abstract concepts. For example, the C++ data type int, together with the operators +, -, *, /, etc., provides a (restricted) implementation of the mathematical concept of integers. Such concepts typically include a set of operators representing basic operations on objects in a terse, convenient, and conventional way. Unfortunately, only very few such concepts can be directly supported by a programming language. For example, ideas such as complex arithmetic, matrix algebra, logic signals, and strings receive no direct support in C++. Classes provide a facility for specifying a representation of nonprimitive objects in C++ together with a set of operations that can be performed on such objects. Defining operators to operate on class objects sometimes allows a programmer to provide a more conventional and convenient notation for manipulating class objects than could be achieved using only the basic functional notation. For example,

```
class complex {
    double  re, im;
public:
    complex(double r, double i) { re=r; im=i; }
    friend complex operator+(complex, complex);
    friend complex operator*(complex, complex);
};
```

defines a simple implementation of the concept of complex numbers, where a number is represented by a pair of double precision floating point numbers manipulated (exclusively) by the operators + and *. The programmer provides a meaning for + and * by defining functions named `operator+` and `operator*`. For example, given b and c of type `complex`, b+c means (by definition) `operator+(b,c)`. It is now possible to approximate the conventional interpretation of complex expressions. For example:

```
void f()
{
    complex a = complex(1, 3.1);
    complex b = complex(1.2, 2);
    complex c = b;

    a = b+c;
    b = b+c*a;
    c = a*b+complex(1,2);
}
```

The usual precedence rules hold, so the second statement means `b=b+(c*a)`; not `b=(b+c)*a`.

6.2 Operator Functions

Functions defining meanings for the following operators can be declared:

```
+      -      *      /      %      ^      &      !      ~      !
=      <      >      +=     -=     *=     /=     %=     ^=     &=
!=     <<     >>     >>=    <<=    ==     !=     <=     >=     &&
||     ++     --     []     ()     new    delete
```

The last four are subscript (§6.7), function call (§6.8), free store allocation, and free store de-allocation (§3.2.6). It is not possible to change the precedence of these operators, nor can the expression syntax be changed. For example, it is not possible to define a unary % or a binary !. It is not possible to define new operator tokens, but you can use the function call notation when this set of operators is not adequate. For example, use `pow()`, not `**`. These restrictions may seem draconian, but more flexible rules can very easily lead to ambiguities. For example, defining an operator ** to mean exponentiation may seem an obvious and easy task at first glance, but think again. Should ** bind to the left (as in Fortran) or to the right (as in Algol)? Should the expression a**p be interpreted a*(*p) or (a)**(p)?

The name of an operator function is the keyword operator followed by the operator itself, for example operator<<. An operator function is declared and can be called like any other function; a use of the operator is only a shorthand for an explicit call of the operator function. For example

```
void f(complex a, complex b)
{
    complex c = a + b;          // shorthand
    complex d = operator+(a,b); // explicit call
}
```

Given the preceding declaration of complex, the two initializers are synonymous.

6.2.1 Binary and Unary Operators

A binary operator can be defined by either a member function taking one argument or a friend function taking two arguments. Thus, for any binary operator @, aa@bb can be interpreted as either aa.operator@(bb) or operator@(aa,bb). If both are defined, aa@bb is an error. A unary operator, whether prefix or postfix, can be defined by either a member function taking no arguments or a friend function taking one argument. Thus, for any unary operator @, both aa@ and @aa can be interpreted as either aa.operator@() or operator@(aa). If both are defined, aa@ and @aa are errors. Consider these examples:

```
class X {
// friends:

    friend X operator-(X);       // unary minus
    friend X operator-(X,X);     // binary minus
    friend X operator-();        // error: no operand
    friend X operator-(X,X,X);   // error: ternary

// members (with implicit first argument: this):

    X* operator&();              // unary & (address of)
    X operator&(X);              // binary & (and)
    X operator&(X,X);            // error: ternary
};
```

When the operators ++ and -- are overloaded, it is not possible to distinguish prefix application from postfix application.

6.2.2 Predefined Meanings for Operators

No assumptions are made about the meaning of a user-defined operator. In particular, since an overloaded = is not assumed to implement assignment to its first operand, no test is made to ensure that that operand is an lvalue (§r.6).

The meanings of some built-in operators are defined to be equivalent to some combination of other operators on the same arguments. For example, if a is an int, ++a means a+=1, which in turn means a=a+1. Such relations do not hold for user-defined operators unless the user happens to define them that way. For example, the definition of operator+=() for a type complex cannot be deduced from the definitions of complex::operator+() and complex::operator=().

Because of historical accident, the operators = and & have predefined meanings when applied to class objects. There is no elegant way of "undefining" these two operators. They can, however, be disabled for a class X. One might, for example, declare X::operator&() without providing a definition for it. If somewhere the address of an object of class X is taken, the linker will detect the missing definition†. Alternatively, X::operator&() might be defined to cause a run-time error.

6.2.3 Operators and User-defined Types

An operator function must either be a member or take at least one class object argument (functions redefining the new and delete operators need not). This rule ensures that a user cannot change the meaning of any expression not involving a user-defined data type. In particular, it is not possible to define an operator function that operates exclusively on pointers.

An operator function intended to accept a basic type as its first operand cannot be a member function. For example, consider adding a complex variable aa to the integer 2: aa+2 can with a suitably declared member function be interpreted as aa.operator+(2), but 2+aa cannot be since there is no class int for which to define + to mean 2.operator+(aa). Even if there were, two different member functions would be needed to cope with 2+aa and aa+2. Since the compiler does not know the meaning of a user-defined +, it cannot assume that it is commutative and interpret 2+aa as aa+2. This example is trivially handled using friend functions.

All operator functions are, by definition, overloaded. An operator function provides a new meaning for an operator in addition to the built-in definition, and there can be several operator functions with the same name as long as they differ sufficiently in their argument types for the compiler to tell them apart (see §4.6.7).

---

† On some systems, the linker is so "smart" that it complains even when an unused function is not defined. On such systems this technique cannot be used.

6.3   User-defined Type Conversion

The implementation of complex numbers presented in the introduction is too restrictive to please anyone, so it must be extended. This is mostly a trivial repetition of the techniques previously presented. For example:

```
class complex {
    double  re, im;
public:
    complex(double r, double i) { re=r; im=i; }

    friend complex operator+(complex, complex);
    friend complex operator+(complex, double );
    friend complex operator+(double, complex );

    friend complex operator-(complex, complex);
    friend complex operator-(complex, double );
    friend complex operator-(double, complex );
    complex operator-();          // unary -

    friend complex operator*(complex, complex);
    friend complex operator*(complex, double );
    friend complex operator*(double, complex );

    // ...
};
```

With this declaration of `complex`, we can now write:

```
void f()
{
    complex a(1,1), b(2,2), c(3,3), d(4,4), e(5,5);
    a = -b-c;
    b = c*2.0*c;
    c = (d+e)*a;
}
```

However, writing a function for each combination of `complex` and `double`, as for `operator*()` above, is unbearably tedious. Furthermore, a realistic facility for complex arithmetic must provide at least a dozen such functions; see, for example, the type `complex` as declared in `<complex.h>`.

6.3.1 Constructors

An alternative to using several (overloaded) functions is to declare a constructor that given a `double` creates a `complex`. For example,

```
class complex {
    // ...
    complex(double r) { re=r; im=0; }
};
```

A constructor requiring a single argument need not be called explicitly:

```
complex z1 = complex(23);
complex z2 = 23;
```

Both z1 and z2 will be initialized by calling complex(23,0).

A constructor is a prescription for creating a value of a given type. When a value of a type is expected, and when such a value can be created by a constructor, given the value to be assigned, the constructor will be used. For example, class complex could be declared like this:

```
class complex {
    double re, im;
public:
    complex(double r, double i =0) { re=r; im=i; }

    friend complex operator+(complex, complex);
    friend complex operator*(complex, complex);
};
```

and operations involving complex variables and integer constants would be legal. An integer constant will be interpreted as complex with the imaginary part zero. For example, a=b*2 means

```
a=operator*( b, complex( double(2), double(0) ) )
```

A user-defined conversion is implicitly applied only if it is unique (§6.3.3).

An object constructed by explicit or implicit use of a constructor is automatic and will be destroyed at the first opportunity, typically immediately after the statement in which it was created.

6.3.2 Conversion Operators

Using a constructor to specify type conversion is convenient, but has implications that can be undesirable:

[1] There can be no implicit conversion from a user-defined type to a basic type (since the basic types are not classes);

[2] It is not possible to specify a conversion from a new type to an old one without modifying the declaration for the old one; and

[3] It is not possible to have a constructor with a single argument without also having a conversion.

The last does not appear to be a serious problem, and the first two problems can be coped with by defining a *conversion operator* for the source type. A member function X::operator T(), where T is a type name, defines a conversion from X to T. For example, one could define a type tiny that can take on values in the range 0..63 only but still mix freely with integers in arithmetic operations:

```
class tiny {
    char v;
    int assign(int i)
    { return v = (i&~63) ? (error("range error"),0) : i; }
public:
    tiny(int i)              { assign(i); }
    tiny(tiny& t)            { v = t.v; }
    int operator=(tiny& t)   { return v = t.v; }
    int operator=(int i)     { return assign(i); }
    operator int()           { return v; }
};
```

The range is checked whenever a tiny is initialized by an int and whenever
an int is assigned to one. One tiny can be assigned to another without a
range check. To enable the usual integer operations on tiny variables,
tiny::operator int(), the implicit conversion from tiny to int, is
defined. Whenever a tiny appears where an int is needed, the appropriate
int is used. For example:

```
void main()
{
    tiny c1 = 2;
    tiny c2 = 62;
    tiny c3 = c2 - c1;   // c3 = 60
    tiny c4 = c3;        // no range check (not necessary)
    int i = c1 + c2;     // i = 64
    c1 = c2 + 2 * c1;    // range error: c1 = 0 (not 66)
    c2 = c1 - i;         // range error: c2 = 0
    c3 = c2;             // no range check (not necessary)
}
```

A type *vector of tiny* would appear to be more useful since it would also
save space; the subscript operator [ ] can be used to make such a type convenient to use.

Another use of user-defined conversion operators is types providing nonstandard representations of numbers (base 100 arithmetic, fixed point arithmetic, Binary Coded Decimal representation, etc.); this will typically involve
redefinition of operators such as + and *.

Conversion functions appear to be particularly useful for handling data
structures when reading (implemented by a conversion operator) is trivial,
whereas assignment and initialization are distinctly less trivial.

The istream and ostream types rely on a conversion function to make
statements such as

```
while (cin>>x) cout<<x;
```

possible. The input operation cin>>x above returns an istream&. That
value is implicitly converted to a value indicating the state of cin, and this
value can then be tested by the while (see §8.4.2). However, it is typically

not a good idea to define an implicit conversion from one type to another in such a way that information is lost in the conversion.

6.3.3 Ambiguities

An assignment to (or initialization of) an object of class **X** is legal if either the assigned value is an **X** or there is a unique conversion of the assigned value to type **X**.

In some cases, a value of the desired type can be constructed by repeated use of constructors or conversion operators. This must be handled by explicit use; only one level of user-defined implicit conversion is legal. In some cases, a value of the desired type can be constructed in more than one way. Such cases are illegal. For example:

```
class x { /* ... */ x(int); x(char*); };
class y { /* ... */ y(int); };
class z { /* ... */ z(x); };

overload f;
x f(x);
y f(y);

z g(z);

f(1);           // illegal: ambiguous f(x(1)) or f(y(1))
f(x(1));
f(y(1));
g("asdf");      // illegal: g(z(x("asdf"))) not tried
g(z("asdf"));
```

User-defined conversions are only considered if a call cannot be resolved without them. For example:

```
class x { /* ... */ x(int); };
overload h(double), h(x);
h(1);
```

The call could be interpreted as either `h(double(1))` or `h(x(1))` and would appear to be illegal according to the uniqueness rule. However, the first interpretation uses only a standard conversion and will be chosen under the rules presented in §4.6.7.

The rules for conversion are neither the simplest to implement, the simplest to document, nor the most general that could be devised. Consider the requirement that a conversion must be unique to be legal. A simpler approach would allow the compiler to use any conversion it could find; thus it would not be necessary to consider all possible conversions before declaring an expression legal. Unfortunately, this would mean that the meaning of a program depended on which conversion was found. In effect, the meaning of a program would in some way depend on the order of the declaration of the conversions. Since these will often reside in different source files (written by different programmers), the meaning of a program would depend on the order in which its parts were merged together. Alternatively, implicit conversions could be disallowed. Nothing could be simpler, but this rule leads to either inelegant user interfaces or an explosion of overloaded functions as seen in the class `complex` in the previous section.

The most general approach would take all available type information into account and consider all possible conversions. For example, using the preceding declarations, `aa=f(1)` could be handled because the type of `aa` determines a unique interpretation. If `aa` is an `x`, `f(x(1))` is the only one yielding the `x` needed in the assignment; if `aa` is a `y`, `f(y(1))` will be used instead. The most general approach would also cope with `g("asdf")` because `g(z(x("asdf")))` is a unique interpretation. The problem with this approach is that it requires extensive analysis of a complete expression to determine the interpretation of each operator and function call. This leads to slow compilation and also to surprising interpretations and error messages as the compiler considers conversions defined in libraries, etc. With this approach, the compiler takes more information into account than the programmer writing the code can be expected to know!

6.4   Constants

It is not possible to define constants of a class type in the sense that `1.2` and `12e3` are constants of type `double`. However, constants of the basic types can often be used instead if class member functions are used to provide an interpretation for them. Constructors taking a single argument provide a general mechanism for this. When constructors are simple and inline substituted, it is quite reasonable to think of constructor invocations as constants. For example, given the declaration of class `complex` in `<complex.h>`, the expression `zz1*3+zz2*complex(1,2)` will cause two function calls and not five. The two `*` operations will cause real function calls, but the `+` operation and the constructor called to create `complex(3)` and `complex(1,2)` will be inline expanded.

6.5   Large Objects

For each use of a `complex` binary operator as previously declared, a copy of each operand is passed as an argument to the function implementing the operator. The overhead of copying two `double`s is noticeable, but probably quite acceptable. Unfortunately, not all classes have a conveniently small representation. To avoid excessive copying, one can declare functions to take reference arguments. For example:

```
class matrix {
    double m[4][4];
public:
    matrix();
    friend matrix operator+(matrix&, matrix&);
    friend matrix operator*(matrix&, matrix&);
};
```

References allow the use of expressions involving the usual arithmetic operators for large objects without excessive copying. Pointers can not be used because it is not possible to redefine the meaning of an operator when applied to a pointer. The plus operator could be defined like this:

```
matrix operator+(matrix& arg1, matrix& arg2)
{
    matrix sum;
    for (int i=0; i<4; i++)
        for (int j=0; j<4; j++)
            sum.m[i][j] = arg1.m[i][j] + arg2.m[i][j];
    return sum;
}
```

This `operator+()` accesses the operands of + through references, but returns an object value. Returning a reference would appear to be more efficient:

```
class matrix {
    // ...
    friend matrix& operator+(matrix&, matrix&);
    friend matrix& operator*(matrix&, matrix&);
};
```

This is legal, but causes a memory allocation problem. Since a reference to the result will be passed out of the function as reference to the return value, it cannot be an automatic variable. Since an operator is often used more than once in an expression, the result cannot be a `static` local variable. It would typically be allocated on the free store. Copying the return value is often cheaper (in execution time, code space, and data space) and simpler to program.

6.6   Assignment and Initialization

Consider a very simple class `string`:

```
struct string {
    char* p;
    int size;    // of vector pointed to by p

    string(int sz) { p = new char[size=sz]; }
    ~string() { delete p; }
};
```

A string is a data structure consisting of a pointer to a vector of characters and the size of that vector. The vector is created by the constructor and deleted by the destructor. However, as shown in §5.10, this can cause trouble. For example:

```
void f()
{
    string s1(10);
    string s2(20);
    s1 = s2;
}
```

will allocate two character vectors, but the assignment `s1=s2` will destroy the pointer to one of them and duplicate the other. The destructor will be called for `s1` and `s2` on exit from `f()` and then delete the same vector twice with predictably disastrous results. The solution to this problem is to define assignment of `string` objects appropriately.

```
struct string {
    char* p;
    int size;     // of vector pointed to by p

    string(int sz) { p = new char[size=sz]; }
    ~string() { delete p; }
    void operator=(string&);
};

void string::operator=(string& a)
{
    if (this == &a) return;      // beware of s=s;
    delete p;
    p=new char[size=a.size];
    strcpy(p,a.p);
}
```

This definition of `string` will ensure that the preceding example will work as intended. However, a small modification to `f()` will cause the problem to reappear in a different guise:

```
void f()
{
    string s1(10);
    string s2 = s1;
}
```

Now only one `string` is constructed, but two are destroyed. A user-defined assignment operator is not applied to an uninitialized object. A quick look at `string::operator=()` shows why that would be unreasonable: the pointer `p` would contain an undefined and effectively random value. An assignment operator often relies on its arguments being initialized. For an initialization such as the preceding one this is by definition not so. Consequently, a similar, but separate, function must be defined to cope with initialization:

```
struct string {
    char* p;
    int size;    // of vector pointed to by p

    string(int sz) { p = new char[size=sz]; }
    ~string() { delete p; }
    void operator=(string&);
    string(string&);
};

void string::string(string& a)
{
    p=new char[size=a.size];
    strcpy(p,a.p);
}
```

For a type X, the constructor X(X&) takes care of initialization by an object of the same type X. It cannot be overemphasized that *assignment and initialization are different operations*. This is especially important when a destructor is declared. If a class X has a destructor that performs a nontrivial task, such as free store de-allocation, it is very likely that it needs the full complement of functions for completely avoiding bitwise copying of objects:

```
class X {
    // ...
    X(something);   // constructor: create objects
    X(X&);          // constructor: copy in initialization
    operator=(X&);  // assignment: cleanup and copy
    ~X();           // destructor: cleanup
};
```

There are two more cases when an object is copied: as a function argument and as a function return value. When an argument is passed a hitherto uninitialized variable, the formal argument, is initialized. The semantics are identical to those of other initializations. The same is the case for function return, though that is less obvious. In both cases, X(X&) will, if defined, be applied:

```
string g(string arg)
{
    return arg;
}

main ()
{
    string s = "asdf";
    s = g(s);
}
```

Clearly, the value of s ought to be "asdf" after the call of g(). Getting a copy of the value of s into the argument arg is not difficult; it takes a call of string(string&). Getting a copy of that value out of g() takes another call of string(string&); this time, the variable initialized is a temporary one, which is then assigned to s. Such temporary variables are, of course, destroyed properly using string::~string() as soon as possible.

6.7   Subscripting

An operator[] function can be used to give subscripts a meaning for class objects. The second argument (the subscript) of an operator[] function may be of any type. This makes it possible to define associative arrays, etc. As an example, let us recode the example from §2.3.10 in which an associative array is used to write a small program for counting the number of occurrences of words in a file. There a function is used. Here a proper associative array type is defined:

```
struct pair {
    char* name;
    int val;
};

class assoc {
    pair* vec;
    int max;
    int free;
public:
    assoc(int);
    int& operator[](char*);
    void print_all();
};
```

An assoc keeps a vector of pairs of size max. The index of the first unused vector element is kept in free. The constructor looks like this:

```
assoc::assoc(int s)
{
    max = (s<16) ? s : 16;
    free = 0;
    vec = new pair[max];
}
```

The implementation uses the same trivial and inefficient search method as in §2.3.10. However, an assoc grows in case of overflow:

```
#include <string.h>

int& assoc::operator[](char* p)
/*
    maintain a set of "pair"s:
    search for p,
    return a reference to the integer part of its "pair"
    make a new "pair" if "p" has not been seen
*/
{
    register pair* pp;

    for (pp=&vec[free-1]; vec<=pp; pp-- )
        if (strcmp(p,pp->name)==0) return pp->val;

    if (free==max) {      // overflow: grow the vector
        pair* nvec = new pair[max*2];
        for (int i=0; i<max; i++) nvec[i] = vec[i];
        delete vec;
        vec = nvec;
        max = 2*max;
    }

    pp = &vec[free++];
    pp->name = new char[strlen(p)+1];
    strcpy(pp->name,p);
    pp->val = 0;          // initial value: 0
    return pp->val;
}
```

Since the representation of an `assoc` is hidden, we need a way of printing it. The next section will show how a proper iterator can be defined. Here we will just use a simple print function:

```
void assoc::print_all()
{
    for (int i = 0; i<free; i++)
        cout << vec[i].name << ": " << vec[i].val << "\n";
}
```

Finally we can write the trivial main program:

```
main()  // count the occurrences of each word on input
{
    const MAX = 256; // larger than the largest word
    char buf[MAX];
    assoc vec(512);
    while (cin>>buf) vec[buf]++;
    vec.print_all();
}
```

6.8   Function Call

Function call, that is, the notation *expression(expression-list)*, can be interpreted as a binary operation, and the call operator ( ) can be overloaded in the same way as other operators. An argument list for an `operator()` function is evaluated and checked according to the usual argument passing rules. Over-loading function call seems to be useful primarily for defining types with only a single operation, and for types for which one operation is so predominant that others can be ignored in most contexts.

We did not define an iterator for the associative array type `assoc`. This could be done by defining a class `assoc_iterator` with the job of presenting elements from an `assoc` in some order. The iterator needs access to the data stored in an `assoc` and it is therefore made a `friend`:

```
class assoc {
friend class assoc_iterator;
    pair* vec;
    int max;
    int free;
public:
    assoc(int);
    int& operator[](char*);
};
```

The iterator can be defined as:

```
class assoc_iterator {
    assoc* cs;   // current assoc array
    int i;       // current index
public:
    assoc_iterator(assoc& s) { cs = &s; i = 0; }
    pair* operator()()
        { return (i<cs->free)? &cs->vec[i++] : 0; }
};
```

An `assoc_iterator` must be initialized for an `assoc` array, and will return a pointer to (new) a `pair` from that array each time it is activated using the ( ) operator. When it reaches the end of the array, it returns 0:

```
main()  // count the occurrences of each word on input
{
    const MAX = 256; // larger than the largest word
    char buf[MAX];
    assoc vec(512);
    while (cin>>buf) vec[buf]++;
    assoc_iterator next(vec);
    pair* p;
    while ( p = next() )
        cout << p->name << ": " << p->val << "\n";
}
```

An iterator type like this has the advantage over a set of functions doing the same job: it has its own private data for keeping track of the iteration. It is typically also important that many iterators of such a type can be active simultaneously.

Naturally, this use of objects to represent iterators has nothing in particular to do with operator overloading. Many people like iterators with operations such as `first()`, `next()`, and `last()`.

6.9   A String Class

Here is a more realistic version of class `string`. It counts the references to a string to minimize copying and uses standard C++ character strings as constants.

```
#include <stream.h>
#include <string.h>

class string {
    struct srep {
        char* s;        // pointer to data
        int   n;        // reference count
    };
    srep *p;

public:
    string(char *);     // string x = "abc"
    string();           // string x;
    string(string &);   // string x = string ...
    string& operator=(char *);
    string& operator=(string &);
    ~string();
    char& operator[](int i);

    friend ostream& operator<<(ostream&, string&);
    friend istream& operator>>(istream&, string&);

    friend int operator==(string &x, char *s)
        { return strcmp(x.p->s, s) == 0; }

    friend int operator==(string &x, string &y)
        { return strcmp(x.p->s, y.p->s) == 0; }

    friend int operator!=(string &x, char *s)
        { return strcmp(x.p->s, s) != 0; }

    friend int operator!=(string &x, string &y)
        { return strcmp(x.p->s, y.p->s) != 0; }
};
```

The constructors and the destructor are (as usual) trivial:

```
string::string()
{
    p = new srep;
    p->s = 0;
    p->n = 1;
}

string::string(char* s)
{
    p = new srep;
    p->s = new char[ strlen(s)+1 ];
    strcpy(p->s, s);
    p->n = 1;
}

string::string(string& x)
{
    x.p->n++;
    p = x.p;
}

string::~string()
{
    if (--p->n == 0) {
        delete p->s;
        delete p;
    }
}
```

As usual, the assignment operators are very similar to the constructors. They must handle cleanup of their first (left-hand) operand:

```
string& string::operator=(char* s)
{
    if (p->n > 1) {          // disconnect self
        p->n--;
        p = new srep;
    }
    else if (p->n == 1)
        delete p->s;

    p->s = new char[ strlen(s)+1 ];
    strcpy(p->s, s);
    p->n = 1;
    return *this;
}
```

It is wise to make sure that assignment of an object to itself works correctly:

```
string& string::operator=(string& x)
{
    x.p->n++;
    if (--p->n == 0) {
        delete p->s;
        delete p;
    }
    p = x.p;
    return *this;
}
```

The output operator is intended for demonstrating the use of reference counting. It echos each input string (using the << operator, defined below):

```
ostream& operator<<(ostream& s, string& x)
{
    return s << x.p->s << " [" << x.p->n << "]\n";
}
```

The input operation uses the standard character string input function (§8.4.1).

```
istream& operator>>(istream& s, string& x)
{
    char buf[256];
    s >> buf;
    x = buf;
    cout << "echo: " << x << "\n";
    return s;
}
```

The subscript operator is provided for access to individual characters. The index is checked:

```
void error(char* p)
{
    cerr << p << "\n";
    exit(1);
}
```

```
char& string::operator[](int i)
{
    if (i<0 || strlen(p->s)<i) error("index out of range");
    return p->s[i];
}
```

The main program simply exercises the string operators a bit. It reads words from input into strings and then prints the strings. It continues to do so until the string done is recognized, it runs out of strings to store words in, or it finds the end of file. Then it prints out all the strings in reverse order and terminates.

```
main()
{
    string x[100];
    int n;

    cout << "here we go\n";
    for (n = 0; cin>>x[n]; n++) {
        string y;
        if (n==100) error("too many strings");
        cout << (y = x[n]);
        if (y=="done") break;
    }
    cout << "here we go back again\n";
    for (int i=n-1; 0<=i; i--) cout << x[i];
}
```

6.10   Friends and Members

Finally, it is possible to discuss when to use members and when to use friends
to access the private part of a user-defined type. Some operations must be
members: constructors, destructors, and virtual functions (see next chapter),
but typically there is a choice.

Consider a simple class X:

```
class X {
    // ...
    X(int);
    int m();
    friend int f(X&);
}
```

Superficially there is no reason for choosing a friend f(X&) over a member
X::m() (or vice versa) for implementing an operation on an object of class X.
However, the member X::m() can be invoked only for a "real object"
whereas the friend f(X&) might be called for an object created by an implicit
type conversion. For example:

```
void g()
{
    1.m();      // error
    f(1);       // f(X(1));
}
```

An operation modifying the state of a class object should therefore be a
member, not a friend. Operators that require lvalue operands for the fundamental types (=, *=, ++, etc.) are most naturally defined as members for
user-defined types.

Conversely, if implicit type conversion is desired for all operands of an operation, the function implementing it must be a friend, not a member. This is often the case for the functions implementing operators that do not require lvalue operands when applied to fundamental types (+, -, ¦ ¦, etc.).

If no type conversions are defined, there appears to be no compelling reason to choose a member over a friend taking a reference argument or vice versa. In some cases the programmer may have a preference for one call syntax over another. For example, most people seem to prefer the notation inv(m) for inverting a matrix m to the alternative m.inv(). Naturally, if inv() really does invert m itself, rather than simply return a new matrix that is the inverse of m, it should be a member.

All other things considered equal, choose a member: It is not possible to know if someone some day will define a conversion operator. It is not always possible to predict if a future change may require changes to the state of the object involved. The member function call syntax makes it clear to the user that the object may be modified; a reference argument is far less obvious. Furthermore, expressions in a member can be noticeably shorter than the equivalent expressions in a friend. The friend function must use an explicit argument, whereas the member can use this implicitly. Unless overloading is used, member names tend to be shorter than the names of friends.

6.11 Caveat

Like most programming language features, operator overloading can be both used and misused. In particular, the ability to define new meanings for old operators can be used to write programs that are well nigh incomprehensible. Imagine, for example, the problems facing a reader of a program in which the operator + has been made to denote subtraction.

The mechanism presented here should protect the programmer/reader from the worst excesses of overloading by preventing a programmer from changing the meaning of operators for basic data types such as int, and by preserving the syntax of expressions and the precedence of operators.

It is probably wise to use operator overloading primarily to mimic conventional use of operators. The function call notation can be used when such conventional use of operators is not established or when the set of operators available for overloading in C++ is not adequate to mimic conventional usage.

6.12 Exercises

1. (*2) Define an iterator for class string. Define a concatenate operator + and an "add to the end" operator +=. What other operations would you like to be able to do on a string?
2. (*1.5) Provide a substring operator for a string class by overloading ( ).

3. (*3) Design class `string` so that the substring operator can be used on the left-hand side of an assignment. First write a version in which a string can be assigned to a substring of the same length, then a version in which the lengths may be different.

4. (*2) Design a class `string` so that it has value semantics for assignment, argument passing, etc; that is, where the string representation, not just the controlling data structure in class `string`, is copied.

5. (*3) Modify the class `string` from the previous example to copy strings only when necessary. That is, keep a shared representation of two strings until one of the strings is modified. Do not try to have a substring operator that can be used on the left-hand side at the same time.

6. (*4) Design a class `string` with value semantics, delayed copy, and a substring operator that can be used on the left-hand side.

7. (*2) In the following program, which conversions are used in each expression?

```
struct X {
    int i;
    X(int);
    operator+(int);
};

struct Y {
    int i;
    Y(X);
    operator+(X);
    operator int();
};

X operator* (X, Y);
int f(X);

X x = 1;
Y y = x;
int i = 2;

main()
{
    i + 10;
    y + 10;
    y + 10 * y;
    x + y + i;
    x * x + i;
    f(7);
    f(y);
    y + y;
    106 + y;
}
```

Define both X and Y to be integer types. Modify the program so that it will run and print the values of each legal expression.

8. (∗2) Define a class INT that behaves exactly like an int. Hint: define INT::operator int().

9. (∗1) Define a class RINT that behaves like an int except that the only operations allowed are + (unary and binary), − (unary and binary), ∗, /, %. Hint: do not define INT::operator int().

10. (∗3) Define a class LINT that behaves like a RINT except that it has at least 64 bits of precision.

11. (∗4) Define a class implementing arbitrary precision arithmetic. Hint: you will need to manage storage in a way similar to what was done for class string.

12. (∗2) Write a program that has been rendered unreadable through use of operator overloading and macros. An idea: define + to mean − and vice versa for INTs; then use a macro to define int to mean INT. Redefining popular functions, using reference type arguments, and a few misleading comments can also create great confusion.

13. (∗3) Swap the result of the previous exercise with a friend. Figure out what your friend's program does without running it. When you have completed this exercise you'll know what to avoid.

14. (∗2) Re-write the complex example (§6.3.1), the tiny example (§6.3.2), and the string example (§6.9) without use of friend functions. Use only member functions. Test each of the new versions. Compare them with the versions using friend functions. Review Exercise 5.3.

15. (∗2) define a type vec4 as a vector of four floats. Define operator[] for vec4. Define operators +, −, ∗, /, =, +=, −=, ∗=, /= for combinations of vectors and floating point numbers.

16. (∗3) Define a class mat4 as a vector of four vec4s. Define operator[] returning a vec4 for mat4. Define the usual matrix operations for this type. Define a function doing Gaussian elimination for a mat4.

17. (∗2) Define a class vector similar to vec4, but with a the size given as an argument to the constructor vector::vector(int).

18. (∗3) Define a class matrix similar to mat4, but with the dimensions given as arguments to the constructor matrix::matrix(int,int).

Chapter 7

Derived Classes

Do not multiply objects without necessity.
– W.Occam

This chapter describes the C++ concept of derived classes. Derived classes provide a simple, flexible, and efficient mechanism for specifying an alternative interface for a class and for defining a class by adding facilities to an existing class without reprogramming or recompilation. Using derived classes, one can also provide a common interface for several different classes so that objects of those classes can be manipulated identically by other parts of a program. This typically involves placing type information in each object so that such objects can be used appropriately in contexts in which their type cannot be known at compile time; the concept of a virtual function is provided to handle such run-time type dependencies safely and elegantly. Fundamentally, derived classes exist to make it easier for a programmer to express commonality.

7.1 Introduction

Consider writing some general facility (for example, a linked list type, a symbol table, or a scheduler for a simulation system) intended to be used by many different people in many different contexts. There is clearly no shortage of candidates for such facilities and the benefits of having them standardized are enormous. Every experienced programmer seems to have written (and debugged) a dozen variations of set types, hash tables, sort functions, etc., but each programmer and each program appears to have a separate version of these concepts, making programs unnecessarily hard to read, hard to debug, and hard to change. Furthermore, in a large program there may very well be several copies of (nearly) identical code for handling such basic concepts.

The reason for this chaos is partly that it is conceptually difficult to present such general purpose facilities in a programming language, and partly that facilities of sufficient generality typically impose space and/or time overheads that make them unsuitable for the simplest and most heavily used facilities (linked lists, vectors, etc.) where they would be most useful. The C++ concept of a derived class, presented in §7.2, does not provide a general solution for all of these problems, but it provides a way of coping with quite a few important special cases. For example, it will be shown how to define an efficient generic linked-list class so that all versions of it share code.

Writing general purpose facilities is nontrivial, and the emphasis in the design is often somewhat different from the emphasis in the design of a special purpose program. Clearly, there is no sharp dividing line between general purpose and special purpose facilities, and the techniques and language facilities presented in this chapter can be seen as increasingly useful as the size and complexity of the program to be written increases.

7.2   Derived Classes

To separate the problems of understanding the language mechanisms and the techniques for using them, the concept of derived classes is introduced in three stages. First, the language features themselves (notation and semantics) will be described using small examples that are not intended to be realistic. After that, some nontrivial uses of derived classes are demonstrated, and finally, a complete program is presented.

7.2.1   Deriving

Consider building a program dealing with people employed by a firm. Such a program might have a data structure like this:

```
struct employee {
    char*       name;
    short       age;
    short       department;
    int         salary;
    employee*   next;
    // ...
};
```

The `next` field would be a link in a list of similar employees. Now let us try to define a manager:

```
struct manager {
    employee emp;          // manager's employee record
    employee* group;       // people managed
    // ...
};
```

A manager is also an employee; the `employee` data is stored in the `emp` member of a `manager` object. This may be obvious to a human reader, but there is nothing that distinguishes the emp member to the compiler. A pointer to a manager (`manager*`) is not a pointer to an employee (`employee*`), so one cannot simply use the one where the other is required. In particular, one cannot put a manager onto a list of employees without writing special code. One could either use explicit type conversion on a `manager*` or put the address of the emp member onto a list of employees, but both are inelegant and can be quite obscure. The correct approach is to state that a manager *is* an employee with a few pieces of information added:

```
struct manager : employee {
    employee* group;
    // ...
};
```

The `manager` is *derived* from `employee`, and conversely, `employee` is a *base class* for `manager`. The class `manager` has the members of class `employee` (name, age, etc.) in addition to the member `group`.

With this definition of `employee` and `manager`, we can now create a list of employees, some of whom are managers. For example:

```
void f()
{
    manager m1, m2;
    employee e1, e2;
    employee* elist;
    elist = &m1;        // put m1, e1, m2, and e2 on elist
    m1.next = &e1;
    e1.next = &m2;
    m2.next = &e2;
    e2.next = 0;
}
```

Since a manager is an employee, a `manager*` can be used as a `employee*`. However, an employee is not necessarily a manager, so an `employee*` cannot be used as a `manager*`. This is explained in detail §7.2.4.

7.2.2 Member Functions

Simple data structures, such as `employee` and `manager`, are really not that interesting and often not particularly useful, so consider adding functions to them. For example:

```
class employee {
    char* name;
    // ...
public:
    employee* next;
    void print();
    // ...
};

class manager : public employee {
    // ...
public:
    void print();
    // ...
};
```

Some questions must be answered. How can a member function of the derived class `manager` use members of its base class `employee`? What members of the base class `employee` can the member functions of the derived class `manager` use? What members of the base class `employee` can a nonmember function use on an object of type `manager`? In what way can the programmer affect the answer to those questions to suit the application?

Consider:

```
void manager::print()
{
    cout << " name is " << name << "\n";
    // ...
}
```

A member of a derived class can use a public name of its base class in the same way as other members, that is, without specifying an object. The object pointed to by `this` is assumed, so `name` (correctly) refers to `this->name`. However, the function `manager::print` will not compile; a member of a derived class has no special permission to access private members of its base class, so `name` is not accessible to it.

This comes as a surprise to many, but consider the alternative: that a member function could access the private members of its base class. The concept of a private member would be rendered meaningless by a facility allowing a programmer to gain access to the private part of a class simply by deriving a new class from it. Furthermore, one could no longer find all uses of a private name by looking at the functions declared as members and friends of that class. One would have to examine every source file of the complete program for derived classes, then examine every function of those classes, then find every class derived from these classes, etc. This is at best tedious, and typically impractical.

On the other hand, it is possible to use the `friend` mechanism to grant such access to either specific functions or every function of a specific class (as described in §5.3). For example:

```
class employee {
friend void manager::print();
    // ...
};
```

would solve the problem for `manager::print()`, and

```
class employee {
friend class manager;
    // ...
};
```

would make every member of class `employee` accessible to every function of class `manager`. In particular, it would make `name` accessible to `manager::print()`.

An alternative, and sometimes cleaner, solution is for the derived class to use only the public members of its base class. For example:

```
void manager::print()
{
    employee::print();    // print employee information
    // ...                // print manager information
}
```

Note that `::` must be used because `print()` has been redefined in `manager`. Such reuse of names is typical. The unwary might write this:

```
void manager::print()
{
    print();              // print employee information
    // ...                // print manager information
}
```

and find the program in an unexpected sequence of recursive calls when `manager::print()` is called.

7.2.3 Visibility

Class `employee` was made a *public* base class of class `manager` by the declaration:

```
class manager : public employee {
    // ...
};
```

This means that a public member of class `employee` is also a public member of class `manager`. For example:

```
void clear(manager* p)
{
    p->next = 0;
}
```

will compile since `next` is a public member of both `employee` and `manager`. Alternatively, one can declare a *private* base class by simply leaving out the word `public` in the class declaration:

```
class manager : employee {
    // ...
};
```

This means that a public member of class `employee` is a private member of class `manager`. That is, `manager`'s member functions can use the public members of `employee` as before, but these members are not accessible to users of class `manager`. In particular, given this declaration of `manager`, the function `clear()` will not compile. Friends of a derived class have the same access to base class members as do member functions.

Since declaring public base classes appears to be more common than declaring private ones, it is a pity that the declaration of a public base class is longer than the declaration of a private one. It is also a source of confusing errors for the beginner.

When a derived `struct` is declared, its base class is by default a `public` base class. That is,

```
struct D : B { ...
```

means

```
class D : public B { public: ...
```

This implies that if you do not find the data hiding provided by use of `class`, `public`, and `friend` useful, you can simply avoid those keywords and stick to `struct`. Language facilities such as member functions, constructors, and operator overloading are independent of the data-hiding mechanism.

It is also possible to declare some, but not all, of the public members of a base class public members of a derived class. For example:

```
class manager : employee {
    // ...
public:
    // ...
    employee::name;
    employee::department;
};
```

The notation

```
class-name :: member-name ;
```

does not introduce a new member but simply makes a public member of a base class public for a derived class. Now, name and department can be used for a manager, but salary and age cannot. Naturally, it is not possible to make a private member of a base class a public member of a derived class. It is not possible to make overloaded names public using this notation.

To sum up, along with providing features in addition to those found in its base class, a derived class can be used to make features (names) of a class inaccessible to a user. In other words, a derived class can be used to provide transparent, semitransparent, and nontransparent access to its base class.

7.2.4 Pointers

If a class derived has a public base class base, then a pointer to derived can be assigned to a variable of type pointer to base without use of explicit type conversion. The opposite conversion, for pointer to base to pointer to derived, must be explicit. For example:

```
class base { /* ... */ };
class derived : public base { /* ... */ };

derived m;
base* pb = &m;        // implicit conversion
derived* pd = pb;     // error: a base* is not a derived*
pd = (derived*)pb;    // explicit conversion
```

In other words, an object of a derived class can be treated as an object of its base class when manipulated through pointers. The opposite is not true.

Were base a private base class of derived, the implicit conversion of a derived* to a base* would not be done. An implicit conversion cannot be performed in this case because a public member of base can be accessed through a pointer to base but not through a pointer to derived:

```
class base {
    int m1;
public:
    int m2;        // m2 is a public member of base
};

class derived : base {
    // m2 is NOT a public member of derived
};

derived d;
d.m2 = 2;          // error: m2 from private base class
base* pb = &d;     // error (private base)
pb->m2 = 2;        // ok
pb = (base*)&d;    // ok: explicit conversion
pb->m2 = 2;        // ok
```

Among other things, this example shows that by using explicit type casting you can break the protection rules. This is clearly not recommended, and doing it usually earns the programmer a just "reward." Unfortunately, undisciplined use of explicit type conversion can also create hell for innocent victims maintaining a program containing them. Fortunately, there is no way of using casting to enable use of the private name m1. A private member of a class can be used only by members and friends of that class.

7.2.5 Class Hierarchies

A derived class can itself be a base class. For example:

```
class employee { ... };
class secretary : employee { ... };
class manager : employee { ... };
class temporary : employee { ... };
class consultant : temporary { ... };
class director : manager { ... };
class vice_president : manager { ... };
class president : vice_president { ... };
```

Such a set of related classes is traditionally called a class hierarchy. Since one can derive a class from a single base class only, such a hierarchy is a tree and cannot be a more general graph structure. For example:

```
class temporary { ... };
class employee { ... };
class secretary : employee { ... };

// not in C++ :
class temporary_secretary : temporary : secretary { ... };
class consultant : temporary : employee { ... };
```

This is a pity, since a directed acyclic graph of derived classes can be very useful. Such structures cannot be declared, but must be simulated using members of the appropriate types. For example:

```
class temporary { ... };
class employee { ... };
class secretary : employee { ... };

// Alternative:
class temporary_secretary : secretary
{ temporary temp; ... };
class consultant : employee
{ temporary temp; ... };
```

This is not elegant and suffers from exactly the problems derived classes were invented to overcome. For example, since consultant is not derived from temporary, a consultant cannot be put on a list of temporary employees

without special code being written. However, this technique has been successfully applied in many useful programs.

7.2.6 Constructors and Destructors

Some derived classes need constructors. If the base class has a constructor,
then that constructor must be called, and if that constructor needs arguments,
then such arguments must be provided. For example:

```
class base {
    // ...
public:
    base(char* n, short t);
    ~base();
};

class derived : public base {
    base m;
public:
    'derived(char* n);
    ~derived();
};
```

Arguments for the base class's constructor are specified in the definition of a
derived class's constructor. In this respect, the base class acts exactly like an
unnamed member of the derived class (see §5.5.4). For example:

```
derived::derived(char* n) : (n,10), m("member",123)
{
    // ...
}
```

Class objects are constructed from the bottom up: first the base, then the
members, and then the derived class itself. They are destroyed in the opposite
order: first the derived class itself, then the members, and then the base.

7.2.7 Type Fields

To use derived classes as more than a convenient shorthand in declarations, the
following problem must be solved: Given a pointer of type `base*` to which
derived type does the object pointed to really belong? There are three fundamental solutions to the problem:
    [1] Ensure that only objects of a single type are ever pointed to (§7.3.3);
    [2] Place a type field in the base class for the functions to inspect; and
    [3] Use virtual functions (§7.2.8).
    Pointers to base classes are commonly used in the design of *container
classes* such as set, vector, and list. In this case, solution 1 yields homogeneous lists; that is, lists of objects of the same type. Solutions 2 and 3 can be
used to build heterogeneous lists; that is, lists of (pointers to) objects of several

different types. Solution 3 is a special type-secure variation of solution 2.

Let us first examine the simple type-field solution, that is, solution 2. The manager/employee example could be redefined like this:

```
enum empl_type { M, E };

struct employee {
    empl_type type;
    employee* next;
    char*     name;
    short     department;
    // ...
};

struct manager : employee {
    employee* group;
    short     level;
    // ...
};
```

Given this, we can now write a function that prints information about each employee:

```
void print_employee(employee* e)
{
    switch (e->type) {
    case E:
        cout << e->name << "\t" << e->department << "\n";
        // ...
        break;
    case M:
        cout << e->name << "\t" << e->department << "\n";
        // ...
        manager* p = (manager*)e;
        cout << " level " << p->level << "\n";
        // ...
        break;
    }
}
```

and use it to print a list of employees like this:

```
void f(employee* ll)
{
    for (; ll; ll=ll->next) print_employee(ll);
}
```

This works fine, especially in a small program written by a single person, but it has the fundamental weakness that it depends on the programmer manipulating types in a way that cannot be checked by the compiler. This typically leads to two kinds of errors in larger programs. The first is failure to test the type field. The second is failure to place all possible cases in a switch such as the one above. Both are reasonably easy to avoid when a program is first written, and both are very hard to avoid when modifying a nontrivial program, especially a large program written by someone else. These problems are often made harder to avoid because functions such as print() are often organized to take advantage of the commonality of the classes involved. For example:

```
void print_employee(employee* e)
{
    cout << e->name << "\t" << e->department << "\n";
    // ...
    if (e->type == M) {
        manager* p = (manager*)e;
        cout << " level " << p->level << "\n";
        // ...
    }
}
```

Finding all such if statements buried in a large function handling many derived classes can be difficult, and even when they have been found it can be hard to understand what is going on.

7.2.8 Virtual Functions

Virtual functions overcome the problems with the type-field solution by allowing the programmer to declare functions in a base class that can be redefined in each derived class. The compiler and loader will guarantee the correct correspondence between objects and functions applied to them. For example:

```
struct employee {
    employee* next;
    char*     name;
    short     department;
    // ...
    virtual void print();
};
```

The keyword virtual indicates that the function print() can have different versions for different derived classes and that it is the task of the compiler to find the appropriate one for each call of print(). The type of the function is declared in the base class and cannot be redeclared in a derived class. A virtual function *must* be defined for the class in which it is first declared. For example:

```
void employee::print()
{
    cout << name << "\t" << department << "\n";
    // ...
}
```

The virtual function can therefore be used even if no class is derived from its class, and a derived class that does not need a special version of a virtual function need not provide one. When deriving a class, one simply provides an appropriate function if it is needed. For example:

```
struct manager : employee {
    employee* group;
    short      level;
    // ...
    void print();
};

void manager::print()
{
    employee::print();
    cout << "\tlevel " << level << "\n";
    // ...
}
```

The function `print_employee()` is now unnecessary since the `print()` member functions have taken its place and a list of employees can be handled like this:

```
void f(employee* 11)
{
    for (; 11; 11=11->next) 11->print();
}
```

Each employee will be written out according to its type. For example:

```
main()
{
    employee e;
        e.name = "J.Brown";
        e.department = 1234;
        e.next = 0;
    manager m;
        m.name = "J.Smith";
        m.department = 1234;
        m.level = 2;
        m.next = &e;
    f(&m);
}
```

will produce:

```
J.Smith 1234
        level 2
J.Brown 1234
```

Note that this will work even if `f()` was written and compiled before the specific derived class `manager` was even conceived of! Clearly implementing this involves storing some kind of type information in each object of class employee. The space taken (in the current implementation) is just enough to hold a pointer. This space is taken only in objects of a class with virtual functions, not in every class object, or even in every object of a derived class. You pay this overhead only for classes for which you declare virtual functions.

Calling a function using the scope resolution operator :: as is done in manager::print() ensures that the virtual mechanism is not used. Otherwise manager::print() would suffer an infinite recursion. The use of a qualified name has another desirable effect: if a virtual function is also inline (as is not uncommon), then inline substitution can be used where :: is used in a call. This provides the programmer with an efficient way to handle some important special cases in which one virtual function calls another for the same object. Since the type of the object is determined in the call of the first virtual function, it often need not be dynamically determined again for another call for the same object.

7.3 Alternative Interfaces

After presenting the language facilities relating to derived classes, the discussion can now return to the problems they exist to solve. The fundamental idea for the classes described in this section is that they are written once and used later by programmers who cannot modify their definition. The classes will physically consist of one or more header files defining an interface and one or more files defining an implementation. The header files will be placed somewhere from which a user can get a copy using an #include directive. The files specifying the definition are typically compiled and put into a library.

7.3.1 An Interface

Consider writing a class slist for singly linked lists in such a way that the class can be used as a base for creating both heterogeneous and homogeneous lists of objects of types yet to be defined. First we will define a type ent:

```
typedef void* ent;
```

The exact nature of the type ent is unimportant, but it must be able to hold a pointer. Then we define a type slink:

```
class slink {
friend class slist;
friend class slist_iterator;
    slink* next;
    ent e;
    slink(ent a, slink* p) { e=a; next=p; }
};
```

A link can hold a single ent and is used to implement class slist:

```
class slist {
friend class slist_iterator;
    slink* last;          // last->next is head of list
public:
    int insert(ent a);   // add at head of list
    int append(ent a);   // add at tail of list
    ent get();           // return and remove head of list
    void clear();        // remove all links

    slist()       { last=0; }
    slist(ent a) { last=new slink(a,0); last->next=last; }
    ~slist()      { clear(); }
};
```

Although the list is clearly implemented as a linked list, the implementation could be changed to use a vector of ents without affecting users. That is, the use of slinks does not show in the declarations of the slist's public functions, only in the private part and the function definitions.

7.3.2 An Implementation

Implementing the slist functions is basically straightforward. The only real problem is what to do in case of an error, for example, what to do in case a user tries to get() something off an empty list. This will be discussed in §7.3.4. Here are the slist member definitions. Note how storing a pointer to the last element of the circular list enables simple implementation of both an append() and an insert() operation:

```
int slist::insert(ent a)
{
    if (last)
        last->next = new slink(a,last->next);
    else {
        last = new slink(a,0);
        last->next = last;
    }
    return 0;
}

int slist::append(ent a)
{
    if (last)
        last = last->next = new slink(a,last->next);
    else {
        last = new slink(a,0);
        last->next = last;
    }
    return 0;
}
```

```
ent slist::get()
{
    if (last == 0) slist_handler("get from empty slist");
    slink* f = last->next;
    ent r = f->e;
    last = (f==last) ? 0 : f->next;
    delete  f;
    return r;
}
```

Note the way the `slist_handler` is called (its declaration can be found in §7.3.4). This pointer to function name is used exactly as if it was the name of a function. This is a shorthand for the more explicit call notation:

```
(*slist_handler)("get from empty list");
```

Finally, `slist::clear()` removes all elements from a list:

```
void slist::clear()
{
    slink* l = last;
    if (l == 0) return;
    do {
        slink* ll = l;
        l = l->next;
        delete ll;
    } while (l!=last);
}
```

Class `slist` provides no facilities for looking into a list, only the means for inserting and deleting members. However, both class `slist` and class `slink` declare a class `slist_iterator` to be a friend, so we can declare a suitable iterator. Here is one in the style presented in §6.8:

```
class slist_iterator {
    slink* ce;
    slist* cs;
public:
    slist_iterator(slist& s) { cs = &s; ce = 0; }

    ent operator()() {
        slink* ll;
        if (ce == 0)
            ll = ce = cs->last;
        else {
            ce = ce->next;
            ll = (ce==cs->last) ? 0 : ce;
        }
        return ll ? ll->e : 0;
    }
};
```

7.3.3 How to Use It

As it stands, class `slist` is virtually useless. After all, for what can one use a
list of `void*` pointers? The trick is to derive a class from `slist` to get a list
of objects of a type that is of interest in a particular program. Consider a compiler for a language such as C++. Here lists of names will be used extensively; a name is something like this:

```
struct name {
    char* string;
    // ...
};
```

Pointers to names, rather than the name objects themselves, will be put onto
lists. This allows use of the small information field, `e`, of an `slist`, and
allows a name to be on more than one list at a time. Here is a definition of a
class `nlist` trivially derived from class `slist`:

```
#include "slist.h"
#include "name.h"

struct nlist : slist {
    void insert(name* a) { slist::insert(a); }
    void append(name* a) { slist::append(a); }
    name* get()          { return (name*)slist::get(); }
    nlist()              {}
    nlist(name* a) : (a) {}
};
```

The functions of the new class are either inherited directly from `slist` or do
nothing but type conversion. The class `nlist` is nothing but an alternative
interface for class `slist`. Because the type `ent` really is `void*`, it is not
necessary to explicitly convert the `name*` pointers used as actual arguments
(§2.3.4).

Name lists might be used like this in a class representing a class definition:

```
struct classdef {
    nlist friends;
    nlist constructors;
    nlist destructors;
    nlist members;
    nlist operators;
    nlist virtuals;
    // ...
    void add_name(name*);
    classdef();
    ~classdef();
};
```

and names might be added to those lists in approximately this manner:

```
void classdef::add_name(name* n)
{
    if (n->is_friend()) {
        if (find(&friends,n))
            error("friend redeclared");
        else if (find(&members,n))
            error("friend redeclared as member");
        else
            friends.append(n);
    }
    if (n->is_operator()) operators.append(n);
    // ...
}
```

where is_operator() and is_friend() are member functions of class name. The find() function could be written like this:

```
int find(nlist* ll, name* n)
{
    slist_iterator ff(*(slist*)ll);
    ent p;
    while ( p=ff() ) if (p==n) return 1;
    return 0;
}
```

Explicit type conversion is used here to use an slist_iterator for an nlist. A better solution, to make an iterator for nlists, is shown in §7.3.5. An nlist might be printed by a function like this:

```
void print_list(nlist* ll, char* list_name)
{
    slist_iterator count(*(slist*)ll);
    name* p;
    int n = 0;
    while ( count() ) n++;
    cout << list_name << "\n" << n << " members\n";
    slist_iterator print(*(slist*)ll);
    while ( p=(name*)print() ) cout << p->string << "\n";
}
```

7.3.4 Error Handling

There are four approaches to the problem of what to do when a general purpose facility such as slist encounters a run-time error (in C++, where no language facility is provided specifically for run-time error handling):

[1] Return an illegal value, and let the user check for it;
[2] Return an additional status value, and let the user check it;
[3] Call an error function provided as part of the slist class; or
[4] Call an error function that the user is supposed to supply.

For a small program written by a single user, there is really not much reason to choose one of these solutions over another. For a general purpose facility, the situation is quite different.

The first approach, returning an illegal value, is infeasible. There is in general no way of knowing that a particular value is illegal for all uses of an slist.

The second approach, returning a status value, can be used in some cases (a variation of this scheme is used for the standard I/O streams istream and ostream; as is explained in §8.4.2). However, it suffers from the serious problem that unless a facility fails often, users will not bother to check the status value. Furthermore, a facility may be used in hundreds or thousands of places in a program. Checking status in each place would make the program much harder to read.

The third approach, providing an error function, lacks flexibility. There is no way for the implementer of a general purpose facility to know how users would like errors to be handled. For example, a user might prefer error messages written in Danish or Hungarian.

The fourth approach, letting the user provide an error function, has some appeal provided that the implementer presents the class as a library (§4.5) containing default versions of the error handling functions.

Solutions 3 and 4 can be made more flexible (and essentially equivalent) by specifying a pointer to a function, rather than the function itself. This enables the designer of a facility such as slist to provide a default error function, while making it easy for programmers using lists to provide their own if and when needed. For example:

```
typedef void (*PFC)(char*); // pointer to function type
extern PFC slist_handler;
extern PFC set_slist_handler(PFC);
```

The function set_slist_handler() allows the user to replace the default. A conventional implementation provides a default error handling function that first writes a message on cerr and then terminates the program using exit():

```
#include "slist.h"
#include <stream.h>

void default_error(char* s)
{
    cerr << s << "\n";
    exit(1);
}
```

It also declares a pointer to an error function and, for notational convenience, a function for setting it:

```
PFC slist_handler = default_error;

PFC set_slist_handler(PFC handler)
{
    PFC rr = slist_handler;
    slist_handler = handler;
    return rr;
}
```

Note the way `set_slist_handler()` returns the previous `slist_handler`. This makes it convenient for the user to set and reset handlers in a stack fashion. This can be most useful in large programs in which an `slist` might be used in several contexts, each of which can then provide its own error handling routines. For example:

```
{
    PFC old = set_slist_handler(my_handler);

    // code where my_handler will be used
    // in case of errors in slist

    set_slist_handler(old); // re-set
}
```

To gain even finer control, the `slist_handler` could be a member of class `slist`, thus allowing different lists to have different error handlers simultaneously.

7.3.5 Generic Classes

Clearly one could define lists of other types (`classdef*`, `int`, `char*`, etc.) in the same way as class `nlist` was defined: by trivial derivation from class `slist`. The process of defining such new types is tedious (and therefore error-prone), but it can be "mechanized" by using macros. Unfortunately, this too can be quite painful when using the standard C preprocessor (§4.7 and §r.11.1). The resulting macros are, however, quite easy to use.

Here is an example of how a generic `slist`, called a `gslist`, can be provided as a macro. First some tools for writing this kind of macro are included from `<generic.h>`:

```
#include "slist.h"

#ifndef GENERICH
#include <generic.h>
#endif
```

Note how `#ifndef` is used to ensure that `<generic.h>` is not included twice in the same compilation. `GENERICH` is defined in `<generic.h>`.

Then the names for the new generic classes are defined using name2(), a name-concatenator macro from <generic.h>:

```
#define gslist(type) name2(type,gslist)
#define gslist_iterator(type) name2(type,gslist_iterator)
```

Finally, the class gslist(type) and gslist_iterator(type) can be written:

```
#define gslistdeclare(type)                                        \
struct gslist(type) : slist {                                      \
    int insert(type a)                                             \
        { return slist::insert( ent(a) ); }                       \
    int append(type a)                                            \
        { return slist::append( ent(a) ); }                       \
    type get() { return type( slist::get() ); }                   \
    gslist(type)() { }                                            \
    gslist(type)(type a) : (ent(a)) {}                           \
    ~gslist(type)() { clear(); }                                 \
};                                                                \
                                                                  \
struct gslist_iterator(type) : slist_iterator {                   \
    gslist_iterator(type)(gslist(type)& s)                        \
        : ( (slist&)s ) {}                                        \
    type operator()()                                            \
        { return type( slist_iterator::operator()() ); } \
};
```

A trailing \ indicates that the next line is part of the macro being defined.

Using this macro, a list of pointers to name, like class nlist used previously, can be defined like this:

```
#include "name.h"

typedef name* Pname;
declare(gslist,Pname); // declare class gslist(Pname)

gslist(Pname) nl;      // declare a gslist(Pname)
```

The declare macro is defined in <generic.h>. It concatenates its arguments and calls the macro with that name, in this case gslistdeclare, defined above. A type name argument to declare must be a simple name. The macro expansion technique used cannot handle a type name such as name*; thus typedef is used.

Using derivation ensures that all instances of the generic class share code. The technique can be used only to create classes of objects of the same size or smaller than the base class used in the macro. This, however, is ideal for lists of pointers. A gslist is used in §7.6.2.

7.3.6 Restricted Interfaces

Class `slist` is quite a general class. Sometimes such generality is not needed or even desirable. Restricted forms of lists such as stacks and queues are even more common than the general list itself. By not declaring the base class public, one can provide such data structures. For example, a queue of integers can be defined like this:

```
#include "slist.h"

class iqueue : slist { // assume sizeof(int)<=sizeof(void*)
public:
    void put(int a) { slist::append((void*)a); }
    int get()       { return int(slist::get()); }
    iqueue()        {}
};
```

Two logically separate operations are performed by this derivation: The concept of list is restricted to the concept of a queue, and the type `int` is specified to restrict the concept of a queue to the data type queue of integers, `iqueue`. Alternatively, these two operations could be done separately. Here first is a list that is restricted so that it can be used only as a stack:

```
#include "slist.h"

class stack : slist {
public:
    slist::insert;
    slist::get;
    stack() {}
    stack(ent a) : (a) {}
};
```

which can then be used to create the type "stack of pointers to characters":

```
#include "stack.h"

class cpstack : stack {
public:
    void push(char* a) { slist::insert(a); }
    char* pop() { return (char*)slist::get(); }
    nlist() {}
};
```

7.4   Adding to a Class

In the preceding examples, nothing is added to the base class by the derived class. Functions are defined for the derived class only to provide type conversion. Each derived class simply provides an alternative interface to a common set of routines. This is an important special case, but the most common reason for defining a new class as a derived class is that one wants what the base class provides, plus a bit more.

New data and function members can be defined for a derived class, in addition to those inherited from its base class. This provides an alternative strategy for providing a linked list facility. Note that when an item is put on an `slist` as previously defined, an `slink` containing two pointers is created. That creation takes time, and one of the pointers can be dispensed with, provided an object need be on only one list at a time, so that the `next` pointer can be placed in the object itself rather than in the separate `slink` object. The idea is to provide a class `olink` with only a `next` field, and a class `olist` that can manipulate pointers to such links. Objects of any class derived from `olink` can then be manipulated by `olist`. The "o" in the names is there to remind you that an object can be on only one `olist` at a time:

```
struct olink {
    olink* next;
};
```

Class `olist` is very similar to class `slist`. The difference is that a user of class `olist` manipulates objects of class `olink` directly:

```
class olist {
    olink* last;
public:
    void insert(olink* p);
    void append(olink* p);
    olink* get();
    // ...
};
```

We can derive class `name` from class `olink`:

```
class name : public olink {
    // ...
};
```

It is now trivial to make a list of names that can be used with no allocation time or space overhead.

Objects put on an `olist` lose their type. That is, the compiler knows only that they are `olink`s. The proper type can be restored using explicit type conversion of objects taken off an `olist`. For example:

```
void f()
{
    olist ll;
    name nn;
    ll.insert(&nn);                    // type of &nn lost
    name* pn = (name*)ll.get();  // and restored
}
```

Alternatively, the type can be restored by deriving yet another class from `olist` to handle the type conversion:

```
class onlist : public olist {
    // ...
    name* get() { return (name*)olist::get(); }
};
```

A `name` can only be on one `olist` at a time. This may be inappropriate for names, but there is no shortage of classes for which it is wholly appropriate. For example, the class `shape` in the following example uses exactly this technique to maintain a list of all shapes. Note that `slist` could have been defined as a class derived from `olist`, thus unifying the two concepts. However, using base and derived classes at this microscopic level of programming can lead to very contorted code.

7.5 Heterogeneous Lists

The preceding lists are homogeneous. That is, only objects of a single type were put on a list. The derived class mechanism is used to ensure that. Lists need not be homogeneous. A list specified in terms of pointers to a class can hold objects of any class derived from that class. That is, it may be heterogeneous. This is probably the single most important and useful aspect of derived classes, and it is essential in the style of programming presented in the following example. That style of programming is often called *object based* or *object oriented*; it relies on operations applied in a uniform manner to objects on heterogeneous lists. The meaning of such operations depends on the actual type of the objects on the list (known only at runtime), not on just the type of the list elements (known to the compiler).

7.6 A Complete Program

Consider writing a program for drawing geometrical shapes on a screen. It will naturally consist of three parts:

[1] A screen manager: low-level routines and data structures defining the screen; it knows about points and straight lines only;

[2] A shape library: a set of definitions of general shapes such as rectangle and circle and standard routines for manipulating them; and

[3] An application program: a set of application-specific definitions and code using them.

Typically, the three parts will be written by different people (in different organizations, at different times). The parts are also typically written in the order they are presented with the added complication that the designers of a lower level have no precise idea of what their code will eventually be used for.

The following example reflects this. To get the example short enough to present, the shape library provides only a few simple services and the application program is trivial. An extremely simple concept of a screen is used so that the reader can try the program even if no graphics facility is available. It should be easy to replace the screen part of the program with something appropriate without changing the code of the shape library or the application program.

7.6.1 The Screen Manager

The intention was to write the screen manager in C (not C++) to emphasize the separation between the levels of the implementation. This turned out to be tedious, so a compromise was made: the style of usage is C (no member functions, virtual functions, user-defined operators, etc.), but constructors are used, function arguments are properly declared and checked, etc. In retrospect, the screen manager looks very much like a C program that has been modified to take advantage of C++ features without being totally rewritten.

The screen is represented as a two-dimensional array of characters, manipulated by functions `put_point()` and `put_line()` using the structure `point` when referring to the screen:

```
// file screen.h.

const XMAX=40, YMAX=24;

struct point {
    int x,y;
    point() {}
    point(int a, int b) { x=a; y=b; }
};

overload put_point;
extern void put_point(int a, int b);
inline void put_point(point p) { put_point(p.x,p.y); }

overload put_line;
extern void put_line(int, int, int, int);
inline void put_line(point a, point b)
    { put_line(a.x,a.y,b.x,b.y); }

extern void screen_init();
extern void screen_refresh();
extern void screen_clear();

#include <stream.h>
```

Before the first use of a put function, the screen must be initialized by `screen_init()`, and changes to the screen data structure are only reflected

on the screen after a call of `screen_refresh()`. The reader will find that
"refresh" is done simply by printing a new copy of the screen array below the
previous version. Here are the functions and data definitions for the screen:

```
#include "screen.h"
#include <stream.h>

enum color { black='*', white=' ' };

char screen[XMAX][YMAX];

void screen_init()
{
    for (int y=0; y<YMAX; y++)
        for (int x=0; x<XMAX; x++)
            screen[x][y] = white;
}
```

Points are written only if they are on the screen:

```
inline int on_screen(int a, int b)
{
    return 0<=a && a<XMAX && 0<=b && b<YMAX;
}

void put_point(int a, int b)
{
    if (on_screen(a,b)) screen[a][b] = black;
}
```

The function `put_line()` is used to draw lines:

```
void put_line(int x0, int y0, int x1, int y1)
/*
    Plot the line (x0,y0) to (x1,y1).
    The line being plotted is b(x-x0) + a(y-y0) = 0.
    minimize abs(eps) where eps = 2*(b(x-x0) + a(y-y0)).
    See Newman and Sproull:
    ``Principles of Interactive Computer Graphics''
    McGraw-Hill, New York, 1979. pp 33-44.
*/
{
    register dx = 1;
    int a = x1 - x0;
    if (a < 0) dx = -1, a = -a;
    register dy = 1;
    int b = y1 - y0;
    if (b < 0) dy = -1, b = -b;
    int two_a = 2*a;
```

```
        int two_b = 2*b;
        int xcrit = -b + two_a;
        register eps = 0;
        for(;;) {
            put_point(x0,y0);
            if(x0==x1 && y0==y1) break;
            if(eps <= xcrit) x0 += dx, eps += two_b;
            if(eps>=a || a<=b) y0 += dy, eps -= two_a;
        }
    }
```

Functions are provided to clear the screen and to refresh it:

```
    void screen_clear() { screen_init(); }

    void screen_refresh()
    {
        for (int y=YMAX-1; 0<=y; y--) {      // top to bottom
            for (int x=0; x<XMAX; x++)       // left to right
                cout.put(screen[x][y]);
            cout.put('\n');
        }
    }
```

The function ostream::put() is used to print characters as characters; ostream::operator<<() prints characters as small integers. You can now imagine that these definitions are available only as compiler output in a library you cannot modify.

7.6.2 The Shape Library

We must define the general concept of a shape. This must be done in such a way that it can be shared (as a base class shape) by all particular shapes (for example, circles and squares), and in such a way that any shape can be manipulated exclusively through the interface provided by class shape:

```
    struct shape {
        shape() { shape_list.append(this); }

        virtual point north() { return point(0,0); }
        virtual point south() { return point(0,0); }
        virtual point east() { return point(0,0); }
        virtual point neast() { return point(0,0); }
        virtual point seast() { return point(0,0); }

        virtual void draw() {};
        virtual void move(int, int) {};
    };
```

The idea is that shapes are positioned by move() and placed on the screen by draw(). Shapes can be positioned relative to each other using the concept of *contact points*, named after points on the compass. Each particular shape defines the meaning of those points for itself, and each defines how it is drawn. To save paper, only the compass points needed in this example are actually defined. The constructor shape::shape() appends the shape to a list of shapes shape_list. This list is a gslist, that is, a version of a generic singly linked list as defined in §7.3.5. It, and a matching iterator, were made like this:

```
typedef shape* sp;
declare(gslist,sp);

typedef gslist(sp) shape_lst;
typedef gslist_iterator(sp) sl_iterator;
```

so that shape_list can be declared like this:

```
shape_lst shape_list;
```

A line can be constructed from either two points or a point and an integer. The latter constructs a horizontal with the length specified by the integer. The sign of the integer indicates whether the point is the left or the right endpoint. Here is the definition:

```
class line : public shape {
/*
    line from "w" to "e"
    north() is defined as ``above the center
    as far north as the northernmost point''
*/
    point w,e;
public:
    point north()
        { return point((w.x+e.x)/2,e.y<w.y?w.y:e.y); }
    point south()
        { return point((w.x+e.x)/2,e.y<w.y?e.y:w.y); }

    void move(int a, int b)
        { w.x += a; w.y += b; e.x += a; e.y += b; }
    void draw() { put_line(w,e); }

    line(point a, point b) { w = a; e = b; }
    line(point a, int l)
        { w = point(a.x+l-1,a.y); e = a; }
};
```

A `rectangle` is defined similarly:

```
class rectangle : public shape {
/*
    nw ---- n ---- ne
    ¦              ¦
    ¦              ¦
    ¦              ¦
    w       c      e
    ¦              ¦
    ¦              ¦
    ¦              ¦
    sw ---- s ---- se
*/
    point sw,ne;
public:
    point north() { return point((sw.x+ne.x)/2,ne.y); }
    point south() { return point((sw.x+ne.x)/2,sw.y); }
    point neast() { return ne; }
    point swest() { return sw; }
    void move(int a, int b)
        { sw.x+=a; sw.y+=b; ne.x+=a; ne.y+=b; }
    void draw();
    rectangle(point, point);
};
```

A `rectangle` is constructed from two points. The code is complicated by the need to figure out the relative position of those points:

```
rectangle::rectangle(point a, point b)
{
    if (a.x <= b.x) {
        if (a.y <= b.y) {
            sw = a;
            ne = b;
        }
        else {
            sw = point(a.x,b.y);
            ne = point(b.x,a.y);
        }
    }
    else {
        if (a.y <= b.y) {
            sw = point(b.x,a.y);
            ne = point(a.x,b.y);
        }
        else {
            sw = b;
            ne = a;
        }
    }
}
```

To draw a rectangle, its four sides are drawn:

```
void rectangle::draw()
{
    point nw(sw.x,ne.y);
    point se(ne.x,sw.y);
    put_line(nw,ne);
    put_line(ne,se);
    put_line(se,sw);
    put_line(sw,nw);
}
```

In addition to the shape definitions, a library of shapes contains functions for manipulating them. For example:

```
void shape_refresh();              // draw all shapes
void stack(shape* p, shape* q);  // put p on top of q
```

The refresh function is needed to cope with our naive screen. It simply re-draws all shapes. Note that it has no idea what kind of shapes it is drawing:

```
void shape_refresh()
{
    screen_clear();
    sl_iterator next(shape_list);
    shape* p;
    while ( p=next() ) p->draw();
    screen_refresh();
}
```

Finally, here is a genuine utility function; it stacks one shape on top of another by specifying that the one's south() should be just above the other's north():

```
void stack(shape* q, shape* p) // put p on top of q
{
    point n = p->north();
    point s = q->south();
    q->move(n.x-s.x,n.y-s.y+1);
}
```

Now imagine that this library is considered proprietary by some company selling software, and that they will sell you only the header file containing the shape definitions and the compiled version of the function definitions. It is still possible for you to define new shapes and take advantage of the utility functions for your own shapes.

7.6.3 The Application Program

The application program is extremely simple. A new shape myshape (looking a little bit like a face when printed) is defined, then a main program is written

that draws such a face wearing a hat. Here first is the declaration of
myshape:

```
#include "shape.h"

class myshape : public rectangle {
    line* l_eye;
    line* r_eye;
    line* mouth;
public:
    myshape(point, point);
    void draw();
    void move(int, int);
};
```

The eyes and the mouth are separate and independent objects created by
myshape's constructor:

```
myshape::myshape(point a, point b) : (a,b)
{
    int ll = neast().x-swest().x+1;
    int hh = neast().y-swest().y+1;
    l_eye = new line(
        point(swest().x+2,swest().y+hh*3/4),2);
    r_eye = new line(
        point(swest().x+ll-4,swest().y+hh*3/4),2);
    mouth = new line(
        point(swest().x+2,swest().y+hh/4),ll-4);
}
```

The eye and mouth objects are refreshed separately by the
shape_refresh() function, and could in principle be manipulated independently from the my_shape object to which they belong. That is one way of
defining features for a hierarchically constructed object such as myshape.
Another way is illustrated by the nose. There is no nose defined; it is simply
added to the picture by the draw() function:

```
void myshape::draw()
{
    rectangle::draw();
    put_point(point(
        (swest().x+neast().x)/2,(swest().y+neast().y)/2));
}
```

A myshape is moved by moving the base rectangle and the secondary
objects l_eye, r_eye, and mouth:

```
void myshape::move(int a, int b)
{
    rectangle::move(a,b);
    l_eye->move(a,b);
    r_eye->move(a,b);
    mouth->move(a,b);
}
```

Finally we can construct a few shapes and move them around a bit:

```
main()
{
    shape* p1 = new rectangle(point(0,0),point(10,10));
    shape* p2 = new line(point(0,15),17);
    shape* p3 = new myshape(point(15,10),point(27,18));
    shape_refresh();
    p3->move(-10,-10);
    stack(p2,p3);
    stack(p1,p2);
    shape_refresh();
    return 0;
}
```

Note again how functions such as `shape_refresh()` and `stack()` manipulate objects of types that were defined long after these functions were written (and possibly compiled).

```
          ***********
          *         *
          *         *
          *         *
          *         *
          *         *
          *         *
          *         *
          *         *
          *         *
          ***********
    ******************
      ************
      *          *
      * **    ** *
      *          *
      *    *     *
      *          *
      * ******** *
      *          *
      ************
```

7.7   Free Store

If you use class `slist`, you might find that your program consumed considerable time allocating and de-allocating objects of class `slink`. Class `slink` is a prime example of a class that could benefit from the programmer taking control of free store management. The optimization technique described in §5.5.6 is ideal for this kind of object. Since every `slink` is created using `new` and destroyed using `delete` by members of class `slist`, there are no problems with other methods of storage allocation.

If a derived class assigns to `this`, the constructor for its base class will be called only after that assignment, and the value of `this` in the base class constructor will be the one assigned by the derived class's constructor. If a base class assigns to `this`, the assigned value will be the one used by the constructor for the derived class. For example:

```
#include <stream.h>

struct base { base(); };

struct derived : base { derived(); };

base::base()
{
    cout << "\tbase 1: this=" << int(this) << "\n";
    if (this == 0) this = (base*)27;
    cout << "\tbase 2: this=" << int(this) << "\n";
}

derived::derived()
{
    cout << "\tderived 1: this=" << int(this) << "\n";
    if (this == 0) this = (derived*)43;
    cout << "\tderived 2: this=" << int(this) << "\n";
}

main()
{
    cout << "base b;\n";
    base b;
    cout << "new base;\n";
    new base;
    cout << "derived d;\n";
    derived d;
    cout << "new derived;\n";
    new derived;
    cout << "at the end\n";
}
```

produced this output

```
base b;
        base 1: this=2147478311
        base 2: this=2147478311
new base;
        base 1: this=0
        base 2: this=27
derived d;
        derived 1: this=2147478310
        derived 2: this=2147478310
new derived;
        derived 1: this=0
        base 1: this=43
        base 2: this=43
        derived 2: this=43
at the end
```

If a destructor for a derived class assigns to `this`, then the value assigned is the one seen by the destructor for its base class.

7.8   Exercises

[1] (*1) Define

```
class base {
public:
    virtual void iam() { cout << "base\n"; }
};
```

Derive two classes from `base`, and for each define `iam()` to write out the name of the class. Create objects of these classes and call `iam()` for them. Assign the address of objects of the derived classes to `base*` pointers and call `iam()` through those pointers.

[2] (*2) Implement the screen primitives (§7.6.1) in a way that is reasonable for your system.

[3] (*2) Define a class `triangle` and a class `circle`.

[4] (*2) Define a function that draws a line connecting two shapes by finding the two closest "contact points" and connecting them.

[5] (*2) Modify the shape example so that `line` is derived from `rectangle`, or vice versa.

[6] (*2) Design and implement a doubly linked list that can be used without an iterator.

[7] (*2) Design and implement a doubly linked list that can be used only through an iterator. The iterator should have operations for moving forwards and backwards, operations for inserting and deleting elements on the list, and a way of accessing a current element.

[8] (*2) Make a generic version of a doubly linked list.

[9] (*4) Make a list in which objects themselves (and not just pointers to objects) are inserted and extracted. Make it work for a class X where `X::X(X&)`, `X::~X()`, and `X::operator=(X&)` have been defined.

[10] (*5) Design and implement a library for writing event-driven simulations. Hint: `<task.h>`. However, that is an old program, and you can do better. There should be a class `task`. An object of class `task` should be able save its state and to have that state restored (you might define `task::save()` and `task::restore()`) so that it can operate as a coroutine. Specific tasks can be defined as objects of classes derived from class `task`. The program to be executed by a task might be specified as a virtual function. It should be possible to pass arguments to a new task as arguments to its constructor(s). There should be a scheduler implementing a concept of virtual time. Provide a function `task::delay(long)` that "consumes" virtual time. Whether the scheduler is part of class `task` or separate will be one of the major design decisions. The tasks will need to communicate. Design a class `queue` for that. Devise a way for a task to wait for input from several queues. Handle run-time errors in a uniform way. How would you debug programs written using such a library?

Chapter 8

Streams

"bad input char: .Ppm{=P!..*@)Z9
A}5!!!!!"syui!!!"!Mp#V6P?p8';!4lf&
− error message (abbreviated)

The C++ language does not provide facilities for input or output. It does not need to; such facilities can be simply and elegantly created using the language itself. The standard stream input/output library described here provides a type-secure, flexible, and efficient method for handling character input and output of integers, floating point numbers, and character strings, and a simple model for extending it to handle user-defined types. Its user interface can be found in <stream.h>. This chapter presents the stream library itself, some ways of using it, and the techniques used to implement it.

8.1 Introduction

Designing and implementing a standard input/output facility for a programming language is notoriously difficult. Traditionally I/O facilities have been designed exclusively to handle a few built-in data types. However, nontrivial C++ programs typically use many user-defined types and input and output of values of those types must also be handled. An I/O facility should clearly be easy, convenient, and safe to use, efficient and flexible, and above all complete. Nobody has come up with a solution that pleases everyone; it should therefore be possible for a user to provide alternative I/O facilities and to extend the standard I/O facilities to cope with special applications.

C++ was designed to enable a user to define new types that are as efficient and convenient to use as built-in types. It is therefore a reasonable requirement that an input/output facility for C++ should be provided in C++ using only facilities available to every programmer. The stream I/O facilities presented here are the result of an effort to meet this challenge.

The <stream.h> I/O facilities are exclusively concerned with the process of converting typed objects into sequences of characters, and vice versa. There are other models for I/O, but this one is fundamental in a UNIX system, and most forms of binary I/O are handled by considering a character as simply a bit pattern and ignoring its conventional correspondence with the alphabet. The key problem for the programmer is then to specify a correspondence between a typed object and an essentially untyped string.

Type-secure and uniform treatment of both built-in and user-defined types can be achieved by using a single overloaded function name for a set of output functions. For example:

```
put(cerr,"x = "); // cerr is the error output stream
put(cerr,x);
put(cerr,"\n");
```

The type of the argument determines which put function will be invoked for each argument. This solution has been used in several languages. However, it is verbose. Overloading the operator << to mean "put to" gives a better notation and lets the programmer put out a sequence of objects in a single statement. For example,

```
cerr << "x = " << x << "\n";
```

where cerr is the standard error output stream. So, if x is an int with the value 123, this statement would print

```
x = 123
```

and a newline onto the standard error output stream. Similarly, if x is of the user-defined type complex with the value (1,2.4), the statement above will print

```
x = (1,2.4)
```

on cerr.

This style can be used as long as x is of a type for which operator << is defined, and a user can trivially define operator << for a new type.

8.2 Output

This section first discusses facilities for both formatted and unformatted output of built-in types. Then the standard way of specifying output operations for used-defined types is presented.

8.2.1 Output of Built-in Types

The class `ostream` is defined with the operator `<<` ("put to") to handle output of the built-in types:

```
class ostream {
    // ...
public:
    ostream& operator<<(char*);
    ostream& operator<<(int i) { return *this<<long(i); }
    ostream& operator<<(long);
    ostream& operator<<(double);

    ostream& put(char);
};
```

An `operator<<` function returns a reference to the `ostream` it was called for, so that another `ostream` can be applied to it. For example,

```
cerr << "x = " << x;
```

where `x` is an `int`, will be interpreted as:

```
(cerr.operator<<("x = ")).operator<<(x);
```

In particular, this implies that when several items are printed by a single output statement, they will be printed in the expected order: left to right.

Having an `operator<<` that takes an `int` is redundant since an `int` can be implicitly converted to a `long`. However, it could also be converted to a `double`. Having `ostream::operator<<(int)` avoids this ambiguity. The function `ostream::put(char)` is provided to write characters as characters; `ostream::operator<<(int)` prints their integer values.

8.2.2 Output of User-defined Types

Consider a user-defined type:

```
class complex {
    double re, im;
public:
    complex(double r = 0, double i = 0) { re=r; im=i; }

    friend double real(complex& a) { return a.re; }
    friend double imag(complex& a) { return a.im; }

    friend complex operator+(complex, complex);
    friend complex operator-(complex, complex);
    friend complex operator*(complex, complex);
    friend complex operator/(complex, complex);
    // ...
};
```

Operator `<<` can be defined for the new type `complex` like this:

```
ostream& operator<<(ostream&s , complex z)
{
    return s << "(" << real(z) << "," << imag(z) << ")";
};
```

and used exactly like a built-in type:

```
complex x(1,2);
// ...
cout << "x = " << x << "\n";
```

producing:

```
x = (1,2)
```

Defining an output operation for a user-defined type does not require modification of the declaration of class `ostream` nor access to the (hidden) data structure maintained by it. The former is fortunate because the declaration of class `ostream` resides among the standard header files to which the general user does not have write access. The latter is also important because it provides protection against accidental corruption of that data structure. It also makes it possible to change the implementation of an `ostream` without affecting user programs.

8.2.3 Some Design Details

An output operator was used to avoid the verbosity that would have resulted from using an output function. But why `<<`?

It is not possible to invent a new lexical token (see §6.2). The assignment operator was a candidate for both input and output, but most people seemed to prefer the input operator to be different from the output operator. Furthermore, = binds the wrong way; that is, `cout=a=b` means `cout=(a=b)`.

The operators `<` and `>` were tried, but the meanings "less than" and "greater than" were so firmly implanted in people's minds that the new I/O statements were for all practical purposes unreadable. Apart from that, "<" is just above "," on most keyboards and people were writing statements like this:

```
cout < x , y , z;
```

It is not easy to give good error messages for such statements.

The operators `<<` and `>>` do not appear to cause that kind of problem. They are asymmetric in a way that can be used to suggest "to" and "from," and the precedence of `<<` is low enough to allow arithmetic expressions as operands without using parentheses. For example:

```
cout << "a*b+c=" << a*b+c << "\n";
```

Naturally, parentheses must be used to write expressions containing operators of lower precedence. For example:

```
cout << "a^b|c=" << (a^b|c) << "\n";
```

The left shift operator can also be used in an output statement:

```
cout << "a<<b=" << (a<<b) << "\n";
```

There are no character valued expressions in C++. In particular, '\n' is an integer (with the value 10 when the ASCII character set is used), so that

```
cout << "x = " << x << '\n';
```

writes the number 10 and not the expected newline. This and similar problems can be alleviated by defining a few macros (using the standard ASCII character names):

```
#define sp << " "
#define ht << "\t"
#define nl << "\n"
```

The example can now be written like this:

```
cout << "x = " << x nl;
```

The functions ostream::put(char) and chr(int) (see §8.2.4) are provided to print characters. Nonsyntactic macros are in some quarters considered the worst kind, but I happen to like these.

Consider also the examples:

```
cout << x << " " << y << " " << z << "\n";
cout << "x = " << x << ", y = " << y << "\n";
```

People find them hard to read because of the number of quotes and because the output operator is visually too imposing. The macros above plus a bit of indentation can help here:

```
cout << x sp << y sp << z nl;
cout << "x = " << x
     << ", y = " << y nl;
```

8.2.4 Formatted Output

Here, << has been used only for unformatted output, and that has indeed been its major use in real programs. There are, however, a few formatting routines that create a string representation of their argument for use as output. Their (optional) second argument specifies the number of character positions to be used.

```
char* oct(long, int =0);    // octal representation
char* dec(long, int =0);    // decimal representation
char* hex(long, int =0);    // hexadecimal representation
```

```
char* chr(int, int =0);     // character
char* str(char*, int =0);   // string
```

Truncation or padding will be done unless a zero-sized field is specified; then (exactly) as many characters as needed are used. For example:

```
cout << "dec(" << x
     << ") = oct(" << oct(x,6)
     << ") = hex(" << hex(x,4)
     << ")";
```

Given x==15, this produces

```
dec(15) = oct(    17) = hex(    f)
```

One can also used a general format string:

```
char* form(char* format ...);
```

Using cout<<form() is equivalent to using the C standard output function printf()†; the return value of form() is a string produced by converting and formatting its arguments after the first under control of the format string format. The format string contains two types of objects: plain characters, which are simply copied to the output stream, and conversion specifications, each of which causes conversion and printing of the next argument. Each conversion specification is introduced by the character %. For example

```
cout<<form("there were %d members present",no_of_members);
```

Here %d specifies that no_of_members is to be treated as an int and printed as the appropriate sequence of decimal digits. With no_of_members==127, the output is

```
there were 127 members present.
```

The set of conversion specifications is quite large and provides a great degree of flexibility. Following the %, there may be:

- –   an optional minus sign that specifies left-adjustment of the converted value in the indicated field;
- *d*   an optional digit string specifying a field width; if the converted value has fewer characters than the field width, it will be blank-padded on the left (or right, if the left-adjustment indicator has been given) to make up the field width; if the field width begins with a zero, zero-padding will be done instead of blank-padding;
- .   an optional period that serves to separate the field width from the next digit string;
- *d*   an optional digit string specifying a precision that specifies the number

---

† The explanation of format strings is a lightly edited version of the specification of printf().

of digits to appear after the decimal point, for e- and f-conversion, or the maximum number of characters to be printed from a string;

*   a field width or precision may be * instead of a digit string. In this case an integer argument supplies the field width or precision;

h   an optional character h, specifying that a following d, o, x, or u corresponds to a short integer argument;

l   an optional character l, specifying that a following d, o, x, or u corresponds to a long integer argument;

%   indicating that the character % is to be printed; no argument is used;

c   a character that indicates the type of conversion to be applied. The conversion characters and their meanings are:

d   The integer argument is converted to decimal notation;

o   The integer argument is converted to octal notation;

x   The integer argument is converted to hexadecimal notation;

f   The float or double argument is converted to decimal notation in the style *[-]ddd.ddd* where the number of d's after the decimal point is equal to the precision specification for the argument. If the precision is missing, 6 digits are given; if the precision is explicitly 0, no digits and no decimal point are printed;

e   The float or double argument is converted to decimal notation in the style *[-]d.ddde+dd* where there is one digit before the decimal point and the number of digits after the decimal point is equal to the precision specification for the argument; when the precision is missing, 6 digits are produced;

g   The float or double argument is printed in style d, in style f, or in style e, whichever gives full precision in minimum space;

c   The character argument is printed. Null characters are ignored;

s   The argument is taken to be a string (character pointer), and characters from the string are printed until a null character or until the number of characters indicated by the precision specification is reached; however, if the precision is 0 or missing, all characters up to a null are printed.

u   The unsigned integer argument is converted to decimal notation;

In no case does a nonexistent or small field width cause truncation of a field; padding takes place only if the specified field width exceeds the actual width.

Here is a more elaborate example:

```
char* src_file_name;
int line;
char* line_format = "\n#line %d \"%s\"\n";
// ...
cout << "int a;\n";
cout << form(line_format,line,src_file_name);
cout << "int b;\n";
```

which produces:

```
int a;

#line 13 "C++/main.c"
int b;
```

Using form() is unsafe in the sense that type checking is not done. For example, here is a well-known way of getting unpredictable output and/or a core dump:

```
char x;
// ...
cout<<form("bad input char: %s",x);
```

It does, however, provide great flexibility in a form that is familiar to C programmers. It is possible to mix stream output with printf-style output.

There is currently no entirely satisfactory facility for providing formatted output of user-defined types. In particular, it will probably be necessary to find a standard way of providing the output function for a user-defined type with information allowing it to determine space limitations, expectations about padding, left or right adjustment, etc., as expressed by its caller. A practical, but not ideal approach, is to provide functions for user-defined types that, like the formatting functions oct(), hex(), etc., produce a suitable string representation of the object for which they are called. For example:

```
class complex {
    float re,im;
public:
    // ...
    char* string(char* format)
        { return form(format,re,im); }
};
// ...
cout << z.string("(%.3f,%.3f)");
```

Store for the strings returned by form(), hex(), etc., comes from a single statically allocated cyclic buffer. It is therefore unwise to save a pointer returned by one of these functions for later use. The characters pointed to will change.

8.2.5 A Virtual Output Function

Sometimes an output function needs to be virtual. Consider the example of class shape providing the general concept of a geometric shape (§1.18):

```
class shape {
    // ...
public:
    // ...
    virtual void draw(ostream& s); // draw "this" on "s"
};

class circle : public shape {
    int radius;
public:
    // ...
    void draw(ostream&);
};
```

That is, a circle has all the attributes of a shape and can be manipulated as a shape, but it also has some special properties that must be taken into account when it is manipulated.

To maintain the standard output paradigm for such classes, the operator `<<` can be defined like this:

```
ostream& operator<<(ostream& s, shape* p)
{
    p->draw(s);
    return s;
}
```

Assuming `next` is an iterator of the kind defined in §7.3.3 a list of shapes can be drawn like this:

```
while ( p = next() ) cout << p;
```

8.3 Files and Streams

Streams are typically connected to files. The standard input stream `cin`, the standard output stream `cout`, and the standard error stream `cerr` are created by the stream library. The programmer can open other files and create streams for them.

8.3.1 Initialization of Output Streams

An `ostream` has the constructors:

```
class ostream {
    // ...
    ostream(streambuf* s);      // bind to stream buffer
    ostream(int fd);            // bind for file
    ostream(int size, char* p); // bind to vector
};
```

The primary job of these constructors is to associate a buffer with the stream. A streambuf is a class managing a buffer; it is described in §8.6, as is class filebuf managing the streambuf for a file. Class filebuf is derived from class streambuf.

The declaration of the standard output streams cout and cerr that can be found in the source code for the stream I/O library look like this:

```
        // declare a suitable amount of buffer space
    char cout_buf[BUFSIZE];

        // make a "filebuf" to manage that space
        // bind it to UNIX output stream 1 (already open)
    filebuf cout_file(1,cout_buf,BUFSIZE);

        // make the ostream providing the user interface
    ostream cout(&cout_file);

    char cerr_buf[1];

        // 0-length, that is unbuffered
        // UNIX output stream 2 (already open)
    filebuf cerr_file(2,cerr_buf,0);

    ostream cerr(&cerr_file);
```

Examples of the use of the other two ostream constructors can be found in §8.3.3 and §8.5.

8.3.2 Closing Output Streams

The destructor for ostream flushes the buffer using a public member function ostream::flush():

```
    ostream::~ostream()
    {
        flush();
    }
```

An ostream can also be flushed explicitly. For example:

```
    cout.flush();
```

8.3.3 Opening Files

The exact details of how files are opened and closed vary among operating systems and are not described in detail here. Because cin, cerr, and cout are available after <stream.h> has been included, many (if not most) programs need not contain code for opening files. However, here is a program that opens two files given as command line arguments and copies the first onto the second:

```
#include <stream.h>

void error(char* s, char* s2)
{
    cerr << s << " " << s2 << "\n";
    exit(1);
}

main(int argc, char* argv[])
{
    if (argc != 3) error("wrong number of arguments","");

    filebuf f1;
    if (f1.open(argv[1],input) == 0)
        error("cannot open input file",argv[1]);
    istream from(&f1);

    filebuf f2;
    if (f2.open(argv[2],output) == 0)
        error("cannot open or create output file",argv[2]);
    ostream to(&f2);

    char ch;
    while (from.get(ch)) to.put(ch);

    if (!from.eof() || to.bad())
        error("something strange happened","");
}
```

The sequence of operations in creating an `ostream` for a named file is the same as was used for the standard streams: (1) first, a buffer is created (here by declaring a `filebuf`); (2) then, the file is connected to it (here by opening the file with the function `filebuf::open()`); and (3) finally, the `ostream` itself is created with the `filebuf` as argument. Input streams are handled similarly.

A file can be opened in one of two modes:

```
enum open_mode { input, output };
```

The `filebuf::open()` operation returns 0 if it cannot open the file as requested. If the user attempts to open a file that does not exist for `output`, one will be created.

Before terminating, the program checks whether the streams are in a reasonable state (see §8.4.2). Open files are implicitly closed when the program terminates.

A file can also be opened for both reading and writing, but when that is necessary the stream paradigm is rarely ideal. It is often better to consider such a file a (giant) vector. One can define a type that allows the program to treat a file as a vector; see Exercises 8-10.

8.3.4 Copying Streams

It is possible to copy a stream. For example:

```
cout = cerr;
```

The result is two variables referring to the same stream. This is primarily useful for making a standard name such as `cin` refer to something different (see §3.1.6 for an example).

8.4 Input

Input is similar to output. There is a class `istream` providing an input operator `>>` ("get from") for a small set of standard types. A function `operator>>` can then be defined for a user-defined type.

8.4.1 Input of Built-in Types

Class `istream` is defined like this:

```
class istream {
    // ...
public:
    istream& operator>>(char*);        // string
    istream& operator>>(char&);        // character
    istream& operator>>(short&);
    istream& operator>>(int&);
    istream& operator>>(long&);
    istream& operator>>(float&);
    istream& operator>>(double&);
    // ...
};
```

The `operator>>` input functions are defined in this style:

```
istream& istream::operator>>(char& c)
{
        // skip whitespace
    int a;
        // somehow read a character into "a"
    c = a;
}
```

Whitespace is defined as the standard C whitespace by a call to `isspace()` as defined in `<ctype.h>` (blank, tab, newline, formfeed, and carriage return). Alternatively one might use the `get()` functions:

```
class istream {
    // ...
    istream& get(char& c);                          // char
    istream& get(char* p, int n, int ='\n');  // string
};
```

They treat whitespace characters like other characters. The function `istream::get(char)` reads a single character into its argument; the other `istream::get` reads at most n characters into a character vector starting at p. The optional third argument is used to specify a terminator. That is, a character that will not be read. If the terminator is found it is left as the first character on the stream. By default, the second `get()` function will read at most n characters, but not more than a line; `'\n'` is the default terminator. The optional third argument specifies a character that will not be read. For example:

```
cin.get(buf,256,'\t');
```

will read at most 256 characters into `buf`; if a tab (`'\t'`) is seen, it will cause `get()` to return. In that case the `'\t'` will be the next character read from `cin`.

The standard header `<ctype.h>` defines several functions that can be useful when processing input:

```
int isalpha(char)    // 'a'..'z' 'A'..'Z'
int isupper(char)    // 'A'..'Z'
int islower(char)    // 'a'..'z'
int isdigit(char)    // '0'..'9'
int isxdigit(char)   // '0'..'9' 'a'..'f' 'A'..'F'
int isspace(char)    // ' ' '\t' return newline formfeed
int iscntrl(char)    // control character
                     // (ASCII 0..31 and 127)
int ispunct(char)    // punctuation: none of the above
int isalnum(char)    // isalpha() | isdigit()
int isprint(char)    // printable: ascii ' '..'~'
int isgraph(char)    // isalpha() | isdigit() | ispunct()
int isascii(char c) { return 0<=c && c<=127; }
```

All but `isascii()` are implemented by a simple lookup, using the character as an index into a table of character attributes. Expressions such as

```
(('a'<=c && c<='z') || ('A'<=c && c<='Z')) // alphabetic
```

are therefore not only tedious to write and error prone (on a machine with the EBCDIC character set, this will accept nonalphabetic characters), they are also less efficient than using a standard function:

```
isalpha(c)
```

8.4.2 Stream States

Every stream (`istream` or `ostream`) has a *state* associated with it, and errors and nonstandard conditions are handled by setting and testing this state appropriately.

A stream can be in one of the following states:

```
enum stream_state { _good, _eof, _fail, _bad };
```

If the state is `_good` or `_eof`, the previous input operation succeeded. If the state is `_good`, the next input operation might succeed; otherwise, it will fail. In other words, applying an input operation to a stream that is not in the `_good` state is a null operation. If one tries to read into a variable v and the operation fails, the value of v should be unchanged (it is unchanged if v is of one of the types handled by `istream` or `ostream` member functions). The difference between the states `_fail` and `_bad` is subtle and only really interesting to implementers of input operations. In the state `_fail`, it is assumed that the stream is uncorrupted and that no characters have been lost. In the state `_bad`, all bets are off.

One can examine the state of a stream like this:

```
switch (cin.rdstate()) {
case _good:
    // the last operation on cin succeeded
    break;
case _eof:
    // at end of file
    break;
case _fail:
    // some kind of formatting error
    // probably not too bad
    break;
case _bad:
    // cin characters possibly lost
    break;
}
```

For any variable z of a type for which the operators `>>` and `<<` have been defined, a copy loop can be written like this:

```
while (cin>>z) cout << z << "\n";
```

For example, if z is a character vector, this loop will take standard input and put it one word (that is, a sequence of nonwhitespace characters) per line onto standard output.

When a stream is used as a condition, the state of the stream is tested and the test *succeeds* (that is, the value of the condition is nonzero) only if the state is `_good`. In particular, the state of the `istream` returned by the `cin>>z` in the preceding loop is tested. To find out why a loop or test failed, one can examine the state. This test of a stream is implemented by a conversion operator (§6.3.2).

It is really not very convenient to test for errors after each input or output operation, and a common cause of error is a programmer failing to do so in a place where it mattered. For example, output operations are typically unchecked, but they can occasionally fail. The stream I/O paradigm is designed so that if/when an exception-handling mechanism is provided for C++ (either as a language facility or as a standard library), it will be easy to apply it to simplify and standardize stream I/O error handling.

8.4.3 Input of User-defined Types

An input operation can be defined for a user-defined type exactly as an output operation was, but for an input operation it is essential that the second argument is of reference type. For example:

```
istream& operator>>(istream& s, complex& a)
/*
    input formats for a complex; "f" indicates a float:
        f
        ( f )
        ( f , f )
*/
{
    double re = 0, im = 0;
    char   c = 0;

    s >> c;
    if (c == '(') {
        s >> re >> c;
        if (c == ',') s >> im >> c;
        if (c != ')') s.clear(_bad);      // set the state
    }
    else {
        s.putback(c);
        s >> re;
    }

    if (s) a = complex(re,im);
    return s;
}
```

Despite the scarcity of error handling code, this will actually handle most kinds of errors. The local variable c is initialized to avoid having its value accidentally '(' after a failed operation. The final check of the stream state ensures that the value of the argument a is changed only if everything went well.

The operation for setting a stream state is called `clear()` because its most common use is to reset the state of a stream to _good; _good is the default argument value for both `istream::clear()` and `ostream::clear()`.

More work is needed on the input operations. In particular, it would be nice if one could specify input in terms of a pattern (as in languages such as Snobol or Icon) and then just test for success and failure of the complete input operation. Such operations would naturally have to provide some extra buffering so that they could restore an input stream to its original state after a failed pattern-match operation.

8.4.4 Initialization of Input Streams

Naturally, constructors are provided for the type `istream` as they were for the type `ostream`:

```
class istream {
    // ...
    istream(streambuf* s, int sk =1, ostream* t =0);
    istream(int size, char* p, int sk =1);
    istream(int fd, int sk =1, ostream* t =0);
};
```

The `sk` argument specifies whether whitespace should be skipped or not. The `t` argument (optionally) specifies a pointer to an `ostream` that the `istream` is *tied to*. For example, `cin` is tied to `cout`; this means that `cin` executes a

```
cout.flush(); // write output buffer
```

before attempting to read characters from its file.

The function `istream::tie()` can be used to tie (or untie, using `tie(0)`) any `ostream` to any `istream`. For example:

```
int y_or_n(ostream& to, istream& from)
/*
        prompt on "to", get a response from "from"
*/
{
    ostream* old = from.tie(&to);
    for (;;) {
        cout << "type Y or N: ";
        char ch = 0;
        if (!cin.get(ch)) return 0;

        if (ch != '\n') {        // skip rest of line
                char ch2 = 0;
                while (cin.get(ch2) && ch2!='\n') ;
        }
```

```
                    switch (ch) {
                    case 'Y':
                    case 'y':
                    case '\n':
                        from.tie(old);       // restore old tie
                        return 1;
                    case 'N':
                    case 'n':
                        from.tie(old);       // restore old tie
                        return 0;
                    default:
                        cout << "sorry, try again: ";
                    }
            }
    }
```

When buffered input is used (as it is by default) the user cannot type the single letter "**y**" and expect a response. A terminating newline is expected by the system; **y_or_n()** looks at the first character of a line and ignores the rest.

A character can be put back into a stream using the function **istream.putback(char)**. This enables a program to "look ahead" on an input stream.

8.5   String Manipulation

One can perform I/O-like operations on a character vector by binding an **istream** or an **ostream** to it. For example, if a vector contains a traditional zero-terminated string of characters, the copy loop presented above can be used to print the words from that vector:

```
void word_per_line(char v[], int sz)
/*
    print "v" of size "sz" one word per line
*/
{
    istream ist(sz,v); // make an istream for v
    char b2[MAX];       // larger than largest word
    while (ist>>b2) cout << b2 << "\n";
}
```

The terminating zero character is interpreted as end-of-file in this case.

An **ostream** can be used to format messages that should not be printed immediately:

```
char* p = new char[message_size];
ostream ost(message_size,p);
do_something(arguments,ost);
display(p);
```

An operation such as do_something can write to the stream ost, pass ost on to its suboperations, etc., using the standard output operations. There is no need to check for overflow since ost knows its size and will go into _fail state when it is full. Finally, display can write the message to a "real" output stream. This technique can be most useful to cope with cases in which the final display operation involves writing to something more complicated than a traditional line-oriented output device. For example, the text from ost could be placed in a fixed-sized area somewhere on a screen.

8.6 Buffering

The I/O operations are specified without any mention of file types, but not all devices can be treated identically with respect to buffering strategies. For example, an ostream bound to a character string needs a different kind of buffer from an ostream bound to a file. These problems are handled by providing different buffer types for different streams at the time of initialization (note the three constructors for class ostream). There is only one set of operations on these buffer types, so the ostream functions do not contain code distinguishing them. However, the functions handling overflow and underflow are virtual. This is sufficient to cope with the buffering strategies needed to date, and a good example of the use of virtual functions to allow uniform treatment of logically equivalent facilities with different implementations. The declaration of a stream buffer in <stream.h> looks like this:

```
struct streambuf {        // manage a stream buffer

        char* base;        // start of buffer
        char* pptr;        // next free char
        char* gptr;        // next filled char
        char* eptr;        // one off the end of buffer
        char  alloc;       // buffer allocated by "new"

        // Empty a buffer:
        // Return EOF on error, 0 on success
    virtual int overflow(int c =EOF);

        // Fill a buffer:
        // Return EOF on error or end of input,
        // next char otherwise
    virtual int underflow();

    int snextc()           // get the next char
    {
        return (++gptr==pptr) ? underflow() : *gptr&0377;
    }
```

```
        // ...

        int allocate();        // allocate some buffer space

        streambuf() { /* ... */ }
        streambuf(char* p, int l) { /* ... */ }
        ~streambuf() { /* ... */ }
};
```

Note that the pointers needed to maintain the buffer are specified here so that
the common per-character operations can be defined (once only) as maximally
efficient inline functions. Only the overflow() and underflow() functions
need to be implemented for each particular buffering strategy. For example:

```
struct filebuf : public streambuf {

    int  fd;               // file descriptor
    char opened;           // file opened

    int overflow(int c =EOF);
    int underflow();

    // ...

        // Open a file:
        // return 0 if failure, "this" if success
    filebuf* open(char *name, open_mode om);
    int close() { /* ... */ }

    filebuf() { opened = 0; }
    filebuf(int nfd) { /* ... */ }
    filebuf(int nfd, char* p, int l) : (p,l) { /* ... */ }
    ~filebuf() { close(); }
};


int filebuf::underflow()           // fill buffer from "fd"
{
    if (!opened || allocate()==EOF) return EOF;

    int count = read(fd, base, eptr-base);
    if (count < 1) return EOF;

    gptr = base;
    pptr = base + count;
    return *gptr & 0377;
}
```

8.7   Efficiency

One might expect that since the <stream.h> I/O is defined using generally available language features, it would be less efficient than a built-in facility. This does not appear to be the case. Inline expanded functions are used for operations such as "put a character into a buffer," so the only function calls needed at this level come from overflow and underflow. Simple objects (integer, string, etc.) require one function call each. This does not appear to be different from other I/O facilities dealing with objects at this level.

8.8   Exercises

1. (*1.5) Read a file of floating point numbers, make complex numbers out of pairs of numbers read, and write out the complex numbers.
2. (*1.5) Define a type `name_and_address`. Define `<<` and `>>` for it. Copy a stream of name_and_address objects.
3. (*2) Design some functions for requesting and reading information of various types. The `y_or_n()` function in §8.4.4. is a trivial example. Ideas: integer, floating point number, file name, mail address, date, personal information, etc. Try to make them foolproof.
4. (*1.5) Write a program that prints (1) all lower case letters, (2) all letters, (3) all letters and digits, (4) all characters that may appear in a C++ identifier on your system, (5) all punctuation characters, (6) the integer value of all control characters, (7) all whitespace characters (8) the integer value of all whitespace characters, and finally (9) all printing characters.
5. (*4) Implement the C standard I/O library (<stdio.h>) using the C++ standard I/O <stream.h>) library.
6. (*4) Implement the C++ standard I/O (<stream.h>) library using the C standard I/O (<stdio.h>) library.
7. (*4) Implement the C and C++ libraries so that they can be used simultaneously.
8. (*2) Implement a class for which [ ] is overloaded to implement random reading of characters from a file.
9. (*3) As Exercise 8, but make [ ] useful for both reading and writing. Hint: make [ ] return an object of a "descriptor type" for which assignment means assign through descriptor to file, and implicit conversion to char means read from file through descriptor.
10. (*2) As Exercise 9, but let [ ] index records of some kind, not characters.
11. (*3) Make a generic version of the class defined in Exercise 10.
12. (*3.5) Design and implement a pattern matching input operation. Use `printf`-style format strings to specify a pattern. It should be possible to try-out several patterns against some input to find the actual format. One might derive a pattern-matching input class from `istream`.
13. (*4) Invent (and implement) a much better kind of pattern.

Reference Manual

1. Introduction

The C++ programming language is C† extended with classes, inline functions, operator overloading, function name overloading, constant types, references, free store management operators, function argument checking, and a new function definition syntax. The differences between C++ and C are summarized in §15. This manual describes the language as of June 1985.

2. Lexical Conventions

There are six classes of tokens: identifiers, keywords, constants, strings, operators, and other separators. Blanks, tabs, new-lines, and comments (collectively, "white space") as described below are ignored except as they serve to separate tokens. Some white space is required to separate otherwise adjacent identifiers, keywords, and constants.

If the input stream has been parsed into tokens up to a given character, the next token is taken to include the longest string of characters which could possibly constitute a token.

2.1 Comments

The characters /* start a comment, which terminates with the characters */. These comments do not nest. The characters // start a comment, which terminates at the end of the line they occur on.

---

† "The C Programming Language" by Brian W. Kernighan and Dennis M. Ritchie, Prentice Hall, 1978. This manual was derived from the UNIX System V "The C Programming Language – Reference Manual" with permission from AT&T Bell Laboratories.

2.2 Identifiers (Names)

An identifier is an arbitrarily long sequence of letters and digits; the first character must be a letter; the underscore _ counts as a letter. Upper- and lower-case letters are different.

2.3 Keywords

The following identifiers are reserved for use as keywords, and may not be used otherwise:

```
asm        auto      break      case      char
class      const     continue   default   delete
do         double    else       enum      extern
float      for       friend     goto      if
inline     int       long       new       operator
overload   public    register   return    short
sizeof     static    struct     switch    this
typedef    union     unsigned   virtual   void
while
```

The identifiers `signed` and `volatile` are reserved for future use.

2.4 Constants

There are several kinds of constants, as listed below. Hardware characteristics that affect sizes are summarized in §2.6.

2.4.1 Integer Constants

An integer constant consisting of a sequence of digits is taken to be octal if it begins with 0 (digit zero), decimal otherwise. The digits 8 and 9 are not octal digits. A sequence of digits preceded by `0x` or `0X` (digit zero) is taken to be a hexadecimal integer. The hexadecimal digits include `a` or `A` through `f` or `F` with values 10 through 15. A decimal constant whose value exceeds the largest signed integer is taken to be `long`; an octal or hexadecimal constant which exceeds the largest unsigned integer is likewise taken to be `long`; otherwise integer constants are taken to be `int`.

2.4.2 Explicit Long Constants

A decimal, octal, or hexadecimal integer constant immediately followed by `l` (letter ell) or `L` is a long constant.

2.4.3 Character Constants

A character constant is a character enclosed in single quotes, as in `'x'`. The value of a character constant is the numerical value of the character in the machine's character set. Character constants are taken to be `int`.

Certain non-graphic characters, the single quote ′, and the backslash \, may be represented according to the following table of escape sequences:

new-line	NL (LF)	\n
horizontal tab	HT	\t
vertical tab	VT	\v
backspace	BS	\b
carriage return	CR	\r
form feed	FF	\f
backslash	\	\\
single quote	′	\′
bit pattern	*0ddd*	*ddd*
bit pattern	*0xddd*	*xddd*

The escape *ddd* consists of the backslash followed by 1, 2, or 3 octal digits which are taken to specify the value of the desired character. A special case of this construction is \0 (not followed by a digit), which indicates the character NUL. The escape *xddd* consists of the backslash followed by x followed by 1, 2, or 3 hexadecimal digits which are taken to specify the value of the desired character. If the character following a backslash is not one of those specified, the backslash is ignored.

2.4.4 Floating Constants

A floating constant consists of an integer part, a decimal point, a fraction part, an e or E, and an optionally signed integer exponent. The integer and fraction parts both consist of a sequence of digits. Either the integer part or the fraction part (not both) may be missing; either the decimal point or the e (E) and the exponent (not both) may be missing. A floating constant has type `double`.

2.4.5 Enumeration Constants

Names declared as enumerators (see §8.10) are constants of type `int`.

2.4.6 Declared Constants

An object (§5) of any type can be specified to have a constant value throughout the scope (§4.1) of its name. For pointers the `*const` declarator (§8.3) is used to achieve this; for non-pointer objects the specifier `const` (§8.2) is used.

2.5 Strings

A string is a sequence of characters surrounded by double quotes, as in "...". A string has type "array of characters" and storage class `static` (see §4 below), and is initialized with the given characters. All strings, even when written identically, are distinct. The compiler places a null byte \0 at the end of each string so that programs which scan the string can find its end. In a string, the double quote character " must be preceded by a \; in addition, the same escapes as described for character constants may be used. Finally, a new-line may occur only immediately following a \; then both the \ and the new-line are ignored.

2.6 Hardware Characteristics

The following table summarizes certain properties that vary from machine to machine.

	DEC VAX ASCII	Motorola 68000 ASCII	IBM 370 EBCDIC	AT&T 3B ASCII
`char`	8 bits	8 bits	8 bits	8 bits
`int`	32	16	32	32
`short`	16	16	16	16
`long`	32	32	32	32
`float`	32	32	32	32
`double`	64	64	64	64
`pointer`	32	32	24	32
`float` range	$\pm 10^{\pm 38}$	$\pm 10^{\pm 38}$	$\pm 10^{\pm 76}$	$\pm 10^{\pm 38}$
`double` range	$\pm 10^{\pm 38}$	$\pm 10^{\pm 38}$	$\pm 10^{\pm 76}$	$\pm 10^{\pm 308}$
field type	signed	unsigned	unsigned	unsigned
field order	right-to-left	left-to-right	left-to-right	left-to-right
`char`	signed	unsigned	unsigned	unsigned

3. Syntax Notation

In the syntax notation used in this manual, syntactic categories are indicated by *italic* type, and literal words and characters in `constant width` type. Alternatives are listed on separate lines. An optional terminal or non-terminal symbol is indicated by the subscript "opt," so that

$$\{ \ expression_{opt} \ \}$$

indicates an optional expression enclosed in braces. The syntax is summarized in §14.

4. Names and Types

A name denotes an object, a function, a type, a value, or a label. A name is introduced into a program by a declaration (§8). A name can only be used within a region of program text called its scope. A name has a type which determines its use. An object is a region of storage. An object has a storage class which determines its lifetime. The meaning of the values found in an object is determined by the type of the name used to access it.

4.1 Scopes

There are three kinds of scope: local, file, and class.

Local: In general, a name declared in a block (§9.2) is local to that block and can only be used in it after the point of declaration and in blocks enclosed by it. However, labels (§9.12) can be used anywhere in the function in which they are declared. Names of formal arguments for a function are treated as if they were declared in the outermost block of that function.

File: A name declared outside any block (§9.2) or class (§8.5) can be used in the file in which it is declared after the point of declaration.

Class: The name of a class member is local to its class and can only be used in a member function of that class (§8.5.2), after a . operator applied to an object of its class (§7.1), or after a -> operator applied to a pointer to an object of its class (§7.1). Static class members (§8.5.1) and function members may also be referred to where the name of their class is in scope by using the :: operator (§7.1). A class declared within a class (§8.5.15) is not considered a member and its name belongs to the enclosing scope.

A name may be hidden by an explicit declaration of that same name in a block or class. A name in a block or class can only be hidden by a name declared in an enclosed block or class. A hidden non-local name can still be used when its scope is specified using the :: operator (§7.1). A class name hidden by a non-type name can still be used if prefixed by class, struct, or union (§8.2). An enum name hidden by a non-type name can still be used if prefixed by enum (§8.2).

4.2 Definitions

A declaration (§8) is a definition unless it declares a function without specifying the body (§10), it contains the extern specifier (1) and no initializer or function body, or it is a class name declaration (§8.8).

4.3 Linkage

A name of file scope that is not explicitly declared static is common to every file in a multi-file program; so is the name of a function. Such names are said to be external. Every declaration of an external name in the program refers to the same object (§5), function (§10), type (§8.7), class (§8.5), enumeration (§8.10), or enumerator value (§8.10).

The types specified in all declarations of an external name must be identical. There may be more than one definition of a type, enumeration, inline function (§8.1), or non-aggregate const (§8.2) provided the definitions are identical, occur in different files, and all initializers are constant expressions (§12). In all other cases, there must be exactly one definition for an external name in a program.

An implementation may require that a non-aggregate `const` used where no definition of the `const` has been seen must be declared explicitly `extern` and must have exactly one definition in the program. The same restriction may be imposed on `inline` functions.

4.4 Storage Classes

There are two declarable storage classes: automatic and static.

> *Automatic* objects are local to each invocation of a block and are discarded upon exit from it.

> *Static* objects exist and retain their values throughout the execution of the entire program.

Some objects are not associated with names and their lifetimes are explicitly controlled using the `new` and `delete` operators; see §7.2 and §9.14.

4.5 Fundamental Types

Objects declared as characters (`char`) are large enough to store any member of the implementation's character set, and if a genuine character from that character set is stored in a character variable, its value is equivalent to the integer code for that character.

Up to three sizes of integer, declared `short int`, `int`, and `long int`, are available. Longer integers provide no less storage than shorter ones, but the implementation may make either short integers, or long integers, or both, equivalent to plain integers. "Plain" integers have the natural size suggested by the host machine architecture; the other sizes are provided to meet special needs.

Each enumeration (§8.10) is a set of named constants. The properties of an `enum` are identical to those of an `int`.

Unsigned integers, declared `unsigned`, obey the laws of arithmetic modulo 2^n where n is the number of bits in the representation.

Single-precision floating point (`float`) and double-precision floating point (`double`) may be synonymous in some implementations.

Because objects of the foregoing types can usefully be interpreted as numbers, they will be referred to as *arithmetic* types. Types `char`, `int` of all sizes, and `enum` will collectively be called *integral* types. `float` and `double` will collectively be called *floating* types.

The void type specifies an empty set of values. The (nonexistent) value of a void object may not be used in any way, and neither explicit nor implicit conversions may be applied. Because a void expression denotes a nonexistent value, such an expression may be used only as an expression statement (§9.1) or as the left operand of a comma expression (§7.15). An expression may be explicitly converted to type void (§7.2).

4.6 Derived Types

There is a conceptually infinite number of derived types constructed from the fundamental types in the following ways:

arrays of objects of a given type;

functions which take arguments of given types and return objects of a given type;

pointers to objects of a given type;

references to objects of a given type;

constants which are values of a given type;

classes containing a sequence of objects of various types, a set of functions for manipulating these objects, and a set of restrictions on the access to these objects and functions;

structures which are classes without access restrictions;

unions which are structures capable of containing objects of different types at different times.

In general these methods of constructing objects can be applied recursively.

A object of type void* (pointer to void) can be used to point to objects of unknown type.

5. Objects and Lvalues

An *object* is a region of storage; an *lvalue* is an expression referring to an object. An obvious example of an lvalue expression is the name of an object. There are operators which yield lvalues: for example, if E is an expression of pointer type, then *E is an lvalue expression referring to the object to which E points. The name "lvalue" comes from the assignment expression E1 = E2 in which the left operand E1 must be an lvalue expression. The discussion of each operator below indicates whether it expects lvalue operands and whether it yields an lvalue.

6. Conversions

A number of operators may, depending on their operands, cause conversion of the value of an operand from one type to another. This section explains the result to be expected from such conversions. §6.6 summarizes the conversions demanded by most ordinary operators; it will be supplemented as required by the discussion of each operator. §8.5.6 describes user-defined conversions.

6.1 Characters and Integers

A character or a short integer may be used wherever an integer may be used. In all cases the value is converted to an integer. Conversion of a shorter integer to a longer always involves sign extension; integers are signed quantities. Whether or not sign-extension occurs for characters is machine dependent; see §2.6. The more explicit type `unsigned char` forces the values to range from 0 to a machine dependent maximum.

On machines that treat characters as signed, the characters of the ASCII set are all positive. However, a character constant specified with an octal escape suffers sign extension and may appear negative; for example, `'\377'` has the value -1.

When a longer integer is converted to a shorter or to a `char`, it is truncated on the left; excess bits are simply discarded.

6.2 Float and Double

Single-precision floating arithmetic may be used for `float` expressions. Conversions between single-precision and double-precision floating-point numbers are as mathematically correct as the hardware allows.

6.3 Floating and Integral

Conversions of floating values to integral type tend to be machine-dependent; in particular the direction of truncation of negative numbers varies from machine to machine. The result is undefined if the value will not fit in the space provided.

Conversions of integral values to floating type are well behaved. Some loss of precision occurs if the destination lacks sufficient bits.

6.4 Pointers and Integers

An expression of integral type may be added to or subtracted from a pointer; in such a case the first is converted as specified in the discussion of the addition operator.

Two pointers to objects of the same type may be subtracted; in this case the result is converted to an `int` or a `long` dependent on the machine; see §7.4.

6.5 Unsigned

Whenever an unsigned integer and a plain integer are combined, the plain integer is converted to unsigned and the result is unsigned. The value is the least unsigned integer congruent to the signed integer (modulo $2^{wordsize}$). In a 2's complement representation, this conversion is conceptual and there is no actual change in the bit pattern.

When an unsigned integer is converted to long, the value of the result is the same numerically as that of the unsigned integer. Thus the conversion amounts to padding with zeros on the left.

6.6 Arithmetic Conversions

A great many operators cause conversions and yield result types in a similar way. This pattern will be called the "usual arithmetic conversions."

First, any operands of type char, unsigned char, or short are converted to int.

Then, if either operand is double, the other is converted to double and that is the type of the result.

Otherwise, if either operand is unsigned long the other is converted to unsigned long and that is the type of the result.

Otherwise, if either operand is long, the other is converted to long and that is the type of the result.

Otherwise, if either operand is unsigned, the other is converted to unsigned and that is the type of the result.

Otherwise, both operands must be int, and that is the type of the result.

6.7 Pointer Conversions

The following conversions may be performed wherever pointers are assigned, initialized, compared, etc.

The constant 0 may be converted to a pointer, and it is guaranteed that this value will produce a pointer distinguishable from a pointer to any object.

A pointer of any type may be converted to a void*.

A pointer to a class may converted to a pointer to a public base class of that class; see §8.5.3.

The name of a vector may be converted to a pointer to its own first element.

An identifier which is declared "function returning ...", when used except in the function-name position of a call, is converted to "pointer to function returning ...".

6.8 Reference Conversions

The following conversion may be performed wherever references are initialized.

A reference to a class may converted to a reference to a public base class of that class; see §8.6.3.

7. Expressions

The precedence of expression operators is the same as the order of the major subsections of this section, highest precedence first. Thus, for example, the expressions referred to as the operands of + (§7.4) are those expressions defined in §§7.1-7.4. Within each subsection, the operators have the same precedence. Left- or right-associativity is specified in each subsection for the operators discussed therein. The precedence and associativity of all the expression operators is summarized in the grammar of §14.

Otherwise the order of evaluation of expressions is undefined. In particular the compiler considers itself free to compute subexpressions in the order it believes most efficient, even if the subexpressions involve side effects. The order in which side effects take place is unspecified. Expressions involving a commutative and associative operator (*, +, &, !, ^) may be rearranged arbitrarily, even in the presence of parentheses; to force a particular order of evaluation an explicit temporary must be used.

The handling of overflow and divide check in expression evaluation is machine-dependent. Most existing implementations of C++ ignore integer overflows; treatment of division by 0, and all floating-point exceptions, varies between machines, and is usually adjustable by a library function.

In addition to the standard meanings described in §7.2-15 operators may be overloaded, that is given meanings when applied to user-defined types; see §7.16.

7.1 Primary Expressions

Primary expressions involving ., ->, ::, subscripting, and function call group left-to-right.

> *expression-list:*
>> *expression*
>> *expression-list , expression*

id:

      identifier
      operator-function-name
      typedef-name :: *identifier*
      typedef-name :: *operator-function-name*

primary-expression:

      id
      :: *identifier*
      constant
      string
      this
      (*expression*)
      primary-expression [*expression*]
      primary-expression (*expression-list$_{opt}$*)
      primary-expression . *id*
      primary-expression -> *id*

An identifier is a primary expression, provided it has been suitably declared (§8). An *operator-function-name* is an identifier with a special meaning; see §7.16 and §8.5.11.

The operator :: followed by an identifier of file scope is the same as the identifier. It allows an object to be referred to even if its identifier has been hidden §4.1).

A *typedef-name* (§8.8) followed by :: followed by an identifier is a primary expression. The *typedef-name* must denote a class (§8.5) and the identifier must denote a member of that class. Its type is specified by the declaration of the identifier. The *typedef-name* may be hidden by a non-type name; in this case the *typedef-name* can still be found and used.

A constant is a primary expression. Its type may be int, long, float, or double depending on its form.

A string is a primary expression. Its type is "array of char". It is typically immediately converted to a pointer to its first character (§6.7).

The keyword this is a local variable in the body of a member function (see §8.5); it is a pointer to the object for which the function was invoked.

A parenthesized expression is a primary expression whose type and value are identical to those of the unadorned expression. The presence of parentheses does not affect whether the expression is an lvalue.

A primary expression followed by an expression in square brackets is a primary expression. The intuitive meaning is that of a subscript. Usually, the primary expression has type "pointer to ...", the subscript expression is int, and the type of the result is "...". The expression E1[E2] is identical (by definition) to *((E1)+(E2)). All the clues needed to understand this notation are contained in this section together with the discussions in §§ 7.1, 7.2, and 7.4 on identifiers, *, and + respectively; §8.4.2 below summarizes the implications.

A function call is a primary expression followed by parentheses containing a possibly empty, comma-separated list of expressions which constitute the actual arguments to the function. The primary expression must be of type "function returning ..." or "pointer to function returning ...", and the result of the function call is of type "...".

Each formal argument is initialized (§8.6) with its actual argument. Standard (§6.6-8) and user-defined (§8.5.6) conversions are performed. A function may change the values of its formal arguments, but these changes cannot affect the values of the actual arguments except where a formal argument is of reference type (§8.4).

A function may be declared to accept fewer arguments or more arguments than are specified in the function declaration (§8.4). Any actual argument of type float for which there is no formal argument is converted to double before the call; any of type char or short is converted to int; and as usual, array names are converted to pointers. The order of evaluation of arguments is undefined by the language; take note that compilers differ.

Recursive calls to any function are permitted.

A primary expression followed by a dot followed by an identifier (or an identifier qualified by a typedef-name using the :: operator) is an expression. The first expression must be a class object, and the identifier must name a member of that class. The value is the named member of the object, and it is an lvalue if the first expression is an lvalue. Note that "class objects" can be structures (§8.5.12) and unions (§8.5.13).

A primary expression followed by an arrow (->) followed by an identifier (or an identifier qualified by a typedef-name using the :: operator) is an expression. The first expression must be a pointer to a class object and the identifier must name a member of that class. The result is an lvalue referring to the named member of the class to which the pointer expression points. Thus the expression E1->MOS is the same as (*E1).MOS. Classes are discussed in §8.5.

If an expression has the type "reference to ..." (see §8.4 and §8.6.3) the value of the expression is the object denoted by the reference. A reference can be thought of as a name of an object; see §8.6.3.

7.2 Unary Operators

Expressions with unary operators group right-to-left.

>   *unary-expression:*
>
>> *unary-operator expression*
>> *expression* **++**
>> *expression* **−−**
>> **sizeof** *expression*
>> **sizeof** (*type-name*)
>> (*type-name*) *expression*
>> *simple-type-name* (*expression-list*)
>> **new** *type-name initializer*$_{opt}$
>> **new** (*type-name*)
>> **delete** *expression*
>> **delete** [*expression*] *expression*
>
>   *unary-operator:* one of
>> *   &   + −   !   ~   ++   −−

The unary * operator means *indirection*: the expression must be a pointer, and the result is an lvalue referring to the object to which the expression points. If the type of the expression is "pointer to . . .", the type of the result is ". . .".

The result of the unary & operator is a pointer to the object referred to by the operand. The operand must be an lvalue. If the type of the expression is ". . .", the type of the result is "pointer to . . .".

The result of the unary + operator is the value of its operand after the usual arithmetic conversions have been performed. The operand must be of arithmetic type.

The result of the unary − operator is the negative of its operand. The operand must be of arithmetic type. The usual arithmetic conversions are performed. The negative of an unsigned quantity is computed by subtracting its value from 2^n, where n is the number of bits in an int.

The result of the logical negation operator ! is 1 if the value of its operand is 0, 0 if the value of its operand is non-zero. The type of the result is int. It is applicable to any arithmetic type or to pointers.

The ~ operator yields the one's complement of its operand. The usual arithmetic conversions are performed. The type of the operand must be integral.

7.2.1 Increment and Decrement

The operand of prefix ++ is incremented. The operand must be an lvalue. The value is the new value of the operand, but is not an lvalue. The expression ++x is equivalent to x+=1. See the discussions of addition (§7.4) and assignment operators (§7.14) for information on conversions.

The operand of prefix -- is decremented analogously to the prefix ++ operator.

The value obtained by applying a postfix ++ is the value of the operand. The operand must be an lvalue. After the result is noted, the object is incremented in the same manner as for the prefix ++ operator. The type of the result is the same as the type of the operand.

The value obtained by applying a postfix -- is the value of the operand. The operand must be an lvalue. After the result is noted, the object is decremented in the manner as for the prefix -- operator. The type of the result is the same as the type of the operand.

7.2.2 Sizeof

The sizeof operator yields the size, in bytes, of its operand. (A *byte* is undefined by the language except in terms of the value of sizeof. However, in all existing implementations a byte is the space required to hold a char.) When applied to an array, the result is the total number of bytes in the array. The size is determined from the declarations of the objects in the expression. This expression is semantically an unsigned constant and may be used anywhere a constant is required.

The sizeof operator may also be applied to a parenthesized type name. In that case it yields the size, in bytes, of an object of the indicated type.

7.2.3 Explicit Type Conversion

An optionally parenthesized *simple-type-name* (§8.2) followed by a parenthesized expression (or an *expression-list* if the type is a class with a suitably declared constructor §8.5.5) causes the value of the expression to be converted to the named type. To express conversion to a type that does not have a simple name the *type-name* (§8.7) must be parenthesized. If the type name is parenthesized the expression need not be parenthesized. This construction is called a *cast*.

A pointer may be explicitly converted to any of the integral types large enough to hold it. Whether an int or long is required is machine dependent. The mapping function is also machine dependent, but is intended to be unsurprising to those who know the addressing structure of the machine. Details for some particular machines were given in §2.6.

An object of integral type may be explicitly converted to a pointer. The mapping always carries an integer converted from a pointer back to the same pointer, but is otherwise machine dependent.

A pointer to one type may be explicitly converted to a pointer to another type. The resulting pointer may cause addressing exceptions upon use if the subject pointer does not refer to an object suitably aligned in storage. It is guaranteed that a pointer to an object of a given size may be converted to a pointer to an object of a smaller size and back again without change. Different machines may differ in the number of bits in pointers and in alignment requirements for objects. Aggregates are aligned on the strictest boundary required by any of their constituents.

An object may be converted to a class object only if an appropriate constructor or conversion operator has been declared (§8.5.6).

An object may be explicitly converted to a reference type X& if a pointer to that object may be explicitly converted to an X*.

7.2.4 Free Store

The new operator creates an object of the *type-name* (see §8.7) to which it is applied. The lifetime of an object created by new is not restricted to the scope in which it is created. The new operator returns a pointer to the object it created. When that object is an array a pointer to its first element is returned. For example, both new int and new int[10] return an int*. An initializer may be supplied for certain class objects (§8.6.2). To obtain storage the new operator (§7.2) will call the function

```
void* operator new(long);
```

The argument specifies the number of bytes required. The store will be uninitialized. If operator new() cannot find the amount of store required it will return zero.

The delete operator destroys an object created by the new operator. The result is void. The operand of delete must be a pointer returned by new. The effect of applying delete to a pointer not obtained from the new operator is undefined. However, deleting a pointer with the value zero is harmless. To free the store pointed to the delete operator will call the function

```
void operator delete(void*);
```

In the form

```
delete [ expression ] expression
```

the second expression points to a vector and the first expression gives the number of elements of that vector. Specifying the number of elements is redundant except when deleting vectors of certain classes; see§8.5.8.

7.3 Multiplicative Operators

The multiplicative operators *, /, and % group left-to-right. The usual arithmetic conversions are performed.

> *multiplicative-expression:*
> > *expression* * *expression*
> > *expression* / *expression*
> > *expression* % *expression*

The binary * operator indicates multiplication. The * operator is associative and expressions with several multiplications at the same level may be rearranged by the compiler.

The binary / operator indicates division. When positive integers are divided truncation is toward 0, but the form of truncation is machine-dependent if either operand is negative. On all machines covered by this manual, the remainder has the same sign as the dividend. It is always true that (a/b)*b + a%b is equal to a (if b is not 0).

The binary % operator yields the remainder from the division of the first expression by the second. The usual arithmetic conversions are performed. The operands must not be floating.

7.4 Additive Operators

The additive operators + and – group left-to-right. The usual arithmetic conversions are performed. There are some additional type possibilities for each operator.

> *additive-expression:*
> > *expression* + *expression*
> > *expression* – *expression*

The result of the + operator is the sum of the operands. A pointer to an object in an array and a value of any integral type may be added. The latter is in all cases converted to an address offset by multiplying it by the length of the object to which the pointer points. The result is a pointer of the same type as the original pointer, and which points to another object in the same array, appropriately offset from the original object. Thus if P is a pointer to an object in an array, the expression P+1 is a pointer to the next object in the array.

No further type combinations are allowed for pointers.

The + operator is associative and expressions with several additions at the same level may be rearranged by the compiler.

The result of the – operator is the difference of the operands. The usual arithmetic conversions are performed. Additionally, a value of any integral type may be subtracted from a pointer, and then the same conversions as for addition apply.

If two pointers to objects of the same type are subtracted, the result is converted (by division by the length of the object) to an integer representing the number of objects separating the pointed-to objects. Depending on the machine the resulting integer may be of type int or type long; see §2.6. This conversion will in general give unexpected results unless the pointers point to objects in the same array, since pointers, even to objects of the same type, do not necessarily differ by a multiple of the object-length.

7.5 Shift Operators

The shift operators << and >> group left-to-right. Both perform the usual arithmetic conversions on their operands, each of which must be integral. Then the right operand is converted to int; the type of the result is that of the left operand. The result is undefined if the right operand is negative, or greater than or equal to the length of the object in bits.

> *shift-expression:*
> > *expression* << *expression*
> > *expression* >> *expression*

The value of E1 << E2 is E1 (interpreted as a bit pattern) left-shifted E2 bits; vacated bits are 0-filled. The value of E1 >> E2 is E1 right-shifted E2 bit positions. The right shift is guaranteed to be logical (0-fill) if E1 is unsigned; otherwise it may be arithmetic (fill by a copy of the sign bit).

7.6 Relational Operators

The relational operators group left-to-right, but this fact is not very useful; a<b<c does not mean what it seems to.

> *relational-expression:*
> > *expression* < *expression*
> > *expression* > *expression*
> > *expression* <= *expression*
> > *expression* >= *expression*

The operators < (less than), > (greater than), <= (less than or equal to) and >= (greater than or equal to) all yield 0 if the specified relation is false and 1 if it is true. The type of the result is int. The usual arithmetic conversions are performed. Two pointers may be compared; the result depends on the relative locations in the address space of the pointed-to objects. Pointer comparison is portable only when the pointers point to objects in the same array.

7.7 Equality Operators

equality-expression:
     expression == *expression*
     expression != *expression*

The == (equal to) and the != (not equal to) operators are exactly analogous to the relational operators except for their lower precedence. (Thus a<b == c<d is 1 whenever a<b and c<d have the same truth-value.)

A pointer may be compared to 0.

7.8 Bitwise AND Operator

and-expression:
     expression & *expression*

The & operator is associative and expressions involving & may be rearranged. The usual arithmetic conversions are performed; the result is the bitwise AND function of the operands. The operator applies only to integral operands.

7.9 Bitwise Exclusive OR Operator

exclusive-or-expression:
     expression ^ *expression*

The ^ operator is associative and expressions involving ^ may be rearranged. The usual arithmetic conversions are performed; the result is the bitwise exclusive OR function of the operands. The operator applies only to integral operands.

7.10 Bitwise Inclusive OR Operator

inclusive-or-expression:
     expression ¦ *expression*

The ¦ operator is associative and expressions involving ¦ may be rearranged. The usual arithmetic conversions are performed; the result is the bitwise inclusive OR function of its operands. The operator applies only to integral operands.

7.11 Logical AND Operator

logical-and-expression:
     expression && *expression*

The && operator groups left-to-right. It returns 1 if both its operands are non-zero, 0 otherwise. Unlike &, && guarantees left-to-right evaluation; moreover the second operand is not evaluated if the first operand is 0.

The operands need not have the same type, but each must have one of the fundamental types or be a pointer. The result is always `int`.

7.12 Logical OR Operator

> *logical-or-expression:*
>> *expression* ¦¦ *expression*

The ¦¦ operator groups left-to-right. It returns 1 if either of its operands is non-zero, and 0 otherwise. Unlike ¦, ¦¦ guarantees left-to-right evaluation; moreover, the second operand is not evaluated if the value of the first operand is non-zero.

The operands need not have the same type, but each must have one of the fundamental types or be a pointer. The result is always `int`.

7.13 Conditional Operator

> *conditional-expression:*
>> *expression* ? *expression* : *expression*

Conditional expressions group right-to-left. The first expression is evaluated and if it is non-zero, the result is the value of the second expression, otherwise that of third expression. If possible, the usual arithmetic conversions are performed to bring the second and third expressions to a common type. If possible the pointer conversions are performed to bring the second and third expressions to a common type. The result has the common type; only one of the second and third expressions is evaluated.

7.14 Assignment Operators

There are a number of assignment operators, all of which group right-to-left. All require an lvalue as their left operand, and the type of an assignment expression is that of its left operand; this lvalue may not refer to a constant (array name, function name, or `const`). The value is the value stored in the left operand after the assignment has taken place.

> *assignment-expression:*
>> *expression assignment-operator expression*

> *assignment-operator:* one of
>> =   +=   -=   *=   /=   %=   >>=   <<=   &=   ^=   ¦=

In the simple assignment with =, the value of the expression replaces that of the object referred to by the left hand operand. If both operands have arithmetic type, the right operand is converted to the type of the left preparatory to the assignment. If the left hand argument has pointer type the right hand operand must be of the same type or a type that can be converted to it; see §6.7. Both operands may be objects of the same class. Objects of some derived classes cannot be assigned; see §8.5.3.

Assignment to a object of type "reference to ..." assigns to the object denoted by the reference.

The behavior of an expression of the form E1 *op*= E2 may be inferred by taking it as equivalent to E1 = E1 *op* (E2); however, E1 is evaluated only once. In += and -=, the left operand may be a pointer, in which case the (integral) right operand is converted as explained in §7.4; all right operands and all non-pointer left operands must have arithmetic type.

7.15 Comma Operator

> *comma-expression:*
>> *expression* , *expression*

A pair of expressions separated by a comma is evaluated left-to-right and the value of the left expression is discarded. The type and value of the result are the type and value of the right operand. This operator groups left-to-right. In contexts where comma is given a special meaning, for example in lists of actual arguments to functions (§7.1) and lists of initializers (§8.6), the comma operator as described in this section can only appear in parentheses; for example,

```
f(a, (t=3, t+2), c)
```

has three arguments, the second of which has the value 5.

7.16 Overloaded Operators

Most operators may be *overloaded*, that is declared to accept class objects as operands (see §8.5.11). It is not possible to change the precedence of operators, nor to change the meaning of operators applied to non-class objects. The pre-defined meaning of the operators = and (unary) & applied to class objects may be changed.

Identities among operators applied to basic types (for example a++ ≡ a+=1) need not hold for operators applied to class types. Some operators, for example assignment, require an operand to be an lvalue when applied to basic types; this is not required when the operators are declared for class types.

7.16.1 Unary Operators

A unary operator, whether prefix or postfix, may be defined by a member function (see §8.5.4) taking no arguments or a friend function (see §8.5.10) taking one argument, but not both. Thus, for any unary operator @, both x@ and @x can be interpreted as either x.operator@() or operator@(x). When the operators ++ and -- are overloaded, it is not possible to distinguish prefix application from postfix application.

7.16.2 Binary Operators

A binary operator may be defined either by a member function taking one
argument or by a `friend` function taking two arguments, but not both. Thus,
for any binary operator `@`, `x@y` can be interpreted as either `x.operator@(y)`
or `operator@(x,y)`.

7.16.3 Special Operators

Function call

>   *primary-expression* `(` *expression-list*$_{opt}$ `)`

and subscripting

>   *primary-expression* `[` *expression* `]`

are considered binary operators. The names of the defining functions are
`operator()` and `operator[]`, respectively. Thus, a call `x(arg)` is
interpreted as `x.operator()(arg)` for a class object `x`. A subscripting
`x[y]` is interpreted as `x.operator[](y)`.

8. Declarations

Declarations are used to specify the interpretation given to each identifier; they
do not necessarily reserve storage associated with the identifier. Declarations
have the form

>   *declaration:*
>   *decl-specifiers*$_{opt}$ *declarator-list*$_{opt}$ `;`
>   *name-declaration*
>   *asm-declaration*

The declarators in the declarator-list contain the identifiers being declared.
Only in external function definitions (§10) or external function declarations
may the *decl-specifiers* be omitted. Only when declaring a class (§8.5) or
enumeration (§8.10), that is, when the *decl-specifiers* is a *class-specifier* or
enum-specifier, may the *declarator-list* be empty. Name-declarations are
described in §8.8; asm declarations are described in §8.11.

>   *decl-specifier;*
>   *sc-specifier*
>   *type-specifier*
>   *fct-specifier*
>   `friend`
>   `typedef`

decl-specifiers:
> *decl-specifier decl-specifiers*_{opt}

The list must be self-consistent in the way described below.

8.1 Storage Class Specifiers

The "storage class" specifiers are:

sc-specifier:
>   auto
>   static
>   extern
>   register

Declarations using the `auto`, `static`, and `register` specifiers also serve as definitions in that they cause an appropriate amount of storage to be reserved. If an `extern` declaration is not a definition §4.2 there must be a definition for the given identifiers somewhere else.

A `register` declaration is best thought of as an `auto` declaration, together with a hint to the compiler that the variables declared will be heavily used. The hint may be ignored. The address-of operator & cannot be applied to them.

The `auto` or `register` specifiers can only be used for names of objects declared in a block and for formal arguments. There can be no `static` functions within a block, nor any `static` formal arguments.

At most one *sc-specifier* may be given in a declaration. If the *sc-specifier* is missing from a declaration, the storage class is taken to be automatic inside a function and static outside. Exception: functions are never automatic.

The `static` and `extern` specifiers can only be used for names of objects or functions.

Some specifiers can only be used in function declarations:

fct-specifiers:
>   overload
>   inline
>   virtual

The `overload` specifier enables a single name to be used to denote several functions; see §8.9.

The `inline` specifier is only a hint to the compiler, does not affect the meaning of a program, and may be ignored. It indicates that inline substitution of the function body is to be preferred to the usual function call implementation. A function (§8.5.2 and §8.5.10) defined within the declaration of a class is `inline` by default.

The `virtual` specifier may only be used in declarations of class members; see §8.5.4.

The `friend` specifier is used to override the name hiding rules for class members and can only be used within a class declaration; see §8.5.10.

The `typedef` specifier is used to introduce a name for a type; see §8.8.

8.2 Type Specifiers

The type-specifiers are

> *type-specifier:*
> > *simple-type-name*
> > *class-specifier*
> > *enum-specifier*
> > *elaborated-type-specifier*
> > `const`

The word `const` may be added to any legal type-specifier. Otherwise, at most one type-specifier may be given in a declaration. An object of `const` type is not an lvalue. If the type-specifier is missing from a declaration, it is taken to be `int`.

> *simple-type-name:*
> > *typedef-name*
> > `char`
> > `short`
> > `int`
> > `long`
> > `unsigned`
> > `float`
> > `double`
> > `void`

The words `long`, `short`, and `unsigned` may be thought of as adjectives. They may be applied to `int`; `unsigned` may also be applied to `char`, `short`, and `long`.

Class and enumeration specifiers are discussed in §8.5 and §8.10, respectively.

> *elaborated-type-specifier:*
> > *key typedef-name*
> > *key identifier*

key:

```
class
struct
union
enum
```

An elaborated type specifier may be used to refer to a class or enumeration name where the name may have been hidden by a local name. For example:

```
class x { ... };

void f(int x)
{
        class x a;
        // ...
}
```

If the class or enumeration name has not been previously declared, the *elaborated-type-specifier* acts as a *name-declaration*; see §8.8.

8.3 Declarators

The declarator-list appearing in a declaration is a comma-separated sequence of declarators, each of which may have an initializer.

declarator-list:
    init-declarator
    init-declarator , *declarator-list*

init-declarator:
    declarator initializer$_{opt}$

Initializers are discussed in §8.6. The specifiers in the declaration indicate the type and storage class of the objects to which the declarators refer. Declarators have the syntax:

declarator:
    dname
    (*declarator*)
    * const$_{opt}$ *declarator*
    & const$_{opt}$ *declarator*
    declarator (*argument-declaration-list*)
    declarator [*constant-expression*$_{opt}$]

> *dname:*
>> *simple-dname*
>> *typedef-name* : : *simple-dname*
>
> *simple-dname:*
>> *identifier*
>> *typedef-name*
>> ~ *typedef-name*
>> *operator-function-name*
>> *conversion-function-name*

The grouping is the same as in expressions.

8.4 Meaning of Declarators

Each declarator is taken to be an assertion that when a construction of the same form as the declarator appears in an expression, it yields an object of the indicated type and storage class. Each declarator contains exactly one *dname*; it specifies the identifier that is declared. Except for the declarations of some special functions (see §8.5.2) a *dname* will be a simple *identifier*.

If an unadorned identifier appears as a declarator, then it has the type indicated by the specifier heading the declaration.

A declarator in parentheses is identical to the unadorned declarator, but the binding of complex declarators may be altered by parentheses; see the examples below.

Now imagine a declaration

        T D1

where `T` is a type-specifier (like `int`, etc.) and `D1` is a declarator. Suppose this declaration makes the identifier have type "... `T`," where the "..." is empty if `D1` is just a plain identifier (so that the type of `x` in "`int x`" is just `int`). Then if `D1` has the form

        *D

the type of the contained identifier is "... pointer to `T`."

If `D1` has the form

        * const D

the type of the contained identifier is "... constant pointer to `T`" that is, the same type as `*D`, but the contained identifier is not an lvalue.

If `D1` has the form

&D

or

```
& const D
```

the type of the contained identifier is "... reference to T." Since a reference by definition cannot be an lvalue, use of const is redundant. It is not possible to have a reference to void (a void&).

If D1 has the form

D(*argument-declaration-list*)

then the contained identifier has the type "... function taking arguments of type *argument-declaration-list* and returning T."

>*argument-declaration-list:*
>>*arg-declaration-list*$_{opt}$ ... $_{opt}$

>*arg-declaration-list:*
>>*arg-declaration-list* , *argument-declaration*
>>*argument-declaration*

>*argument-declaration:*
>>*decl-specifiers declarator*
>>*decl-specifiers declarator* = *expression*
>>*decl-specifiers abstract-declarator*
>>*decl-specifiers abstract-declarator* = *expression*

If the *argument-declaration-list* terminates with an ellipsis the number of arguments is only known to be equal to or greater than the number of argument types specified; if it is empty the function takes no arguments. All declarations for a function must agree exactly both in the type of the value returned and in the number and type of arguments.

The *argument-declaration-list* is used to check and convert actual arguments in calls and to check pointer-to-function assignments. If an expression is specified in an argument declaration this expression is used as a default argument. Default arguments will be used in calls where trailing arguments are missing. A default argument cannot be redefined by a later declaration. However, a declaration may add default arguments not given in previous declarations.

An identifier can optionally be provided as an argument name; if present in a function declaration, it cannot be used since it immediately goes out of scope; if present in a function definition (§10) it names a formal argument.

If D1 has the form

      D[*constant-expression*]

or

      D[ ]

then the contained identifier has type "... array of T." In the first case the constant expression is an expression whose value is determinable at compile time, and whose type is int. (Constant expressions are defined in §12.) When several "array of" specifications are adjacent, a multi-dimensional array is created; the constant expressions which specify the bounds of the arrays may be missing ˙only for the first member of the sequence. This elision is useful when the array is external and the actual definition, which allocates storage, is given elsewhere. The first constant-expression may also be omitted when the declarator is followed by initialization. In this case the size is calculated from the number of initial elements supplied.

An array may be constructed from one of the basic types, from a pointer, from a structure or union, or from another array (to generate a multi-dimensional array).

Not all the possibilities allowed by the syntax above are permitted. The restrictions are: functions may not return arrays or functions, although they may return pointers to such things; there are no arrays of functions, although there may be arrays of pointers to functions.

8.4.1 Examples

The declaration

      `int i, *pi, f( ), *fpi( ), (*pif)( );`

declares an integer i, a pointer pi to an integer, a function f returning an integer, a function fpi returning a pointer to an integer, and a pointer pif to a function which returns an integer. It is especially useful to compare the last two. The binding of *fpi( ) is *(fpi( )), so that the declaration suggests, and the same construction in an expression requires, the calling of a function fpi, and then using indirection through the (pointer) result to yield an integer. In the declarator (*pif)( ), the extra parentheses are necessary to indicate that indirection through a pointer to a function yields a function, which is then called. The functions f and fpi are declared to take no arguments, and pif to point to a function which takes no argument.

The declaration

      `const a = 10, *pc = &a, *const cpc = pc;`
      `int b, *const cp = &b;`

declares a: a constant integer, pc: a pointer to a constant integer, cpc: a constant pointer to a constant integer, b: an integer, and cp: a constant pointer to integer. The value of a, cpc, and cp cannot be changed after initialization. The value of pc can be changed, and so can the object pointed to by cp. Examples of illegal operations are:

```
a = 1; a++; *pc = 2; cp = .&a; cpc++;
```

Examples of legal operations are:

```
b = a; *cp = a; pc++; pc = cpc;
```

The declaration

```
fseek(FILE*, long, int);
```

declares a function taking three arguments of the specified types. Since no return value type is specified it is taken to be int (§8.2). The declaration

```
point(int = 0, int = 0);
```

declares a function which can be called with zero, one or two arguments of type int. It may be called in any of these ways:

```
point(1,2);  point(1);  point();
```

The declaration

```
printf(char* ...);
```

declares a function which can be called with varying number and types of arguments. For example:

```
printf("hello world");
printf("a=%d b=%d", a, b);
```

However, it must always have a char* as its first argument.

The declaration

```
float fa[17], *afp[17];
```

declares an array of float numbers and an array of pointers to float numbers. Finally,

```
static int x3d[3][5][7];
```

declares a static three-dimensional array of integers, with rank 3×5×7. In complete detail, x3d is an array of three items; each item is an array of five arrays; each of the latter arrays is an array of seven integers. Any of the expressions x3d, x3d[i], x3d[i][j], x3d[i][j][k] may reasonably appear in an expression.

8.4.2 Arrays, Pointers, and Subscripting

Every time an identifier of array type appears in an expression, it is converted into a pointer to the first member of the array. Because of this conversion, arrays are not lvalues. Except where it has been declared for a class (§7.16.3), the subscript operator [ ] is interpreted in such a way that E1[E2] is identical to *((E1)+(E2)). Because of the conversion rules which apply to +, if E1 is an array and E2 an integer, then E1[E2] refers to the E2-th member of E1. Therefore, despite its asymmetric appearance, subscripting is a commutative operation.

A consistent rule is followed in the case of multi-dimensional arrays. If E is an n-dimensional array of rank $i \times j \times \cdots \times k$, then E appearing in an expression is converted to a pointer to an $(n-1)$-dimensional array with rank $j \times \cdots \times k$. If the * operator, either explicitly or implicitly as a result of subscripting, is applied to this pointer, the result is the pointed-to $(n-1)$-dimensional array, which itself is immediately converted into a pointer.

For example, consider

```
int x[3][5];
```

Here x is a 3×5 array of integers. When x appears in an expression, it is converted to a pointer to (the first of three) 5-membered arrays of integers. In the expression x[i], which is equivalent to *(x+i), x is first converted to a pointer as described; then x+i is converted to the type of x, which involves multiplying i by the length the object to which the pointer points, namely 5 integer objects. The results are added and indirection applied to yield an array (of 5 integers) which in turn is converted to a pointer to the first of the integers. If there is another subscript the same argument applies again; this time the result is an integer.

It follows from all this that arrays in C++ are stored row-wise (last subscript varies fastest) and that the first subscript in the declaration helps determine the amount of storage consumed by an array but plays no other part in subscript calculations.

8.5 Class Declarations

A class is a type. Its name becomes a *typedef-name* (see §8.8) which can be used even within the class specifier itself. Objects of a class consist of a sequence of members.

>   *class-specifier:*
>   class-head { *member-list*$_{opt}$ }
>   class-head { *member-list*$_{opt}$ public : *member-list*$_{opt}$ }

class-head:
      aggr identifier$_{opt}$
      aggr identifier : `public`$_{opt}$ *typedef-name*

aggr:
      `class`
      `struct`
      `union`

Class objects may be assigned, passed as arguments to functions, and returned by functions (except objects of some derived classes; see §8.5.3). Other plausible operators, such as equality comparison, can be defined by the user; see §8.5.11.

A structure is a class with all members public; see §8.5.9. A union is a structure which holds only one member at a time; see §8.5.13. A *member-list* may declare data, function, class, enum, field members (§8.5.14), and friends (§8.5.10). A *member-list* may also contain declarations adjusting the visibility of member names; see §8.5.9.

member-list:
      member-declaration member-list$_{opt}$

member-declaration:
      decl-specifiers$_{opt}$ *member-declarator* ;
      function-definition ;$_{opt}$

member-declarator:
      declarator
      identifier$_{opt}$: *constant-expression*

Members that are class objects must be objects of previously declared classes. In particular, a class `cl` may not contain an object of class `cl`, but it may contain a pointer to an object of class `cl`.

A simple example of a struct declaration is

```
struct tnode {
        char tword[20];
        int count;
        tnode *left;
        tnode *right;
};
```

which contains an array of 20 characters, an integer, and two pointers to similar structures. Once this declaration has been given, the declaration

```
tnode s, *sp;
```

declares s to be a tnode and sp to be a pointer to a tnode. With these declarations

```
sp->count
```

refers to the count field of the structure to which sp points;

```
s.left
```

refers to the left subtree pointer of the structure s; and

```
s.right->tword[0]
```

refers to the first character of the tword member of the right subtree of s.

8.5.1 Static Members

A data member of a class may be static; function members may not. Members may not be auto, register, or extern. There is only one copy of a static member shared by all objects of the class in a program. A static member mem of class cl can be referred to as cl::mem, that is, without referring to an object. It exists even if no objects of class cl have been created. No initializer can be specified for a static member, and it cannot be of a class with a constructor.

8.5.2 Member Functions

A function declared as a member (without the friend specifier (§8.5.10) is called a member function, and is called using the class member syntax (§7.1). For example:

```
struct tnode {
        char tword[20];
        int count;
        tnode *left;
        tnode *right;
        void set(char*, tnode* l, tnode* r);
};

tnode n1, n2;
n1.set("asdf",&n2,0);
n2.set("ghjk",0,0);
```

The definition of a member function is considered to be within the scope of its class. This means that it can use names of its class directly. If the definition of a member function is lexically outside the class declaration the member function name must be qualified by the class name using the :: operator. Function definitions are discussed in §10. For example:

```
void tnode::set(char* w, tnode* l, tnode* r) {
        count = strlen(w);
        if (sizeof(tword)<=count)
                error("tnode string too long");
        strcpy(tword,w);
        left = l;
        right = r;
}
```

The notation `tnode::set` specifies that the function `set` is a member of and in the scope of class `tnode`. The member names `tword`, `count`, `left`, and `right` refer to the object for which the function was called. Thus, in the call `n1.set("abc",0,0)`, `tword` refers to `n1.tword`, and in the call `n2.set("def",0,0)` it refers to `n2.tword`. The functions `strlen`, `error`, and `strcpy` are assumed to be declared elsewhere; see §10.

In a member function, the keyword `this` is a pointer to the object for which the function is called.

A member function may be defined (§10) in the class declaration, in which case it is `inline` (§8.1). Thus

```
struct x {
        int  f() { return b; }
        int  b;
};
```

is equivalent

```
struct x {
        int  f();
        int  b;
};
inline x::f() { return b; }
```

It is legal to apply the address-of operator to a member function. However, the type of the resulting pointer to function is undefined, so that any use of it is implementation dependent.

8.5.3 Derived Classes

In the construct

$$aggr \; identifier \; : \; \texttt{public}_{opt} \; typedef\text{-}name$$

the *typedef-name* must denote a previously declared class, which is called a base class for the class being declared. The class is said to be derived from its base class. For the meaning of `public` see §8.5.9. Members of the base class can be referred to as if they were members of the derived class, except when a base member name has been re-defined in the derived class; in this case the : : operator (§7.1) can be used to refer to the hidden name. A derived class can itself be used as a base class. It is not possible to derive from a union (§8.5.13). A pointer to a derived class may be implicitly converted to a pointer to a public base class (§6.7).

Assignment is not implicitly defined (see §7.14 and §8.5) for objects of a class derived from a class for which operator= has been defined (§8.5.11).

For example:

```
class base {
public:
        int a, b;
};

class derived : public base {
public:
        int b, c;
};

derived d;
d.a = 1;
d.base::b = 2;
d.b = 3;
d.c = 4;
base* bp = &d;
```

assigns to the four members of d and makes bp a pointer to d.

8.5.4 Virtual Functions

If a base class base contains a virtual (§8.1) function vf, and a derived class derived also contains a function vf then both functions must have the same type, and a call of vf for an object of class derived invokes derived::vf. For example:

```
struct base {
        virtual void vf();
                void f();
};

class derived : public base {
public:
        void vf();
        void f();
};
```

```
derived d;
base* bp = &d;
bp->vf();
bp->f();
```

The calls invoke `derived::vf` and `base::f`, respectively, for the class `derived` object named d. That is, the interpretation of the call of a virtual function depends on the type of the object for which it is called, whereas the interpretation of a call of a non-virtual member function depends only on the type of the pointer denoting that object.

A virtual function cannot be a `friend` (§8.5.10). A function f in a class derived from a class which has a virtual function f is itself considered virtual. A virtual function in a base class must be defined. A virtual function which has been defined in a base class need not be defined in a derived class. In that case, the function defined for the base class is used in all calls.

8.5.5 Constructors

A member function with the same name as its class is called a constructor; it is used to construct values of its class type. If a class has any constructor each object of that class must be initialized before any use is made of the object; see §8.6.

A constructor may not be `virtual` or `friend`.

If a class has a base class or member objects with constructors, their constructors are called before the constructor for the derived class. The constructor for the base class is called first. See §10 for an explanation of how arguments can be specified for such constructors, and see §8.5.8 for an explanation of how constructors can be used for free storage management.

An object of a class with a constructor cannot be a member of a union.

No return value type can be specified for a constructor, nor can a return statement be used in the body of a constructor.

A constructor can be used explicitly to create new objects of its type, using the syntax

>   *typedef-name* (*argument-list*$_{opt}$)

For example,

```
complex zz = complex(1,2.3);
cprint( complex(7.8,1.2) );
```

Objects created in this way are unnamed (unless the constructor was used as an initializer as for zz above), with their lifetime limited to the scope in which they are created.

8.5.6 Conversions

A constructor taking a single argument specifies a conversion from its argument type to the type of its class. Such conversions are used implicitly in addition to the standard conversions (§6.6-7). An assignment to an object of class X is legal if the type T of assigned value is X, or if a conversion has been declared from T to X. Constructors are used similarly for conversion of initializers (§8.6), function arguments (§7.1), and function return values (§9.10). For example:

```
class X { ... X(int); };
f(X arg) {
        X a = 1;        // a = X(1)
        a = 2;          // a = X(2)
        f(3);           // f(X(3))
}
```

When no constructor for class X accepts the assigned type, no attempt is made to find other constructors to convert the assigned value into a type acceptable to a constructor for class X. For example:

```
class X { ... X(int); };
class Y { ... Y(X); };
Y a = 1;                // illegal: Y(X(1)) not tried
```

A member function of a class X with a name of the form

> *conversion-function-name:*
> 　　operator *type*

specifies a conversion from X to *type*. The *type* may not contain [ ] "vector of" or ( ) "function returning" declarators. It will be used implicitly like the constructors above (only if it is unique: §8.9), or it can be called explicitly using the cast notation. For example:

```
class X {
        // ...
        operator int();
};

X a;
int i = int(a);
i = (int)a;
i = a;
```

In all three cases the value assigned will be converted by X::operator int(). User defined conversions are not restricted to be used in assignments and initializations only. For example

```
X a, b;
// ...
int i = (a) ? 1+a : 0;
int j = (a&&b) ? a+b : i;
```

8.5.7 Destructors

A member function of class cl named ~cl is called a destructor; it takes no arguments, and no return value can be specified for it; it is used to destroy values of type cl immediately before the object containing them is destroyed. A destructor cannot be called explicitly.

The destructor for a base class is executed after the destructor for its derived class. Destructors for member objects are executed after the destructor for the object they are members of. See §8.5.8 for an explanation of how destructors can be used for free storage management.

An object of a class with a destructor cannot be a member of a union.

8.5.8 Free Store

When a class object is created using the new operator the constructor will (implicitly) use operator new to obtain the store needed (§7.1). By assigning to the this pointer before any use of a member a constructor can implement its own storage allocation. By assigning a zero value to this, a destructor can avoid the standard deallocation operation for objects of its class. For example:

```
class cl {
        int v[ 10];
        cl() { this = my_allocator( sizeof(cl) ); }
        ~cl() { my_deallocator( this ); this = 0; }
}
```

On entry into a constructor this is non-zero if allocation has already taken place (as is the case for auto, static, and member objects) and zero otherwise.

Calls to constructors for a base class and for member objects will take place after an assignment to this. If a base class's constructor assigns to this, the new value will also be used by the derived class's constructor (if any).

The number of elements must be specified when deleting a vector of objects of a class with a destructor. For example:

```
class X { ... ~X(); };
X* p = new X[size];
delete[size] p;
```

8.5.9 Visibility of Member Names

The members of a class declared with the keyword `class` are private, that is, their names can only be used by member functions (§8.5.2) and friends (see §8.5.10), unless they appear after the "`public:`" label; in that case they are public. A public member can be used in any function. A `struct` is a class with all members public; see §8.5.12.

If a derived class is declared `struct` or if the keyword `public` precedes the base class name in the declaration of the derived class the public members of the base class are public for the derived class; otherwise, they are private. A public member `mem` of a private base class `base` can be declared to be public for the derived class by a declaration of the form

> *typedef-name* `::` *identifier* `;`

where the *typedef-name* denotes the base class and the *identifier* is the name of a member of the base class. Such a declaration must occur in the public part of the derived class. Consider

```
class base {
        int a;
public:
        int b, c;
        int bf();
};

class derived : base {
        int d;
public:
        base::c;
        int e;
        int df();
};


        int ef(derived&);
```

The external function `ef` can use only the names c, e, and df. Being a member of `derived`, the function df can use the names b, c, bf, d, e, and df, but not a. Being a member of `base`, the function bf can use the members a, b, c, and bf.

8.5.10 Friends

A friend of a class is a non-member function which may use the private member names from the class. A friend is not in the scope of the class and is not called using the member selection syntax (unless it is a member of another class). The following example illustrates the differences between members and friends:

```
class private {
        int a;
        friend void friend_set(private*, int);
public:
        void member_set(int);
};

void friend_set(private* p, int i) { p->a = i; }
void private::member_set(int i) { a = i; }

private obj;
friend_set(&obj,10);
obj.member_set(10);
```

When a `friend` declaration refers to an overloaded name or operator only the function specified by the argument types becomes a friend. A member of a class `cl1` can be the friend of a class `cl2`. For example

```
class cl2 {
        friend char* cl1::foo(int);
        //'...
};
```

All the functions of a class `cl1` can be made friends of a class `cl2` by a single declaration

```
class cl2 {
        friend class cl1 ;
        // ...
};
```

A `friend` function defined (§10) in a class declaration is `inline`.

8.5.11 Operator Functions

Most operators can be overloaded to take class object operands.

operator-function-name:
        operator *operator*

operator: one of
        new   delete

+	−	*	/	%	^	&	¦	~
!	=	<	>	+=	−=	*=	/=	%=
^=	&=	¦=	<<	>>	>>=	<<=	==	!=
<=	>=	&&	¦¦	++	−−	( )	[ ]	

The last two operators are function call and subscripting. An operator function (except `operator new` and `operator delete`; see §7.2) must either be a member function or take at least one class argument. See also §7.16.

8.5.12 Structures

A structure is a class with all members public. That is

        struct s { ... };

is equivalent to

        class s { public: ... };

A structure may have member functions (including constructors and destructors). The base of a derived `struct` is public. That is

        struct s : b { ... };

is equivalent to

        class s : public b { public: ... };

8.5.13 Unions

A union may be thought of as a structure all of whose member objects begin at offset 0 and whose size is sufficient to contain any of its member objects. At most one of the member objects can be stored in a union at any time. A union may have member functions (including constructors and destructors). It is not possible to derive a class from a union. An object of a class with a constructor or a destructor cannot be a member of a union.

A union of the form

        union { *member-list* } ;

is called an anonymous union; it defines an unnamed object. The names of the members of an anonymous union must be distinct from other names in the scope where the union is declared; they can be used directly in that scope without using the usual member access syntax (§8.5). For example

        union { int a; char* p; };
        a = 1;
        // ...
        p = "asdf";

Here a and p are used like ordinary (non-member) variables, but since they are union members they have the same address.

8.5.14 Bit Fields

A *member-declarator* of the form

$$identifier_{opt} \; : \; constant\text{-}expression$$

specifies a field; its length is set off from the field name by a colon. Fields are packed into machine integers; they do not straddle words. A field which does not fit into the space remaining in an integer is put into the next word. No field may be wider than a word. Fields are assigned right-to-left on some machines, left-to-right on other machines; see §2.6.

An unnamed field is useful for padding to conform to externally-imposed layouts. As a special case, an unnamed field with a width of 0 specifies alignment of the next field at a word boundary.

Implementations are not required to support any but integer fields. Moreover, even int fields may be considered to be unsigned. For these reasons, it is recommended that fields be declared as unsigned. The address-of operator & may not be applied to them, so that there are no pointers to fields.

Fields may not be union members.

8.5.15 Nested Classes

A class may be declared within another class. That, however, is only a notational convenience since the inner class belongs to the enclosing scope. For example:

```
int x;

class enclose {
        int x;
        class inner {
                int y;
                void f(int);
        };
        int g(inner*);
};

inner a;
void inner::f(int i) { x = i; } // assign to ::x
int enclose::g(inner* p) { return p->y; } // error
```

8.6 Initialization

A declarator may specify an initial value for the identifier being declared.

initializer:
>   = *expression*
>   = { *initializer-list* , $_{opt}$ }
>   (*expression-list*)

> *initializer-list:*
>> *expression*
>> *initializer-list* , *initializer-list*
>> { *initializer-list* }

All expressions in an initializer for a static variable must be constant expressions, which are described in §12, or expressions which reduce to the address of a previously declared variable, possibly offset by a constant expression. Automatic or register variables may be initialized by arbitrary expressions involving constants, previously declared variables and functions.

Static and external variables which are not initialized are guaranteed to start off as 0; automatic and register variables which are not initialized are guaranteed to start off as garbage.

When an initializer applies to a *scalar* (a pointer or an object of arithmetic type), it consists of a single expression, perhaps in braces. The initial value of the object is taken from the expression; the same conversions as for assignment are performed.

Note that since ( ) is not an initializer, X a( ); is not the declaration of an object of class X, but the declaration of a function taking no argument and returning an X.

8.6.1 Initializer Lists

When the declared variable is an *aggregate* (a class or an array) then the initializer may consist of a brace-enclosed, comma-separated list of initializers for the members of the aggregate, written in increasing subscript or member order. If the array contains subaggregates, this rule applies recursively to the members of the aggregate. If there are fewer initializers in the list than there are members of the aggregate, then the aggregate is padded with 0's.

Braces may be elided as follows. If the initializer begins with a left brace, then the succeeding comma-separated list of initializers initializes the members of the aggregate; it is erroneous for there to be more initializers than members. If, however, the initializer does not begin with a left brace, then only enough elements from the list are taken to account for the members of the aggregate; any remaining members are left to initialize the next member of the aggregate of which the current aggregate is a part.

For example,

```
int x[] = { 1, 3, 5 };
```

declares and initializes x as a 1-dimensional array which has three members, since no size was specified and there are three initializers.

```
float y[4][3] = {
      { 1, 3, 5 },
      { 2, 4, 6 },
      { 3, 5, 7 },
};
```

is a completely-bracketed initialization: 1, 3, and 5 initialize the first row of the array y[0], namely y[0][0], y[0][1], and y[0][2]. Likewise the next two lines initialize y[1] and y[2]. The initializer ends early and therefore y[3] is initialized with 0's. Precisely the same effect could have been achieved by

```
float y[4][3] = {
      1, 3, 5, 2, 4, 6, 3, 5, 7
};
```

The initializer for y begins with a left brace, but that for y[0] does not, therefore three elements from the list are used. Likewise the next three are taken successively for y[1] and y[2]. Also,

```
float y[4][3] = {
      { 1 }, { 2 }, { 3 }, { 4 }
};
```

initializes the first column of y (regarded as a two-dimensional array) and leaves the rest 0.

8.6.2 Class Objects

An object with private members cannot be initialized using an initializer list; neither can a union object. An object of a class with a constructor must be initialized. If a class has a constructor which does not take arguments, that constructor is used for objects which are not explicitly initialized. An argument list for a constructor can be appended to the name in a declaration or to the type in a new expression. The following initializations all yield the same value (§8.4):

```
struct complex {
      float re, im;
      complex(float r, float i = 0) { re=r; im=i; }
};

complex zz1(1, 0);
complex zz2(1);
complex* zp1 = new complex(1,0);
complex* zp2 = new complex(1);
```

Class objects can also be initialized by explicit use of the = operator. For example:

```
complex zz3 = complex(1,0);
complex zz4 = complex(1);
complex zz5 = 1;
complex zz6 = zz3;
```

If a constructor taking a reference to an object of its own class exists, it will be invoked when an object is initialized with another object of that class, but not when an object is initialized with a constructor.

An object can be a member of an aggregate only (1) if the object's class does not have a constructor, or (2) if one of its constructors takes no arguments, or (3) if the aggregate is a class with a constructor that specifies a member initialization list(see §10). In case 2 that constructor is called when the aggregate is created. If the aggregate is a class (but not if it is a vector) default arguments can be used for the constructor call. If a member of an aggregate has a destructor then that destructor is called when the aggregate is destroyed.

Constructors for non-local static objects are called in the order they occur in a file; destructors are called in reverse order. It is undefined whether the constructor and destructor for a local static object are called if the function in which the object is declared is not called. If the constructor for a local static object is called, it is called after the constructors for global objects lexically preceding it. If the destructor for a local static object is called, it is called before the destructors for global objects lexically preceding it.

8.6.3 References

When a variable is declared to be a `T&`, that is "reference to type `T`", it must be initialized by an object of type `T` or by an object that can be converted into a `T`. The reference becomes an alternative name for the object. For example:

```
int i;
int& r = i;
r = 1;              // the value of i becomes 1
int* p = &r;        // p points to i
```

The value of a reference cannot be changed after initialization. Note that initialization of a reference is treated very differently from assignment to it.

If the initializer for a reference to type `T` is not an lvalue an object of type `T` will be created and initialized with the initializer. The reference then becomes a name for that object. The lifetime of an object created in this way is the scope in which it is created. For example:

```
double& rr = 1;
```

is legal and rr will point to a double containing the value 1.0.

Note that a reference to a class B can be initialized by an object of a class D provided B is a public base class of D (in that case a D is a B).

References are particularly useful as formal arguments. For example:

```
struct B { ... };
struct D : B { ... };
int f(B&);
D a;
f(a);
```

8.6.4 Character Arrays

A char array may be initialized by a string; successive characters of the string initialize the members of the array. For example,

```
char msg[] = "Syntax error on line %s\n";
```

shows a character array whose members are initialized with a string. Note that sizeof(msg)==25.

8.7 Type Names

Sometimes (to specify type conversions explicitly, and as an argument of sizeof or new) it is desired to supply the name of a data type. This is accomplished using a *type-name*, which in essence is a declaration for an object of that type which omits the name of the object.

> *type-name:*
> > *type-specifier abstract-declarator*

> *abstract-declarator:*
> > *empty*
> > ∗ *abstract-declarator*
> > *abstract-declarator (argument-declaration-list)*
> > *abstract-declarator [constant-expression$_{opt}$]*
> > *(abstract-declarator)*

It is possible to identify uniquely the location in the abstract-declarator where the identifier would appear if the construction were a declarator in a declaration. The named type is then the same as the type of the hypothetical identifier. For example,

```
int
int *
int *[3]
int (*)[3]
int *()
int (*)()
```

name respectively the types "integer," "pointer to integer," "array of 3 pointers to integers," "pointer to array of 3 integers," "function returning pointer to integer," and "pointer to function returning an integer."

8.8 Typedef

Declarations containing the *decl-specifier* typedef define identifiers which can be used later as if they were type keywords naming fundamental or derived types.

>   *typedef-name:*
>   *identifier*

Within the scope of a declaration involving typedef, each identifier appearing as part of any declarator therein becomes syntactically equivalent to the type keyword naming the type associated with the identifier in the way described in §8.4. The *decl-specifier* typedef may not be used for a class member. The name of a class or an enum is also a *typedef-name*. For example, after

```
typedef int MILES, *KLICKSP;
struct complex { double re, im; };
```

the constructions

```
MILES distance;
extern KLICKSP metricp;
complex z, *zp;
```

are all legal declarations; the type of distance is int, that of metricp is "pointer to int".

typedef does not introduce new types, only synonyms for types which could be specified in another way. Thus in the example above distance is considered to have exactly the same type as any other int object.

A class declaration, however, does introduce a new type. For example:

```
struct X { int a; };
struct Y { int a; };
X a1;
Y a2;
int a3;
```

declares three variables of three different types.

A declaration of the form

> *name-declaration:*
>   *aggr identifier* ;
>   enum *identifier* ;

specifies that an identifier is the name of some (possibly not yet defined) class
or enumeration. Such declarations allows declaration of classes which refer to
each other. For example:

```
class vector;

class matrix {
        // ...
        friend vector operator*(matrix&, vector&);
};

class vector {
        // ...
        friend vector operator*(matrix&, vector&);
};
```

8.9 Overloaded Function Names

When several (different) function declarations are specified for a single name,
that name is said to be overloaded. When that name is used, the correct
function is selected by comparing the types of the actual arguments with the
formal argument types.

Finding which function to call is done in three separate steps:

> Look for an exact match and use it if found.

> Look for a match using standard conversions (§6.6-8) and use any one
> found.

> Look for a match using user-defined conversions (§8.5.6). If a unique
> set of conversions is found use it.

A zero, a char, or a short is considered an exact match for a formal
argument of type int. A float is considered an exact match for a formal
argument of type double.

Only the following conversions will be applied for an argument to an overloaded function: int to long, int to double, and the pointer and reference conversions (§6.7-8).

To overload the name of a function other than a member or operator function an overload declaration must precede any declaration of the function; see §8.1. For example:

```
overload abs;
double   abs(double);
int      abs(int);

abs(1);        // call abs(int);
abs(1.0);      // call abs(double);
```

For example:

```
class X { ... X(int); };
class Y { ... Y(int); };
class Z { ... Z(char*); };

overload int f(X), f(Y);
overload int g(X), g(Z);

f(1);           // illegal: f(X(1)) or f(Y(1))
g(1);           // g(X(1))
g("asdf");      // g(Z("asdf"))
```

The address-of operator & may only be applied to an overloaded name in an assignment or an initialization where the type expected determines which function to take the address of. For example:

```
int operator=(matrix&, matrix&);
int operator=(vector&, vector&);
int (*pfm)(matrix&, matrix&) = &operator=;
int (*pfv)(vector&, vector&) = &operator=;
int (*pfx)(...) = &operator=;                       // error
```

8.10 Enumeration Declarations

Enumerations are int types with named constants.

> *enum-specifier:*
>> enum *identifier*$_{opt}$ { *enum-list* }
>
> *enum-list:*
>> *enumerator*
>> *enum-list* , *enumerator*

enumerator:
    identifier
    identifier = *constant-expression*

The identifiers in an enum-list are declared as constants, and may appear wherever constants are required. If no enumerators with = appear, then the values of the corresponding constants begin at 0 and increase by 1 as the declaration is read from left-to-right. An enumerator with = gives the associated identifier the value indicated; subsequent identifiers continue the progression from the assigned value.

The names of enumerators must be distinct from those of ordinary variables. The names of enumerators with different constants must also be distinct. The values of the enumerators need not be distinct.

The role of the identifier in the enum-specifier is entirely analogous to that of the class name; it names a particular enumeration. For example,

```
enum color { red, yellow, green=20, blue };
color col = red;
color* cp = &col;
if (*cp == blue) // ...
```

makes `color` the name of a type describing various colors, and then declares `col` as an object of that type, and `cp` as a pointer to an object of that type. The possible values are drawn from the set {0, 1, 20, 21}.

8.11 Asm Declaration

An asm declaration has the form

    asm (*string*) ;

The meaning of an asm declaration is not defined. Typically it is used to pass information through the compiler to an assembler.

9. Statements

Except as indicated, statements are executed in sequence.

9.1 Expression Statement

Most statements are expression statements, which have the form

    expression ;

Usually expression statements are assignments or function calls.

9.2 Compound Statement, or Block

So that several statements can be used where one is expected, the compound statement (also, and equivalently, called "block") is provided:

> *compound-statement:*
> > { *statement-list*_{*opt*} }
>
> *statement-list:*
> > *statement*
> > *statement statement-list*

Note that a declaration is an example of a statement (§9.14).

9.3 Conditional Statement

The two forms of the conditional statement are

> `if` (*expression*) *statement*
> `if` (*expression*) *statement* `else` *statement*

The expression must be of arithmetic or pointer type or of a class type for which a conversion to arithmetic or pointer type is defined (see §8.5.6). The expression is evaluated and if it is non-zero, the first substatement is executed. If `else` is used the second substatement is executed if the expression is 0. As usual the "else" ambiguity is resolved by connecting an `else` with the last encountered `else`-less `if`.

9.4 While Statement

The `while` statement has the form

> `while` (*expression*) *statement*

The substatement is executed repeatedly so long as the value of the expression remains non-zero. The test takes place before each execution of the statement. The expression is handled as in a conditional statement (§9.3).

9.5 Do Statement

The `do` statement has the form

> `do` *statement* `while` (*expression*) ;

The substatement is executed repeatedly until the value of the expression becomes zero. The test takes place after each execution of the statement. The expression is handled as in a conditional statement (§9.3).

9.6 For Statement

The `for` statement has the form

`for` (*statement-1 expression-1*$_{opt}$; *expression-2*$_{opt}$) *statement-2*

This statement is equivalent to

> *statement-1*
> `while` (*expression-1*) {
> > *statement-2*
> > *expression-2* ;
>
> }

except that a `continue` in *statement-2* will execute *expression-2* before re-evaluating *expression-1*. Thus the first statement specifies initialization for the loop; the first expression specifies a test, made before each iteration, such that the loop is exited when the expression becomes 0; the second expression often specifies an incrementing that is performed after each iteration.

Either or both of the expressions may be dropped. A missing *expression-1* makes the implied `while` clause equivalent to `while(1)`. Note that if *statement-1* is a declaration, the scope of the name declared extends to the end of the block enclosing the for-statement.

9.7 Switch Statement

The `switch` statement causes control to be transferred to one of several statements depending on the value of an expression. It has the form

> `switch` (*expression*) *statement*

The type of the expression must be of arithmetic or pointer type. Any statement within the statement may be labeled with one or more case labels as follows:

> `case` *constant-expression* :

where the constant expression must be of the same type as the switch expression; the usual arithmetic conversions are performed. No two of the case constants in the same switch may have the same value. Constant expressions are defined in §12.

There may also be at most one label of the form

> `default` :

When the `switch` statement is executed, its expression is evaluated and compared with each case constant. If one of the case constants is equal to the value of the expression, control is passed to the statement following the matched case label. If no case constant matches the expression, and if there is a `default` label, control passes to the labeled statement. If no case matches and if there is no `default` then none of the statements in the switch is executed.

case and default labels in themselves do not alter the flow of control, which continues unimpeded across such labels. To exit from a switch, see break, §9.8.

Usually the statement that is the subject of a switch is compound. Declarations may appear at the head of this statement, but initializations of automatic or register variables are ineffective.

9.8 Break Statement

The statement

        break ;

causes termination of the smallest enclosing while, do, for, or switch statement; control passes to the statement following the terminated statement.

9.9 Continue Statement

The statement

        continue ;

causes control to pass to the loop-continuation portion of the smallest enclosing while, do, or for statement; that is to the end of the loop. More precisely, in each of the statements

```
while ( ... ) {      do {                for ( ... ) {
   ...                  ...                 ...
contin: ;            contin: ;           contin: ;
}                    } while ( ... );    }
```

a continue is equivalent to goto contin. (Following the contin: is a null statement, §9.13.)

9.10 Return Statement

A function returns to its caller by means of the return statement, which has one of the forms

        return ;
        return *expression* ;

The first form can be used only in functions which does not return a value, that is, a function with the return value type void. The second form can be used only in functions returning a value; the value of the expression is returned to the caller of the function. If required, the expression is converted, as in an initialization, to the type of the function in which it appears. Flowing off the end of a function is equivalent to a return with no returned value.

9.11 Goto Statement

Control may be transferred unconditionally by means of the statement

> goto *identifier* ;

The identifier must be a label (§9.12) located in the current function. It is not possible to transfer control past a declaration with an (implicit or explicit) initializer, except by transferring control past an inner block without entering it.

9.12 Labeled Statement

Any statement may be preceded by label of the form

> *identifier* :

which serve to declare the identifier as a label. The only use of a label is as a target of a goto. The scope of a label is the current function, excluding any sub-blocks in which the same identifier has been redeclared. See §4.1.

9.13 Null Statement

The null statement has the form

> ;

A null statement is useful to carry a label just before the } of a compound statement or to supply a null body to a looping statement such as while.

9.14 Declaration Statement

A declaration statement is used to introduce a new identifier into a block; it has the form

> *declaration-statement:*
>   *declaration*

If an identifier introduced by a declaration were previously declared in an outer block, the outer declaration is hidden for the duration of the block, after which it resumes its force.

Any initializations of auto or register variables are performed each time their *declaration-statement* is executed. It is possible to transfer into a block, but not in a way that causes initializations not to be performed; see §9.11. Initializations of variables with storage class *static* (§4.4) are performed only once when the program begins execution.

10. Function Definitions

A program consists of a sequence of declarations. Only outside any block and within class declarations may the code for functions be given. Function definitions have the form

    function-definition:
        decl-specifiers_{opt} fct-declarator base-initializer_{opt} fct-body

The *decl-specifiers* `register`, `auto`, `typedef` may not be used, and `friend`, and `virtual` may only be used within a class declaration (§8.5). A function declarator is a declarator for a "function returning ... " (§8.4). The formal arguments are in the scope of the outermost block of the *function-body*. Function declarators have the form

    fct-declarator:
        declarator (*argument-declaration-list*)

If an argument is specified `register`, the corresponding actual argument will be copied, if possible, into a register at the outset of the function. If a constant expression is specified as initializer for an argument this value is used as a default argument value.

The function body has the form

    fct-body:
        compound-statement

A simple example of a complete function definition is

```
int max(int a, int b, int c)
{
        int m = (a > b) ? a : b;
        return (m > c) ? m : c;
}
```

Here `int` is the type-specifier; `max(int a, int b, int c)` is the fct-declarator; `{ ... }` is the function body.

Since in expression context an array name (in particular as an actual argument) is taken to mean a pointer to the first element of the array, declarations of formal arguments declared "array of ..." are adjusted to read "pointer to ...".

Initializers for a base class and for members may be specified in the definition of a constructor. This is most useful for class objects, constants, and references where the semantics of initialization and assignment differ. A base-initializer has the form

    base-initializer:
        : *member-initializer-list*

> *member-initializer-list:*
>> *member-initializer*
>> *member-initializer* , *member-initializer-list*
>
> *member-initializer:*
>> *identifier*$_{opt}$ (*argument-list*$_{opt}$)

If the *identifier* is present in a *member-initializer* the argument list is used to initialize that named member; if not, the argument list is used for the base class. For example:

```
struct base { base(int); ... };

struct derived : base {
        derived(int);
        base b;
        const c;
};
derived::derived(int a) : (a+1), b(a+2), c(a+3)
{ /* ... */ }

derived d(10);
```

First, the base class's constructor `base::base()` is called for the object `d` with the argument 11; then the constructor for the member `b` is called with the argument 12 and the constructor for the member `c` is called with the argument 13; then the body of `derived::derived()` is executed (see §8.5.5). The order in which constructors are called for members is unspecified. If the base class has a constructor that can be invoked without arguments, no argument list need be provided. If a member's class has a constructor that can be invoked without arguments, no argument list need be provided for that member.

11. Compiler Control Lines

The compiler contains a preprocessor capable of macro substitution, conditional compilation, and inclusion of named files. Lines beginning with **#** communicate with this preprocessor. These lines have syntax independent of the rest of the language; they may appear anywhere and have effect which lasts (independent of scope) until the end of the source program file.

Note that `const` and `inline` definitions provide alternatives to many uses of `#define`.

11.1 Token Replacement

A compiler-control line of the form

> #define *identifier token-string*

causes the preprocessor to replace subsequent instances of the identifier with the given string of tokens. Semicolons in, or at the end of, the token-string are part of that string. A line of the form

> #define *identifier*(*identifier* , ... , *identifier*) *token-string*

where there is no space between the first identifier and the (, is a macro definition with arguments. Subsequent instances of the first identifier followed by a (, a sequence of tokens delimited by commas, and a) are replaced by the token string in the definition. Each occurrence of an identifier mentioned in the formal argument list of the definition is replaced by the corresponding token string from the call. The actual arguments in the call are token strings separated by commas; however commas in quoted strings or protected by parentheses do not separate arguments. The number of formal and actual arguments must be the same. Strings and character constants in the token-string are scanned for formal arguments, but strings and character constants in the rest of the program are not scanned for defined identifiers.

In both forms the replacement string is rescanned for more defined identifiers. In both forms a long definition may be continued on another line by writing \ at the end of the line to be continued. A control line of the form

> #undef *identifier*

causes the identifier's preprocessor definition to be forgotten.

11.2 File Inclusion

A compiler control line of the form

> #include *"filename"*

causes the replacement of that line by the entire contents of the file *filename*. The named file is searched for first in the directory of the original source file, and then in a sequence of specified or standard places. Alternatively, a control line of the form

> #include *<filename>*

searches only the specified or standard places, and not the directory of the source file. (How the places are specified is not part of the language.)

#include's may be nested.

11.3 Conditional Compilation

A compiler control line of the form

> #if *expression*

checks whether the expression evaluates to non-zero. The expression must be a constant expression (§12). In addition to the usual C++ operations a unary operator **defined** can be used. When applied to an identifier, its value is non-zero if that identifier has been defined using #define and not later undefined using #undef; otherwise its value is 0. A control line of the form

> #ifdef *identifier*

checks whether the identifier is currently defined in the preprocessor; that is, whether it has been the subject of a #define control line. A control line of the form

> #ifndef *identifier*

checks whether the identifier is currently undefined in the preprocessor.

All three forms are followed by an arbitrary number of lines, possibly containing a control line

> #else

and then by a control line

> #endif

If the checked condition is true then any lines between #else and #endif are ignored. If the checked condition is false then any lines between the test and an #else or, lacking an #else, the #endif, are ignored.

These constructions may be nested.

11.4 Line Control

For the benefit of other preprocessors which generate C++ programs, a line of the form

> #line *constant* "*filename*"

causes the compiler to believe, for purposes of error diagnostics, that the line number of the next source line is given by the constant and the current input file is named by the identifier. If the identifier is absent the remembered file name does not change.

12. Constant Expressions

In several places C++ requires expressions which evaluate to a constant: as array bounds (§8.4), as `case` expressions (§9.7), as default function arguments (§8.4), and in initializers (§8.6). In the first case, the expression can involve only integer constants, character constants, enumeration constants, non-aggregate `const` values initialized with constant expressions, and `sizeof` expressions, possibly connected by the binary operators

```
+    -    *    /    %    &    ¦    ^    <<
>>   ==   !=   <    >    <=   >=   &&   ¦¦
```

or by the unary operators

```
+    -    ~    !
```

or by the ternary operator

```
?:
```

Parentheses can be used for grouping, but not for function calls.

In the other cases constant expressions may also contain the unary & operator applied to external or static objects or to external or static arrays subscripted with a constant expression. The unary & can be applied implicitly by appearance of unsubscripted arrays and functions. The basic rule is that initializers must evaluate either to a constant or to the address of a previously declared external or static object plus or minus a constant.

Less latitude is allowed for constant expressions after `#if`; names declared `const`, `sizeof` expressions, and enumeration constants are not permitted.

13. Portability Considerations

Certain parts of C++ are inherently machine dependent. The following list of potential trouble spots is not meant to be all-inclusive, but to point out the main ones.

Purely hardware issues like word size and the properties of floating point arithmetic and integer division have proven in practice to be not much of a problem. Other facets of the hardware are reflected in differing implementations. Some of these, particularly sign extension (converting a negative character into a negative integer) and the order in which bytes are placed in a word, are a nuisance that must be carefully watched. Most of the others are only minor problems.

The number of `register` variables that can actually be placed in registers varies from machine to machine, as does the set of valid types. Nonetheless, the compilers all do things properly for their own machine; excess or invalid `register` declarations are ignored.

The order of evaluation of function arguments is not specified by the language. It is right-to-left on some machines left-to-right on others. The order in which side effects take place is also unspecified.

Since character constants are really objects of type `int`, multi-character character constants may be permitted. The specific implementation is very machine dependent, however, because the characters are assigned to a word left-to-right on some machines and right-to-left on others.

14. Syntax Summary

This summary of C++ syntax is intended to be an aid to comprehension. It is not an exact statement of the language.

14.1 Expressions

> *expression:*
>> *term*
>> *expression binary-operator expression*
>> *expression* **?** *expression* **:** *expression*
>> *expression-list*
>
> *expression-list:*
>> *expression*
>> *expression-list* **,** *expression*
>
> *term:*
>> *primary-expression*
>> *unary-operator term*
>> *term* **++**
>> *term* **--**
>> `sizeof` *expression*
>> `sizeof` **(** *type-name* **)**
>> **(** *type-name* **)** *expression*
>> *simple-type-name* **(** *expression-list* **)**
>> `new` *type-name initializer*_{opt}
>> `new` **(** *type-name* **)**
>> `delete` *expression*
>> `delete` **[** *expression* **]** *expression*

primary-expression:
      id
      `: :` *identifier*
      constant
      string
      `this`
      `(` *expression* `)`
      primary-expression`[` *expression* `]`
      primary-expression `(` *expression-list*$_{opt}$ `)`
      primary-expression `.` *id*
      primary-expression `->` *id*

id:
      identifier
      operator-function-name
      typedef-name `: :` *identifier*
      typedef-name `: :` *operator-function-name*

operator:
      unary-operator
      binary-operator
      special-operator
      free-store-operator

Binary operators have precedence decreasing as indicated:

binary-operator: `one of`
      `*   /   %`
      `+   -`
      `<<  >>`
      `<   >`
      `==  !=`
      `&`
      `^`
      `|`
      `&&`
      `||`
      assignment-operator

assignment-operator: `one of`
      `=    +=   -=   *=   /=   %=   ^=   &=   |=   >>=   <<=`

unary-operator: `one of`
      `*    &    +    -    ~    !    ++   --`

special-operator: one of
　　　() []

free-store-operator: one of
　　　new   delete

type-name:
　　　decl-specifiers abstract-declarator

abstract-declarator:
　　　empty
　　　* *abstract-declarator*
　　　abstract-declarator (*argument-declaration-list*)
　　　abstract-declarator [*constant-expression*$_{opt}$]

simple-type-name:
　　　typedef-name
　　　char
　　　short
　　　int
　　　long
　　　unsigned
　　　float
　　　double
　　　void

typedef-name:
　　　identifier

14.2 Declarations

declaration:
　　　decl-specifiers$_{opt}$ *declarator-list*$_{opt}$;
　　　name-declaration
　　　asm-declaration

name-declaration:
　　　aggr identifier ;
　　　enum *identifier* ;

aggr:
　　　class
　　　struct
　　　union

asm-declaration:
　　　asm (*string*) ;

decl-specifiers:
>   *decl-specifier decl-specifiers*$_{opt}$

decl-specifier:
>   *sc-specifier*
>   *type-specifier*
>   *fct-specifier*
>   `friend`
>   `typedef`

type-specifier
>   *simple-type-name*
>   *class-specifier*
>   *enum-specifier*
>   *elaborated-type-specifier*
>   `const`

sc-specifier:
>   `auto`
>   `extern`
>   `register`
>   `static`

fct-specifier:
>   `inline`
>   `overload`
>   `virtual`

elaborated-type-specifier:
>   *key typedef-name*
>   *key identifier*

key:
>   `class`
>   `struct`
>   `union`
>   `enum`

declarator-list:
>   *init-declarator*
>   *init-declarator , declarator-list*

init-declarator:
>   *declarator initializer*$_{opt}$

declarator:
    dname
    (*declarator*)
    $*$ `const`$_{opt}$ *declarator*
    `&` `const`$_{opt}$ *declarator*
    declarator (*argument-declaration-list*)
    declarator [*constant-expression*$_{opt}$]

dname:
    simple-dname
    typedef-name `::` *simple-dname*

simple-dname:
    identifier
    typedef-name
    ~ *typedef-name*
    operator-function-name
    conversion-function-name

operator-function-name:
    `operator` *operator*

conversion-function-name:
    `operator` *type*

argument-declaration-list:
    arg-declaration-list$_{opt}$ `...`$_{opt}$

arg-declaration-list:
    arg-declaration-list , *argument-declaration*
    argument-declaration

argument-declaration:
    decl-specifiers declarator
    decl-specifiers declarator = *expression*
    decl-specifiers abstract-declarator
    decl-specifiers abstract-declarator = *expression*

class-specifier:
    class-head { *member-list*$_{opt}$ }
    class-head { *member-list*$_{opt}$ `public` : *member-list*$_{opt}$ }

class-head:
    aggr identifier$_{opt}$
    aggr identifier : `public`$_{opt}$ *typedef-name*

member-list:
>   *member-declaration member-list$_{opt}$*

member-declaration:
>   *decl-specifiers$_{opt}$ member-declarator initializer$_{opt}$;*
>   *function-definition ;$_{opt}$*

member-declarator:
>   *declarator*
>   *identifier$_{opt}$: constant-expression*

initializer:
>   *= expression*
>   *= { initializer-list }*
>   *= { initializer-list , }*
>   *(expression-list)*

initializer-list:
>   *expression*
>   *initializer-list , initializer-list*
>   *{ initializer-list }*

enum-specifier:
>   *enum identifier$_{opt}$ { enum-list }*

enum-list:
>   *enumerator*
>   *enum-list , enumerator*

enumerator:
>   *identifier*
>   *identifier = constant-expression*

14.3 Statements

compound-statement:
>   *{ statement-list$_{opt}$ }*

statement-list:
>   *statement*
>   *statement statement-list*

statement:
    declaration
    compound-statement
    expression$_{opt}$;
    `if` (*expression*) *statement*
    `if` (*expression*) *statement* `else` *statement*
    `while` (*expression*) *statement*
    `do` *statement* `while` (*expression*) ;
    `for` (*statement expression*$_{opt}$; *expression*$_{opt}$) *statement*
    `switch` (*expression*) *statement*
    `case` *constant-expression* : *statement*
    `default` : *statement*
    `break` ;
    `continue` ;
    `return` *expression*$_{opt}$;
    `goto` *identifier* ;
    identifier : *statement*

14.4 External Definitions

program:
    external-definition
    external-definition program

external-definition:
    function-definition
    declaration

function-definition:
    decl-specifiers$_{opt}$ *fct-declarator base-initializer*$_{opt}$ *fct-body*

fct-declarator:
    declarator (*argument-declaration-list*)

fct-body:
    compound-statement

base-initializer:
    : *member-initializer-list*

member-initializer-list:
    member-initializer
    member-initializer , *member-initializer-list*

member-initializer:
    identifier$_{opt}$ (*argument-list*$_{opt}$)

14.5 Preprocessor

```
#define identifier token-string
#define identifier( identifier , ... , identifier ) token-string
#else
#endif
#if expression
#ifdef identifier
#ifndef identifier
#include "filename"
#include <filename>
#line constant "filename"
#undef identifier
```

15. Differences from C

15.1 Extensions

The types of function arguments can be specified (§8.4) and will be checked (§7.1). Type conversions will be performed (§7.1).

Single-precision floating arithmetic may be used for `float` expressions; §6.2.

Function names can be overloaded; §8.9.

Operators can be overloaded; §7.16, §8.5.11.

Functions can be inline substituted; §8.1.

Data objects can be `const`; §8.4.

Objects of reference type can be declared; §8.4, §8.6.3.

A free store is provided by the `new` and `delete` operators; §7.2.

Classes can provide data hiding (§8.5.9), guaranteed initialization (§8.6.2), user-defined conversions (§8.5.6), and dynamic typing through use of virtual functions (§8.5.4).

The name of a class or enumeration is a type name; §8.5.

Any pointer can be assigned to a `void*` without use of a cast; §7.14.

A declaration within a block is a statement; §9.14.

Anonymous unions can be declared; §8.5.13.

15.2 Summary of Incompatibilities

Most constructs in C are legal in C++ with their meaning unchanged. The exceptions are as follows

Programs using one of the new keywords

```
class     const    delete    friend    inline
new       operator overload  public    signed
this      virtual  volatile
```

as identifiers are not legal.

The function declaration f(); means that f takes no arguments, in C it means that f could take arguments of any type at all.

In C an external name may be defined several times, in C++ it must be defined exactly once.

Class names in C++ are in the same name space as other names, so constructs like

```
int s;
struct s { /* ... */ };
f() { s = 1; }
```

cannot be used. However, explicit use of class struct, union, enum (§8.2), or :: (§7.1) can be used to resolve most conflicts. For example

```
int s;
struct s { /* ... */ };
void f() { int s; struct s a; }
void g() { ::s = 1; }
```

15.3 Anachronisms

The extensions presented here may be provided to make it easier to use C programs as C++ programs. Note that each of these features has undesirable aspects. An implementation providing them should also provide a way for the user to ensure that they did not occur in a source file.

A hitherto undefined name can be used as a function name in a call. In this case the name will implicitly be declared as a function returning int with argument type (...).

The keyword void may be used to indicate that a function takes no arguments, thus (void) is equivalent to ().

Programs using the C function definition syntax

old-function-definition:
    decl-specifiers$_{opt}$ *old-function-declarator declaration-list fct-body*

old-function-declarator:
    declarator (parameter-list)

     parameter-list:
        identifier
     .   *identifier* , *identifier*

for example

```
max(a,b) { return (a<b) ? b : a; }
```

may be used. If a function defined like this has not been previously declared its argument type will be taken to be (. . .), that is, unchecked. If it has been declared its type must agree with that of the declaration.

A dot may be used instead of the : : to specify the name in a member function definition. For example:

```
int cl.fct() { /* ... */ }
```

The same name may be declared for both a class or an enumeration and a data object or function in the same scope.

Index

PROGRAMMING LANGUAGE

BJARNE
STROUSTRUP

AT&T Bell Laboratories

Here is the definitive reference and guide to the C++ programming language, which was designed and implemented by author Bjarne Stroustrup. C++ is the result of years of experiments and research at AT&T Bell Laboratories to create a successor to C. It is already heavily used in many AT&T Bell Laboratories projects.

C++ is a superset of C that retains the efficiency and notational convenience of C, while providing facilities for:

- type checking
- data abstraction
- operator overloading
- object-oriented programming

This book contains the tutorial and explanatory material necessary to allow a serious programmer to learn C++ and to complete real projects. The text is intended for computer science students and professional programmers who want to learn about this latest development of the C programming language.

ABOUT THE AUTHOR

Bjarne Stroustrup is the designer and implementer of C++ . He is a member of the Computer Science Research Center at AT&T Bell Laboratories in Murray Hill, New Jersey. Dr. Stroustrup received a master of science degree in computer science and mathematics from the University of Aarhus, Denmark, and his doctorate degree in computer science from Cambridge University, England. His research interests include distributed systems, operating systems, simulation, and programming.

Addison-Wesley Publishing Company, Inc.

ISBN 0-201-12078-X